She is but a Woman

She is but a Woman

Queenship in Scotland, 1424–1463

Fiona Downie

JOHN DONALD

In memory of my father

First published in Great Britain in 2006 by
John Donald, an imprint of Birlinn Ltd

West Newington House
10 Newington Road
Edinburgh
EH9 1QS

www.birlinn.co.uk

ISBN 10: 0 85976 656 X
ISBN 13: 978 0 85976 656 2

British Library Cataloguing-in-Publication Data
A catalogue record for this book is available on request
from the British Library

The publisher acknowledges subsidy from

 Scottish
Arts Council

towards the publication of this volume

Typeset in Janset Text by Koinonia, Bury, Lancashire
Printed and bound by Bell & Bain Ltd, Glasgow

Contents

Illustrations

1. Seal matrix of Joan Beaufort, found at Kinross, Perthshire. ©The Trustees of the National Museums of Scotland (H. NM 163)

2. Genealogy of James II, demonstrating his descent from Saint Margaret through both paternal and maternal lines. From a fifteenth-century manuscript of Bower's *Scotichronicon*. Copyright © The British Library (Royal MS 13.E.x, f.26v)

3. Linlithgow Palace from the south east. ©Crown Copyright reproduced courtesy of Historic Scotland (HS A 3209-6)

4. Ravenscraig Castle from the north east. © Crown Copyright reproduced courtesy of Historic Scotland (HS A 3136–11)

5. Trinity College Church, 1753. Royal Commission on the Ancient and Historical Monuments of Scotland (C 71919)

6. Trinity College Church and Hospital, 1815. Reproduced courtesy of Royal Commission on the Ancient and Historical Monuments of Scotland (C 62936)

7. Margaret of Denmark, from the Trinity Altarpiece by Hugo van der Goes. The Royal Collection © Her Majesty Queen Elizabeth II

8. Saint Catherine presents Isabella Stewart, duchess of Brittany, to the Virgin and child. From a book of hours owned by Isabella. Reproduction by permission of the Syndics of the Fitzwilliam Museum, Cambridge (MS 62, f.20r)

Acknowledgements

Like the queens in this study, I have relied upon a broad network of support for the completion of my work. The PhD thesis on which this book is based could not have been undertaken without the support provided by the Mackie postgraduate studentship for the study of any aspect of Scotland's external relations, offered by the University of Aberdeen. The studentship included a generous travel allowance without which the essential research visits to Edinburgh, London, Paris, Nantes, Lille, Brussels, Turin, Vienna and Innsbruck would have been impossible. I am indebted to the staff of the libraries and archives in each of these cities for their assistance, and am especially grateful to the staff of the Turin archives, who endured my attempts to communicate in Italian with incredible patience and good humour.

The friendship and support of three of my colleagues in the History Department at Aberdeen – Drs Robert Blyth, John Frame and Douglas Hamilton – have been invaluable both during my time in Aberdeen and through the long gestation of this book, and I cannot thank them enough. Thanks are also due to Dr Stephanie Tarbin, who provided long-distance encouragement and advice during my doctoral studies and very generously introduced me to the delights of Walthamstow YMCA in 1994. I am truly grateful! The overwhelming hospitality and support provided by Elizabeth and Richard Chown during my research and recreational visits to Edinburgh deserve their own book of acknowledgements, and I hope they know how much I appreciate everything they have done for me.

Thanks are also due to the large number of people who have encouraged and assisted me during the years it has taken to transform a doctoral thesis into a book. Special mention must be made of Dr Catherine Mann, who read and commented (rigorously) on the complete draft; our friendship has now survived several theses, so must be indestructible. Drs Michael Brown and Roland Tanner read sections of the manuscript and provided invaluable advice, while my biennial discussions with Dr Steve Boardman have been both entertaining and enlightening. Dr Liz Ewan has always provided unfailing support and enthusiasm, for which I am very grateful. Thanks also to my colleagues in the School of Graduate Studies and the Faculty of Architecture Building and Planning at the University of Melbourne, who have been extremely generous with their enthusiasm for a project which must often have seemed a figment of my imagination.

My greatest debt, once again, is to my family. My parents, Bill and Judy, and brothers, Iain and Calum, never once complained about my long absence overseas and excelled themselves at feigning interest in fifteenth-century Scottish queenship. This book is dedicated to all of them, but particularly to my father, who first encouraged me to study Scottish history and who, I think, would have been quite pleased.

Abbreviations and conventions

Abdn. Reg.	*Registrum Episcopatus Aberdonensis*
ADLA	Archives Départmentales de Loire-Atlantique
ADN	Archives Départmentales du Nord
AHR	*American Historical Review*
AN	Archives Nationales
APS	*The Acts of the Parliaments of Scotland*
AS(1)	Archivio di Stato, Sezione Riunite
AS(2)	Archivio di Stato, Direzione e Sezione 1
'Auch. Chron.'	'Auchinleck Chronicle' in McGladdery, *James II*, 160–73
BL	British Library
BN	Bibliothèque Nationale
Cal. Scot. Supp.	*Calendar of Scottish Supplications to Rome*, vol. iv
CDS	*Calendar of Documents Relating to Scotland*
Chron. Wyntoun	*The Original Chronicle of Andrew of Wyntoun*, ed. F.J. Amours
CPR Papal Letters	*Calendar of Entries in the Papal Registers relating to Great Britain and Ireland*
EETS	Early English Text Society
EHR	*English Historical Review*
ER	*The Exchequer Rolls of Scotland*
Foedera	*Foedera, Conventiones, Litterae et Cuiuscunque Generis Acta Publica*
Glas. Reg.	*Registrum Episcopatus Glasguensis, Munimenta Ecclesie Metropolitane Glasguensis*
HHSA	Haus-, Hof- und Staatsarchiv
HMC	*Reports of the Royal Commission on Historical Manuscripts*
IACOB	*Inventaire sommaire des archives départementales de la Côte d'Or. Série B*

IADNB	*Inventaire sommaire des archives départementales du Nord. Série B*
NAS	National Archives of Scotland
Nat. MSS. Scot.	*Facsimiles of the National Manuscripts of Scotland*
NLS	National Library of Scotland
PPC	*Proceedings and Ordinances of the Privy Council of England*
PSAS	*Proceedings of the Society of Antiquaries of Scotland*
RMS	*Registrum Magni Sigilli Regum Scottorum*
Rot. Scot.	*Rotuli Scotiae in Turri Londinensi et in Domo Capitulari Westmonasteriensi Asservati*
Scotichronicon	Bower, W., *Scotichronicon*, ed. Watt, D.E.R.
SHR	*Scottish Historical Review*
TLA	Landesregierungsarchiv für Tirol
Treasure	Pizan, C. de, *The Treasure of the City of Ladies*, trans. S. Lawson
TRHS	*Transactions of the Royal Historical Society*

The letters thorn and yogh are represented by 'th' and 'y'.

The House of Stewart, 1424–63

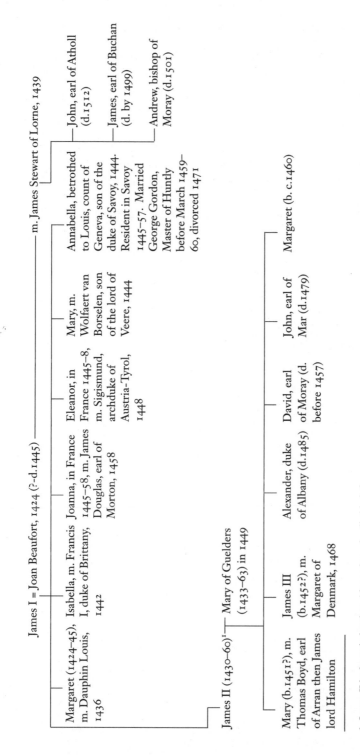

James I = Joan Beaufort, 1424 (?–d.1445) ———————— m. James Stewart of Lorne, 1439

Margaret (1424–45), m. Dauphin Louis, 1436

Isabella, m. Francis I, duke of Brittany, 1442

Joanna, in France 1445–58, m. James Douglas, earl of Morton, 1458

Eleanor, in France 1445–8, m. Sigismund, archduke of Austria-Tyrol, 1448

Mary, m. Wolfaert van Borselen, son of the lord of Veere, 1444

Annabella, betrothed to Louis, count of Geneva, son of the duke of Savoy, 1444. Resident in Savoy 1445–57. Married George Gordon, Master of Huntly before March 1459–60, divorced 1471

John, earl of Atholl (d.1512)

James, earl of Buchan (d. by 1499)

Andrew, bishop of Moray (d.1501)

James II (1430–60)[1] — Mary of Guelders (1433–63) in 1449

Mary (b.1451?), m. Thomas Boyd, earl of Arran then James lord Hamilton

James III (b.1452?), m. Margaret of Denmark, 1468

Alexander, duke of Albany (d.1485)

David, earl of Moray (d. before 1457)

John, earl of Mar (d.1479)

Margaret (b. c.1460)

1 James II had a twin brother, Alexander, who died in infancy.

Introduction

'Sche is but a womman'

On the night of 21 February 1437, a party of assassins entered the monastery of Blackfriars in Perth intending to kill the Scottish king, James I. One of the men attacked the queen, Joan Beaufort, 'wounded her vilaynosly and wolde haue slayne her' had not one of his accomplices stopped him, saying 'What wolle yee do for schame of yourselfe to the queene? Sche is but a womman, lett us goo seche the king.' After finding and killing the king, the regicides had a change of heart about sparing the queen, 'and in their furious cruelte wolde haue slayne her in the same wyesse.' But the queen had 'fledde in her kurtelle and a mantelle aboute her' and survived the attack. In sparing the queen as 'but a womman', the assassins soon realised that they had made a fatal error. Unlike other women, the queen was a political figure by virtue of her relationship to the king and in a position to 'pursewe ... and labour to doo vengaunce upon' her husband's killers. In little over a month after she had run, bleeding, from her attackers, she had orchestrated the capture and execution of the king's assassins and the coronation of her son as James II. Even as he escaped from Blackfriars 'tawardes the countre of the wilde Scottes', one of the murderers anticipated the likely ferocity of the queen's vengeance and asked himself 'Ellas, whi slewe we nott the queene'.[1]

The regicides' indecision about whether to kill Joan Beaufort on the night of 21 February reveals contemporary anxieties about the role and power of the medieval Scottish queen. While the king lived, his queen's primary public role was that of wife, subordinate partner to her husband, and there was little to gain but much to lose by killing her before seeking out and attacking her husband. With the death of the king, however, the queen's importance as a political figure was

---

1 Connolly, M., 'The Dethe of the Kynge of Scotis: A New Edition', SHR, 71 (1992), 59–63.

clearly revealed. Joan was not simply a widow, but a potential guardian of the new king with the desire and ability to punish her husband's murderers and play a leading role in the minority government. Like other medieval Scottish queens, her political role as consort was largely invisible, confined to a private world of persuasion and influence. Under extraordinary circumstances, such as a minority, the enormous potential of the queen's role was revealed.

This book explores the tensions between the invisibility of the queen and the potential of her role in the reigns of Joan Beaufort (d. 1445) and Mary of Guelders (1433–63), queens of James I and James II respectively. It is not an exhaustive biographical study, but an attempt to illuminate broad patterns of behaviour and the limits and potential of fifteenth-century Scottish queenship. Both Joan and Mary played greater roles as consort than their immediate predecessors. Both were able to develop their roles during the minorities of their sons, James II and III. Although their roles during the minorities have received some scholarly attention, Joan and Mary are marginalised in histories of the period, referred to only in discussions of their marriages or times of crisis. Yet their actions and power in the early years of their sons' reigns reveal that they were not hovering on the margins of political life while their husbands ruled. Rather, they were establishing and cultivating relationships with members of the court, learning about Scottish political life and supporting their husbands in the business of government. Their political interests and skills were largely exercised behind the scenes while their husbands lived, but came suddenly into view following their husbands' deaths. This study examines how Joan Beaufort and Mary of Guelders practised the art of queenship throughout their reigns, from their betrothals to their deaths.

Medieval queenship has only relatively recently become the subject of historical scholarship.[2] There have long been biographies of individual queens but the development in the 1980s of an interest in medieval queenship rather than queens was the result of anthropological, socio-logical and feminist studies on the nature of power and authority. In the introduction to the most influential of these studies, *Woman, Culture, and Society*, published in 1974, Michelle Rosaldo argued:

Whether power is exercised through influence or force, it is inherently competitive, whereas authority entails a hierarchical

2 In particular see Parsons, J.C., (ed.), *Medieval Queenship* (Stroud, 1994), Fraden-burg, L.O., (ed.), *Women and Sovereignty* (Edinburgh, 1992), and Stafford, P., *Queens, Concubines and Dowagers. The King's Wife in the Early Middle Ages* (London, 1983).

chain of command and control. Although the idea of authority implies positive actions and duties, the exercise of power has no positive sanctions, only rules that specify 'the conditions of illegality of its operation'.[3]

Rosaldo and later feminist historians departed from a narrow equation of power with authority to develop a broader definition of power encompassing 'the ability to act effectively, to influence people or decisions, and to achieve goals.'[4] Power in this sense can be claimed and exercised by many, while authority is bestowed only on a select few. Power is fluid, constructed in and by competition, while authority is fixed and defined. The differentiation of power and authority facilitated a new understanding of the way in which medieval queens approached their duties and responsibilities. The medieval queen was excluded from authority but she clearly possessed power. She had economic power as a landowner and patron; she could in some kingdoms acquire quasi-official political rights as regent; and she possessed personal influence as the daughter, sister and niece of powerful men and as wife and mother of kings. The many forms of power claimed and exercised by the medieval queen operated simultaneously and varied in potency over her lifetime. The queen's power as a wife – which carried with it the suspicion of undue influence over her husband – was not the same as her revered maternal status, which provided her with the opportunity to exercise power publicly as the child-king's mother in the event of a minority. Unlike the king's authority, set down in a coronation oath, the queen's power was fluid and changing. Her coronation ceremony acknowledged and celebrated her social and political status rather than her responsibilities as queen, her relationship to her husband rather than his kingdom. This new appreciation of the nature of the queen's power enabled the detection of hitherto unrecognised motives and patterns in her behaviour. Her rare appearances in the public record were seen not as proof of her marginal status in political life but as glimpses of the way in which she actively marshalled her power and resources towards defined ends.

3 Rosaldo, M. Z., 'Theoretical Overview' in M.Z. Rosaldo and L. Lamphere, (eds), *Woman, Culture, and Society* (Stanford, 1974), 21 n.2. See also Erler, M., and Kowaleski, M., 'Introduction' in M. Erler and M. Kowaleski, (eds), *Women and Power in the Middle Ages* (Athens, Georgia, 1988), 1–13; Jordan, C., *Renaissance Feminism. Literary Texts and Political Models* (Ithaca, 1990), 4, 209; Weber, M., *The Theory of Social and Economic Organisation*, (New York, 1947), 152–3, 324–9, 341–5; Krieger, L., 'The Idea of Authority in the West', *AHR*, 82 (1977), 249–70.
4 Erler and Kowaleski, 'Introduction', 2.

This modern re-evaluation of the role and power of the medieval queen was also dependent upon the conclusions of gender studies about the ways in which medieval women exercised influence. Excluded from authority and mistrusted in public action, women could not seek power in the same way as men but could exercise power through them.[5] In short, the medieval queen possessed the power to influence. The most obvious channel for the queen's influence was the king – either her husband or son – and the extent of her influence over him was the subject of speculation and debate amongst her contemporaries. Unfortunately, the largely hidden nature of the influence of the royal wife and mother over her husband and son means that it is rarely recorded in traditional historical sources. There is more evidence of the way in which the queen as wife or mother of the king extended her network of influence to encompass the king's chief counsellors and, in the case of foreign queens, other princes. More importantly, the examination of 'how and when women wielded power' has identified the importance of networks of family and friends to the exercise of female influence.[6] Examinations of the family and patronage networks of queens, and of medieval women generally, stress the conscious efforts of women to construct and maintain networks through which they could exert influence and achieve goals, but note that these efforts took place within a male-dominated environment.[7] The interdependence of female networks and male policy is shown most clearly in the involvement of women in arranging the marriages of their children and in preparing their daughters for marriage – a crucial element of medieval diplomacy and social advancement.

The medieval queen's power was in many ways constructed and exercised through competition with the king's male relatives and supporters at court and in government. These men competed with the queen for influence over the king or custody of her son, for the rewards and patronage that the king might see fit to bestow. Like her male competitors in court and government, the politically aware and able queen sought not only to exercise, but also to maximise, her power to influence. She managed her power carefully, according to a strategy or

5 Collier, J.F., 'Women in Politics' in Rosaldo and Lamphere, *Woman, Culture, and Society*, 92.

6 Erler and Kowaleski, 'Introduction', 10.

7 Parsons, J.C., 'Of Queens, Courts, and Books: Reflections on the Literary Patronage of Thirteenth-Century Plantagenet Queens' in J.H. McCash, (ed.), *The Cultural Patronage of Medieval Women* (Athens, Georgia, 1996), 188; Parsons, J.C., and Wheeler, B., (eds), *Medieval Mothering* (New York, 1996).

policy. She carefully selected 'the occasions on which to intervene and the appropriate mode of intervention' rather than expending her influence too freely and risk devaluing her power to persuade. Her actions in managing and maximising her power effectively 'constrain[ed] the choices open to politically active men', just as their actions could limit her options.[8] The queen's power, though largely invisible and overlooked in the extant sources, was therefore an intrinsic part of medieval government and needs to be studied as such. But does recognising the effects of the queen's actions make her just another political player within the male-dominated court and government? Noblemen, particularly relatives of the king, did not rely on influence alone to secure their goals but were able to take direct action and could, in extreme circumstances, make a claim to possessing royal authority itself. The queen could not claim this authority, and was reliant primarily upon her influence as a political tool. In relying upon influence rather than authority, the queen had to persuade individuals with direct power that a particular decision or action was in their interests rather than, or as well as, in her own.[9] In concealing her interests and acting through others, the queen disguised her own power, or indicated that it was utilised solely for the benefit of others. She therefore attempted to maximise her power at the same time as downplaying its importance, a stance which conformed to contemporary views on the unacceptability of female authority and differentiated her from powerful men who sought to claim and advertise public authority.

Studies of medieval queenship have examined the roles of powerful women from Portugal to Hungary and from Denmark to Italy across several centuries. They have revealed the importance of family roles, influence and networks to the exercise of female power and have also underlined the importance of chronology, geography, personality and circumstance to the interplay and effects of these general factors. Considerable work has been done on medieval queens of England and France, but there are no studies of queenship in medieval Scotland, and no in-depth analyses of basic questions such as whether women could succeed in Scotland, how they were crowned or how their households

---

8 Rosaldo and Lamphere, 'Introduction' and Lamphere, L.,'Strategies, Cooperation, and Conflict Among Women in Domestic Groups' in Rosaldo and Lamphere, *Woman, Culture, and Society*; Parsons, T.,'On the Concept of Influence', *Public Opinion Quarterly*, 27 (1963), 52; Collier, T.,'Women in Politics' in Rosaldo and Lamphere, *Woman, Culture, and Society*, 89.
9 Lamphere, 'Strategies, Cooperation, and Conflict', 99–100.

functioned.[10] There is a wealth of studies on sixteenth-century Scottish queens and queenship – a response to the phenomenon of a queen regnant in that century and the amount of evidence generated by the contemporary debate on female rule – but the importance of the fifteenth century to the emergence of this phenomenon has received less attention. The acceptability or otherwise of female rule in sixteenth-century Scotland depended in part upon the earlier experience of female regency under Margaret Tudor and Mary of Guise, and the acceptability of female regency itself was in part the product of the roles played by Joan Beaufort and Mary of Guelders during two fifteenth-century minorities.

While it is currently difficult to situate Joan Beaufort and Mary of Guelders in a broader context of medieval Scottish queenship, their reigns can be examined in the light of considerable recent work on medieval Scottish political history in general and on the Stewart kings in particular.[11] This context is critical to understanding that while both Joan and Mary were politically active as consorts and played leading roles during the minorities of their sons, they could at no stage control the degree of their involvement in political life. The extent of the queen's political role was dependent upon the wishes of her husband, circumstances, and the attitude of the political community – particularly those members of the community who regarded the queen as a competitor for influence over her husband or custody of her son. Above all, the unusual experience of living with active dowager queens – Joan Beaufort and Mary of Guelders were the first queens since the thirteenth century to be alive during their sons' minorities – stimulated contemporary debate and reassessment of the role and power of the Scottish queen. The different experiences of Joan Beaufort and Mary of Guelders were in this sense reflective of fifteenth-century political history.

Their experiences also represented more broadly those of royal and noble women across Western Europe in the late middle ages. A

---

10 See the bibliography for works by Crawford, Dunn, Facinger, Laynesmith, Lee, McCartney, Maurer, Mooney, Myers, Parsons, and Stafford on medieval queenship in England and France.

11 In particular see: Brown, M., *James I* (Edinburgh, 1994); McGladdery, C., *James II* (Edinburgh, 1990); Macdougall, N., *James III. A Political Study* (Edinburgh, 1982); Tanner, R., *The Late Medieval Scottish Parliament. Politics and the Three Estates, 1424–1488* (East Linton, 2001); Grant, A., 'Crown and Nobility in Late Medieval Britain' in. R. A. Mason, (ed.), *Scotland and England, 1286–1815* (Edinburgh, 1987); Wormald, J., 'Taming the Magnates?' in K. J. Stringer, (ed.), *Essays on the Nobility of Medieval Scotland* (Edinburgh, 1985).

secondary theme of this book is the way in which the fifteenth-century European marriage market shaped the careers of these women, making them not simply pawns of medieval diplomacy but also ambassadors, professional networkers and 'peace-weavers'.[12] James II may well have believed himself to have influence on the European stage but he never set foot outside his kingdom. In contrast, his mother, six sisters and wife all mingled with the royalty and nobility of European courts. Their experiences, and the way in which their marital histories linked to create a broad and active network of influential women across Europe, are critical to an understanding of how Joan Beaufort and Mary of Guelders came to be Scottish queens and how they practised the art of queenship in fifteenth-century Scotland.

12 Parsons, J.C., 'Mothers, Daughters, Marriage, Power: Some Plantagenet Evidence, 1150–1500' in Parsons, *Medieval Queenship*, 69.

ONE

Women and power in the fifteenth century
'Royne mere et conffortarresse et advocate'

The Scottish queen in the fifteenth century was a powerful woman or, from the perspective of medieval commentators, a woman who happened to have access to power. Ideas about power are central to medieval ideas about women. The inseparability of power and gender in medieval thought owed a great deal to the theology of the early Church, which based its ideology of women around two extremes: the negative role of Eve in the Creation and Fall of humanity, and the positive role of Mary in humanity's redemption. The dominant interpretation of the Creation story emphasised that man was created first and was closer to God, while woman|was created from man, as an afterthought, a helper, and as fundamentally inferior. This belief in man's superiority was further supported by the Church's interpretation of the Fall, in which the serpent approached the woman as the weaker of the two humans and was able to tempt her to eat the forbidden fruit. At the same time, the seductive power of woman over man enabled her to tempt the man where the serpent could not, as the man asserted in his reply to God that 'It was the woman you put with me; she gave me the fruit, and I ate it'. God confirmed woman's power to weaken man's will and to distract him from God in his punishment of the man: 'Because you listened to the voice of your wife and ate from the tree of which I had forbidden you to eat, accursed be the soil because of you. With suffering shall you get your food from it every day of your life.' Woman's weakness was then responsible for her punishment after the Fall: 'Your yearning shall be for your husband, yet he will lord it over you.'[1] The apparent paradox of woman's fundamental weakness and

1 Genesis 1:27, 2:23, 3:16-7; Turner, J., *One Flesh: Paradisal Marriage and Sexual Relations in the Age of Milton* (Oxford, 1987), 12–21, 24–9, 107; Bloch, R.H., *Medieval Misogyny and the Invention of Western Romantic Love* (Chicago, 1991), 22–7; Bird, P., 'Images of Women in the Old Testament' in R. R. Ruether, (ed.), *Religion and*

inferiority to man and her simultaneous seductive power over him thus justified woman's social, political and economic subordination to man.

Eve became the clerical model of the bad wife, a woman who used her sexual power over her husband to lead him into sin. Mary, by giving birth to the redeemer, removed the stain of Eve, mother of sin, and created the possibility of salvation. Although Mary possessed significant potential power as mother of Christ, her submissive acceptance of her role at the Annunciation – 'I am the handmaid of the Lord,' said Mary, 'let what you have said be done to me' – demonstrated that she would never abuse her influence or attempt to claim authority in her own right.[2] The Annunciation story supports the outcome of the Fall: in choosing to subject herself to the Lord's power, Mary clearly accepts and endorses the subordination of women to men which Eve had caused by abusing her power over her husband. Mary renounced her own power over men and adopted the role of intercessor, a role which emphasised the ultimate authority of God and Christ and allowed her to act only through them. Mary and other biblical intercessors such as Bathsheba, Judith and Esther, were regularly cited as role models for the medieval princess. Their stories emphasised that they derived power from men, and exercised it over them, through the distinctively female roles of wife, mother and seductress.[3] The men over whom they had power were great leaders, who possessed authority in their own right and exercised it by command over other men. The minds and intentions of these leaders were changed by women who used their influence and beauty for the general good. The story of the Fall, however, acted as a constant reminder of the potentially disruptive and dangerous nature of female influence.

While female influence was an ambivalent force, female authority was regarded as fundamentally unnatural. The story of Pope Joan, recounted by the late medieval Scottish chroniclers Wyntoun and Bower, provides a striking example of the perceived absurdity and wrongs of female authority.[4] Joan managed to occupy the most prestigious office in medieval Christendom by pretending to be a man but was finally betrayed by giving birth and dying during a religious procession. Her story illustrates the inseparability of medieval ideas about power and

---

Sexism: Images of Women in the Jewish and Christian Traditions (New York, 1974), 71–7; McLoughlin, E.C., 'Equality of Souls, Inequality of Sexes: Women in Medieval Theology' in R. R. Ruether, *Religion and Sexism*, 216–7; *Scotichronicon*, vii, 339.

2 Luke 1:38.

3 1 Kings 1:11–31, 2:19–20; Judith 10:20–3, 11:8–23, 12:16–20, 13:1–9; Esther 5:1–5.

4 *Chron. Wyntoun*, iv, 166–9; *Scotichronicon*, ii, 305–7.

about women: Joan's sex barred her from the papal office, revealed her deception and justified female exclusion from authority. Under normal circumstances, female power was to be channelled through a man's authority and took the form of influence over male relatives, particularly husbands and sons. The duties of a princess, therefore, were essentially those of any wife and mother, albeit on a larger scale. The fifteenth-century text by Christine de Pizan, *Le Livre des Trois Vertus* (also known as *The Treasure of the City of Ladies*), provides a detailed account of these duties, and the limits and potential of the power of a medieval princess.

Christine de Pizan and a mirror for princesses

In her work *The Treasure of the City of Ladies*, Christine de Pizan provided a comprehensive summary of the ideal day in the life of a princess.[5] The princess was to rise early and hear as many masses as 'accord with her devotion and as time and leisure will permit her.' As she left mass, she was to distribute alms and hear petitions 'with humility and devotion' and, if she could not deal with them all, she was to appoint some charitable gentlemen to assist her and was to supervise their actions. After mass, if her husband had given her 'the responsibility and authority to govern and to be head of the council' in his absence, the princess was to attend council. Christine emphasised that the princess must have

> such a bearing, such a manner and such an expression when she is seated in her high seat that she will indeed seem to be the lady and mistress over all, and everyone will hold her in great reverence as their wise mistress with great authority.

She also had to be attentive, listen to opinions and watch reactions, and to consider her response carefully 'when someone comes to her to speak on a subject' so that 'she cannot be thought simple or ignorant'. The princess had to appoint gentlemen to her council and was to be 'counselled every day by these gentlemen at a certain hour about necessary matters that she has to deal with'. Council was followed by the midday meal at which the princess was to be the perfect hostess, receiving and speaking to her guests according to their rank, age and mood so that 'everyone will say that she is a gracious lady and one who well knows her manners in all places'. In the hours between the meal and vespers, the princess was to rest, work or 'divert herself in private

5 *Treasure*, 59–62.

gatherings' with her ladies. After vespers, at least during summer, she was to walk in the garden and 'if any persons need to see her for any reason they [were to] be allowed to enter and she will hear them'. Christine referred to other pastimes fitting for a princess, such as hunting, but did not write about them in detail, preferring to leave them to 'the preference and desire of their husbands and themselves', while noting that such pastimes should, like everything else, be enjoyed in moderation. At the end of this full and virtuous day, the princess said her prayers and retired to bed.

This programme for the princess' day is an ideal one, but it does illustrate the key features of Christine's thoughts about women and power. Most importantly, the princess did not hold power in her own right. Elsewhere in the work, Christine admonished the proud princess, telling her that she was 'a simple little woman who has no strength, power or authority unless it is conferred upon ... [her] ... by someone else'. Christine's belief that power was ultimately derived from men is also expressed in her frequent references to the importance of male counsel to the princess' decisions and actions.[6] While the power of a princess was derivative and limited, Christine recognised that she was perfectly capable of using it well, and declared that 'Any man is extremely foolish, of whatever class he may happen to be, if he sees that he has a good and wise wife, yet does not give her authority to govern in an emergency'.[7]

When no such emergency existed and her husband was in power, the ideal princess still played an important role in his government as mediator between the prince and his subjects. The subjects were always able 'to come to her and very humbly beseech her to represent them to the prince', and she was to listen patiently and respond wisely, 'excuse her husband and speak well of him'. The subjects had to leave satisfied that the princess would do her best on their behalf, and then she would 'speak to her husband well and wisely'. Similarly, she always attempted to make peace between the prince and his barons and to prevent war. While these duties of mediation and intercession were specifically hers, the princess was to act 'always preserving the honour of her husband'.[8]

The duties of the princess reflected 'natural' female qualities. Christine wrote that 'men are by nature more courageous and more

6 *Treasure*, 41, 49, 52, 60–1, 82.
7 *Treasure*, 80.
8 *Treasure*, 49–52.

hot-headed' while 'women are by nature more timid and also of a sweeter disposition, and for this reason, if they are wise and if they wish to, they can be the best means of pacifying men'.[9] The princess had to cultivate traditionally feminine virtues such as humility, patience, mercy, compassion and charity, virtues which would ensure that she was approached by her subjects to mediate with the prince on their behalf.[10] Christine's description of the behaviour of the princess in council emphasises its passive nature: the princess should listen and respond only 'when someone comes to her to speak on a subject' rather than initiating discussion or otherwise playing an active role. It was her 'bearing ... manner and ... expression' rather than her actions that won the council's regard. The princess had to 'court her subjects' and, while Christine maintained that a prince must be similarly loved by his people, she felt that he should 'keep their affection, not by harshness but in such a way that from this love comes fear, or otherwise his authority is in peril'.[11] The prince's power was thus constant, active and forceful while that of the princess was flexible, supportive and conciliatory. Princes had to be prepared to fight wars and princesses to prevent them.[12] The princess had to lead a virtuous life, go to mass and be on good terms with the clergy, but the prince had to defend the Church actively by overseeing promotions, preventing blasphemy and the like.[13]

There are indications in de Pizan's programme that the ideal princess was not as meek and humble as she pretended. Christine emphasised image over substance: the content of the princess' responses in council was not as important to her power as the effort to avoid being '*thought simple or ignorant*'. Her overall bearing was responsible for making her '*seem* to be the lady and mistress over all', and her conduct as hostess ensured that 'everyone will *say* that she is a gracious lady'.[14] It is difficult to ascertain from these references whether or not Christine was advocating that the princess deliberately obscure her true thoughts and character from public view. There are instances, however, in which it seems that this is exactly what she was proposing. The princess needed to be friendly to her enemies in order to 'make them think that she

9 *Treasure*, 51.
10 *Treasure*, 47–9.
11 *Treasure*, 73–4; de Pizan, C., *The Book of the Body Politic*, ed. and trans. Forhan, K.L., (Cambridge, 1994), 38–9.
12 *The Book of the Body Politic*, 8, 17.
13 *Treasure*, 59–62, 71–3; *The Book of the Body Politic*, 12–4.
14 *Treasure*, 60–1, emphasis added.

regards them highly as her friends and would never believe that they might be otherwise.' Most importantly,

> she should be so wise and circumspect that no one can perceive she does it calculatingly. It would be shameful if at one time she was very cordial and another time gave them furious looks that seemed genuine and were so plain that it was clear her smile was insincere.[15]

The shame did not arise from the insincerity of the princess' behaviour but from revealing that insincerity. This behaviour was quite deliberate and was designed to counteract the activities of her enemies, differentiating it from Christine's more general advice to wives to be patient and forbearing on earth in expectation of rewards in heaven.[16] Instead of enduring in silence, the princess was to call her enemies to ostensibly confidential meetings, pretend to confide in them 'and keep her real thoughts to herself'.

This apparent duplicity was not confined to the court. Christine recommended that the princess 'cultivate' the clergy even more than the nobility so that they would praise her in sermons and protect her from her 'slanderous enemies'.[17] She had to determine which members of the clergy 'will be the most useful and of the greatest authority and in whom, and in whose word, people place the most confidence. Those persons will inspire the others with confidence in her.' She was to treat them well, invite them to dinner, and contribute to their colleges and monasteries in order to win their favour and advice, as well as their support in council. Christine noted that almsgiving should be done in secret to avoid the vice of pride but declared that the princess should ensure that her acts of charity 'will be known and recorded' so that she provided a good example for others to follow. While she acknowledged that such behaviour could be seen as hypocrisy, she felt that it 'may be called a "just hypocrisy", so to speak, for it strives towards good and the avoidance of evil'. The princess was only truly hypocritical if she became overly proud or committed sins in almsgiving, but otherwise the apparent hypocrisy was 'almost necessary, especially to princes and princesses who must rule over others and to whom more reverence is due than to other people'. In these cases, Christine quite openly advocated that the end justified the means, and even the princess' piety

15 *Treasure*, 69.
16 *Treasure*, 62–5.
17 *Treasure*, 71–4.

became simply another instrument deployed to increase her honour.

The Treasure of the City of Ladies thus presents the reader with a princess who is on the one hand passive and silent, and on the other merely pretending to be passive and silent. The work is generally far more practical than its antecedent, *The Book of the City of Ladies*, which focused on defending the abilities and potential of women from misogynist attacks. In the *City of Ladies*, Christine built an allegorical city in which women could live their lives to their full potential in peace and freedom, protected from the outside masculine world by strong tower walls. Her subsequent work concerns women living in the outside world who had to accept dominant modes of behaviour which demanded that a woman be obedient to her husband, chaste, modest and silent.[18] Christine was a pragmatist, and advised princesses to conform at least outwardly to society's expectations of them. Her advice provides an indication of the ambiguity of the princess' role in the first half of the fifteenth century. In theory, the princess could not exercise power in her own right and was limited in the ways in which she could use that power, but in practice she could be involved in every aspect of medieval government.

Christine's treatment of the ambiguity of female power is particularly significant because she wrote with a woman's perspective and had a close working knowledge of the court. The fact that she accepted the basic ideology of the derivative nature of female power, given her otherwise positive views of women, is indicative of the pervasiveness of that ideology. It was not confined to theologians, philosophers, physicians and other learned men, but was part of the *mentalité* of the court, shared by Christine and the princesses for whom she wrote. On the other hand, Christine was aware that this ideology was to some extent culturally determined. She often noted differences between France and other nations or specified that she was writing about French practice and that her views did not universally apply.[19] In addition, her own experience was a constant reminder of those cultural differences. Her father, an Italian physician and astrologer to Charles V of France, had insisted upon her extensive education in opposition to the wishes of her mother. Christine's education in Latin, literature, philosophy and science was far wider than that enjoyed by other women at the French court, and she later became an advocate of education for women as a means of increasing their self-sufficiency in an uncertain world.

18 De Pizan, C., *The Book of the City of Ladies*, trans. Richards, E.J. (New York, 1982).
19 *The Book of the Body Politic*, 33, 54, 92.

Christine had become a professional writer in order to support herself and her family following her husband's death in 1390, and her early difficulties, particularly regarding lawsuits over inheritance, had strengthened her views on women's abilities and on the variability of fortune.[20] In her own account of these years, Christine stated that fortune had made her a man, that she had been forced to take on male characteristics of strength and overcome female characteristics of fear and doubt in order to survive.[21] She was thus aware of the dominant models of male and female behaviour, but also that it was possible to transcend those categories to some degree. Her emphasis on the importance of the princess being seen to conform to expected behaviour in *The Treasure of the City of Ladies* is a reflection of this awareness.

Christine's views on female power also drew on her extensive knowledge of the court. She had personal experience of the fluctuations of fortune following her father's fall from favour after the death of Charles V in 1380, and understood the broader implications of the factionalism of the court in the early fifteenth century when the Burgundians and Armagnacs struggled to control government during Charles VI's bouts of insanity. Christine understood the need for the princess to remain on good terms with the court in its entirety in order to minimise the negative consequences of any changes in the balance of power within the court. More importantly, she was well aware of the princess' role in resolving disputes and mediating between factions. The queen, Isabeau of Bavaria, had been granted power to rule in 1403 with the expectation that she would remain impartial in the struggle. She lost this role in summer 1405 as a result of her extravagance and continuing relationship with the duke of Orléans.[22] Christine, writing *The Treasure of the City of Ladies* at the same time, emphasises the maintenance of reputation as well as the specific duties of a princess who has been given 'authority to govern in an emergency' and her text constitutes

20 Bornstein, D., (ed.), *Ideals for Women and the Works of Christine de Pizan* (Detroit, 1981), 2; Gottlieb, B., 'The Problem of Feminism in the Fifteenth Century' in J. Kirshner, and S. Wemple, (eds), *Women of the Medieval World: Essays in Honour of John H. Mundy* (Oxford, 1985), 345; Gabriel, A.L., 'The Educational Ideas of Christine de Pisan', *Journal of the History of Ideas*, 16 (1955), 3–21; *Treasure*, 18.

21 Bornstein, *Ideals for Women*, 3–4; Willard, C.C., *Christine de Pizan. Her Life and Works* (New York, 1984), 48.

22 Willard, C.C., 'An Autograph Manuscript of Christine de Pizan?', *Studi Francesi*, 9 (1965), 452–7; Hindman, S., *Christine de Pizan's 'Epistre Orthéa': painting and politics at the court of Charles VI*, Studies and Texts, lxxvii (Toronto, 1986), 133–4; Quilligan, M., *The Allegory of Female Authority. Christine de Pizan's 'Cité des Dames'* (Ithaca, 1991), 247–51.

a damning indictment of Isabeau's failures. Christine's question to her royal and noble female readers – 'do you imagine that you are surrounded by luxury and honour so that you can dominate and outdo the whole world at your will?' – might have been directed specifically at the queen.[23]

Christine did not confine herself to implicit criticism of Isabeau's behaviour. She wrote a letter to the queen on 5 October 1405 reminding her of her duties and asking her to make peace between the warring factions.[24] The letter summarises Christine's views on the queen's power and duties, and suggests that Christine saw her advice as being of a practical rather than a theoretical nature. Christine sought to arouse the queen's pity and to encourage her to secure peace by telling her of the misery of the people and the evils of civil war. She urged the queen to feel 'charite, clemence et benignite' for her subjects as these were natural feelings to 'femenines condicions' and more abundant in a great lady than in any other. She reminded the queen that the rewards for her intervention would be the welfare of her soul, the good of her children and their subjects, and the glory of 'perpetuelle memoire'. Christine ended her letter with a warning on the variability of fortune and another request for the queen's intervention. The impression of humility, desperation and loyal concern for the kingdom that the letter attempts to convey is underlined by the incomplete verse, added to one copy of the manuscript, in which Christine stated that she was writing the letter by her own hand at one in the morning because no clerk was available. In addition, the verse indicates that a copy of the letter was also sent to the duke of Orléans to encourage him to make peace with Burgundy. The letter reiterated Christine's belief that the queen must exercise her power for the benefit of others, and focus on her special duties of intercession and mediation, as illustrated by the examples of Esther and Bathsheba.

The most striking aspect of the letter, however, is its stress on the role of the queen as mother. This stress is apparent from the use of the examples of Blanche of Castile and the Virgin, and Christine's reminder to Isabeau that she was mother not only of her own children, but of all her subjects. The close relationship between queenship and mother-

23 *Treasure*, 41, 80.
24 Kennedy, A., 'Christine de Pizan's *Epistre à la Reine* (1405)', *Revue des Langues Romanes*, 92 (1988), 253–64; De Pizan, C., *The Epistle of the Prison of Human Life with An Epistle to the Queen of France and Lament on the Evils of Civil War*, ed. and trans. J. A. Wisman (New York, 1984), 70–83.

hood was further emphasised in the description of a good queen's roles: 'saige et bonne royne mere et conffortarresse et advocate de ses subjiez et de son pueple.' Christine's emphasis on the role of queen as mother appears frequently in her work, and is virtually the only role for the princess in *The Book of the Body Politic*. This does not mean that she believed that the princess should not play a role in public affairs. As this letter indicates, Christine was well aware of the potential of the princess to exert an influence on political life precisely because of the importance of her role as mother. This potential power was stressed in another letter by Christine written in August 1410 in response to the mobilisation of the Armagnac and Burgundian factions in the summer of that year. Christine asked: 'Oh, crowned Queen of France, are you still sleeping?', before reminding her again of her duty to think of the heritage of her children and restrain the princes. Her plea for the queen's assistance ended: 'You, the mother of the noble heirs of France, Revered Princess, who but you can do anything, and who will disobey your sovereignty and authority, if you rightly want to mediate a peace?'[25] The importance and potential power of the queen as mother meant that Isabeau was not simply failing in her political duties by her behaviour but was also failing in her maternal and moral duties.

The Treasure of the City of Ladies was not, however, written solely as a response to Isabeau's failings. The work was dedicated to Margaret of Burgundy, daughter of John the Fearless, on the occasion of her marriage to the dauphin. It is unclear whether Christine wrote the work at her own initiative or if she was requested to do so by the duke, but his gift to Christine after she presented it to him indicates that he was pleased with her work even if he did not commission it. The duke's possible commissioning of the text would not be out of keeping with the Burgundian attitude to the education and abilities of the women of the ducal house. The duke's mother and wife had both been politically active and the latter acted as his representative in his absence. It is likely that the duke expected his daughter to play a similar role at the French court and to represent Burgundian interests there, a particularly important task given the influence of the duke of Orléans at court and his relationship with the queen. In addition, the expectation that the young Burgundian princess would reside at the French court under the guidance of an unsuitable role model, the French queen, may have encouraged the duke to seek other methods of training his daughter for her future responsibilities. He acquired many books of instruc-

25 De Pizan, *Epistle of the Prison of Human Life*, 89.

tion for his library over his lifetime and it would have been logical for him to propose such a book for his daughter. The duke's son, Philip the Good, also held advanced views on the abilities of women, and was praised for his defence of them in *Le Champion des Dames*, a work dedicated to him and written in opposition to misogynist writers such as Jean de Meung.[26]

Burgundian approval of *The Treasure of the City of Ladies* ensured its popularity amongst courts and families associated with the duchy. Copies of it found their way to the libraries of the Cleves and Bourbons following the marriages of Mary and Agnes of Burgundy into those families in 1406 and 1412 respectively. It has further been suggested that many of the surviving manuscripts of the work which were in the possession of 'the rising Middle Class' also originated in areas connected to the daughters of John the Fearless. A study of the miniatures of one of these manuscripts suggests that it was produced in Utrecht or Guelders in c.1430. If the manuscript was produced in Guelders, it could have been influenced by Mary of Burgundy, duchess of Cleves, and her daughter Catherine, duchess of Guelders.[27] The duchess of Burgundy, Isabel of Portugal, was probably responsible for sending a copy of the work to her niece, the queen of Portugal, who requested that it be translated into Portuguese between 1447 and 1455. It has also been argued that the manuscript now held in Vienna was sent to the imperial court by the duchess of Burgundy to another niece, Eleanor of Portugal, who married the Emperor Frederick III in 1452.[28] *The Treasure of the City of Ladies* was well-known in Burgundian circles, indicating that Christine's views on women and power were not regarded as unusual, and that the politically-active Burgundian princesses were well aware of the potential and limitations of their role.

26 Willard, C.C., 'A fifteenth-century view of woman's role in medieval society. Christine de Pizan's *Livre des Trois Vertus*' in R. T. Morewedge, (ed.), *The Role of Woman in the Middle Ages* (London, 1975), 98–9; Willard, C.C., *Christine de Pizan*, 173; Jordan, *Renaissance Feminism*, 93 n.29.

27 Willard, C.C., 'A fifteenth-century view of women's role', 115; Willard, C.C., 'The Manuscript Tradition of the *Livre des Trois Vertus* and Christine de Pizan's Audience', *Journal of the History of Ideas*, 27 (1966), 437–8.

28 Willard, *Christine de Pizan*, 213; Willard, C.C.,'A Portuguese Translation of Christine de Pisan's *Livre des trois vertus*', *Publications of the Modern Language Association*, 78 (1963), 459–64; Bernard, R. B.,'The Intellectual Circle of Isabel of Portugal, Duchess of Burgundy, and the Portuguese Translation of *Le Livre des Trois Vertus*' in G. K. McLeod, (ed.), *The Reception of Christine de Pizan From the Fifteenth Through the Nineteenth Centuries* (Lewiston, 1991), 43–58; Willard, 'The Manuscript Tradition', 439.

Knowledge of Christine's work was widespread on the continent, particularly in French circles. Her writings were patronised by Charles VI, Isabeau of Bavaria, and the dukes of Orléans and Berry, and were praised by other French writers such as Eustache Deschamps and Martin Le Franc.[29] *The Treasure of the City of Ladies* was omitted from the collection of Christine's works presented to Queen Isabeau, but was owned by Isabeau's granddaughter, Jeanne of France, and by two of her successors as queen of France: Charlotte of Savoy and Anne of Brittany. Another of her granddaughters, Yolande, owned copies of at least three works by Christine, but does not seem to have possessed a copy of the *Treasure*.[30] The works owned by Yolande were listed in the late fifteenth-century inventories of the Savoy libraries, but it would seem that Christine's work was known in Savoy prior to Yolande's marriage to the future Amadeus IX of Savoy in 1452. An inventory of the library of Bonne of Savoy in 1432 included a 'romance by Crestina', and Martin Le Franc, secretary to the duke of Savoy, had praised Christine in *Le Champion des Dames*, written between 1440 and 1442. This knowledge of Christine's work may have come via Savoy's contacts with the court of Milan to which Christine had been invited by the duke, Gian Galeazzo Visconti, in 1401.[31] On the other hand, the fact that Le Franc dedicated his work to the duke of Burgundy suggests that knowledge of Christine's work in Savoy may also have been the product of Burgundian influence, perhaps through the marriage of the duke's aunt, Mary of Burgundy, to Amadeus VIII of Savoy in 1403.

The English court was aware of Christine's work as early as 1398, the year in which the earl of Salisbury took Christine's son, Jean, from Paris to England.[32] Jean remained in England until 1402, coming under the protection of Henry IV following Salisbury's execution in 1400. The king also acquired Salisbury's copies of Christine's works and liked them enough to attempt to persuade Christine to join her son in England. She refused, but continued to send copies of her work to Henry in order to remain in favour and persuade him to release

29 De Pizan, *Epistle of the Prison of Human Life*, xviii–xix.
30 Willard, 'The Manuscript Tradition', 439; Mooney, C.,'Queenship in Fifteenth-Century France' (unpublished PhD thesis, University of Ohio, 1977), 124; Mombello, G., 'Christine de Pizan and the House of Savoy' in E. J. Richards, (ed.), *Reinterpreting Christine de Pizan* (Athens, Georgia, 1992), 192.
31 Mombello, 'Christine de Pizan and the House of Savoy', 191; Jordan, *Renaissance Feminism*, 93 n.29; Willard, *Christine de Pizan*, 51, 165.
32 Laidlaw, J.C.,'Christine de Pizan, The Earl of Salisbury and Henry IV', *French Studies*, 36 (1982), 130–43, and Campbell, P.G.C., 'Christine de Pisan en Angleterre', *Revue de Littérature Comparée*, 5 (1925), 659–70.

Jean. Christine had not yet begun writing her more political works at this time, but her early popularity continued and ensured her an English audience for these later and weightier works. Her work grew in popularity later in the century, and survives in seventeen French and English manuscripts now held by the British Library and the Bodleian, including three copies of *The Book of the City of Ladies*, two of *The Treasure of the City of Ladies*, two of the *Book of the Body Politic* and one of the 1405 letter to Queen Isabeau. The copy of the letter to the queen survives in a letter book that was owned by John Stevenes, one of Henry V's chaplains in France in 1415 and later a Canterbury official. The most famous manuscript of Christine's work appeared in England in the middle of the fifteenth century following the 1425 purchase by the duke of Bedford of her collected works presented to Queen Isabeau.[33]

In contrast to French and English reception, there is no surviving evidence of familiarity with Christine's work in fifteenth-century Scotland. Very few manuscripts of any kind from fifteenth-century Scotland survive, but the Scottish court was familiar with the work of writers such as Chaucer, Gower, Hoccleve and Lydgate.[34] The works of these and continental writers may have been brought to Scotland by students and clergy returning from abroad, or by members of the royal family. However, it is likely that Joan Beaufort and James I knew of Christine's work through their contact with the English court, but they may have been unfamiliar with *The Book of the City of Ladies* or *The Treasure of the City of Ladies*. The surviving English evidence of Christine's popularity before the king and queen returned to Scotland in 1424 is confined to the period around the turn of the century, pre-dating the composition of these works. If they did not know Christine's work in Scotland, Joan Beaufort's daughters would have become aware of it in the course of their time in continental courts. Mary of Guelders was almost certainly familiar with Christine's work and views. The possible copying of *The Treasure of the City of Ladies* in Guelders in

33 Campbell, 'Christine de Pisan en Angleterre', 663–4; de Pizan, *Epistle of the Prison of Human Life*, xx; Legge, M.D., *Anglo-Norman Letters and Petitions from All Souls MS.182*, Anglo-Norman Text Society 3 (Oxford, 1941), xii–xvi, 144–50.

34 Lyall, R.J., 'Books and Book Owners in Fifteenth-Century Scotland' in J. Griffiths and D. Pearsall, (eds), *Book Production and Publishing in Britain, 1375–1475* (Cambridge, 1989), 239–41; Bawcutt, P., ' "My bright buke": Women and their Books in Medieval and Renaissance Scotland' in J. Wogan-Browne et al. (eds.), *Medieval Women: Texts and Contexts in Late Medieval Britain. Essays for Felicity Riddy* (Turnhout, 2000), 17–34.

c.1430, Mary's long residence in the household of a woman who sent a copy of the *Treasure* to her niece in Portugal, and the general Burgundian promotion of the work all indicate that Mary knew about the work even if she had not read it herself.

Women and power in medieval Scotland

Like their European contemporaries, fifteenth-century Scottish writers advocated that the power of a princess was derived from that of a prince. The role of a queen regnant was rarely mentioned or discussed. While female succession was theoretically possible in medieval Scotland, the kingdom did not experience the rule of a queen regnant until the sixteenth century. When female succession was raised as an option in 1195 and 1237, 'the Scots ruled [it] out', but it nearly became a reality in 1286.[35] The Maid of Norway technically occupied the Scottish throne between 1286 and 1290, but it is not clear whether or not her succession was representative of the acceptability of female rule to the political community of medieval Scotland.[36] The surviving evidence is not concerned with the nature of female power and the Maid's death *en route* to Scotland for her inauguration makes it impossible to ascertain if female rule would have been accepted in practice or how it might have worked. The theoretical possibility of female succession was later ruled out in the preamble to an entail passed in 1373, which specified that succession be through the male line to avoid the problems that had previously arisen. This carefully specified entail could not, however, provide for the situation that arose in 1437 when there was only one male, the young James II, left in the royal line. His heirs apparent were his sisters Margaret, until her death in 1445, and Isabella. The birth of the future James III ensured that the possibility of female succession was once again averted.[37]

Representations of female power in fifteenth-century Scottish literary and narrative sources reflected the kingdom's political experiences and expectations: queens were either consorts or dowagers. In their references to the derivative nature of female power, these sources utilised the same arguments and models as their European contemporaries.

---

35 Duncan, A.A.M. , *Scotland: The Making of the Kingdom* (Edinburgh, 1975), 611–3.
36 Reid, N., 'Margaret Maid of Norway and Scottish Queenship', *Reading Medieval Studies*, viii (1982), 75–96; Barrow, G.W.S., 'A Kingdom in Crisis: Scotland and the Maid of Norway' (120–41), Helle, K., 'Norwegian Foreign Policy and the Maid of Norway' (142–56), Prestwich, M., 'Edward I and the Maid of Norway' (157–74), all published in *SHR*, 69 (1990).
37 *APS*, i, 549; Edinburgh NAS, SP7/13; Nantes ADLA, E125/8.

Two Scottish translations of French works made by Gilbert Haye in
1456 for the earl of Orkney highlighted the reasons for the exclusion of women from authority. One of the translations, from a work
originally attributed to Aristotle, stated that women were in 'venymous
condicioun mortale, for thai begyn nocht newely to be inymyes to
mankynde', a condition which led them to bring about a prince's
downfall through poison, treason and other means. In short, men 'suld
nocht governe thame be women na trow thair counsale'.[38] The work
stressed the basic link between woman's physical and moral weakness,
and emphasised her capacity for deceit in word and deed, rendering
her incapable of government and untrustworthy in counsel. The other
translation, from a late fourteenth-century text by Bonet, argues that
even if the queen 'in [the king's] absence governand the realme', there
were limits to her power. The queen could not sit in judgement upon
a battle between two knights, for example, because women could not
judge in areas 'that pertenis to jugement of men be thair nature' such
as the masculine world of war and because 'man is of hyar nature and
condicioun' and could not therefore be judged by an inferior.[39] These
problems could be overcome, however, for while women knew little
of war, a queen was always surrounded by 'lordis, barouns, knychtis
and squiaris' who could 'geve hir honourable counsale in sik materis'.
The queen's role was therefore ambiguous: she was expected to act as
her husband's deputy but could never overcome her gender in order
to acquire complete authority. Unlike the king's authority, the queen's
power as deputy or in certain fields would always be questioned. The
debated nature of the queen's status is underlined in the 'Auchinleck
Chronicle' by the criticism of an unspecified queen mother during
the minority of her son. The chronicle states that the king was left 'in
keping with his modere the queen and governing of all the kinrik', a
contentious decision that saw the lords pronounce 'that thai war littill
gud worth bath spirituale and temporall That gaf the keping of the
kinrik till a woman'.[40] Both the 'Auchinleck Chronicle' and Haye's
translation of Bonet imply that a queen was an acceptable regent or
deputy for the king only if she acted as a figurehead and delegated her
power to her male counsellors.

   The inferior nature of female power was also implicit in Bower's

---

38 *Gilbert of the Haye's prose manuscript*, ed. J. H.Stevenson (Scottish Text Society,
   1901–14), i, pp.vii, xxxvi, 2; ii, 108–9.
39 *Gilbert of the Haye*, i, 251–2.
40 'Auch. Chron.', 170.

Scotichronicon. Bower represented Scota, the legendary mother of the Scots, as an apolitical figure. Scota married Gaythelos and bore his children, followed her husband in the search for a new homeland, gave her name to the people of the Scots and became their first queen. She was an important, but in some ways passive, figure in comparison with her husband, the first king of the Scots. Gaythelos led his people through many lands, fought for them and protected them, provided them with laws and with their mission to live in perpetual freedom. Paternal figures thus embraced authority and leadership, while maternal ones emphasised an emotional influence and preeminence. The qualitative aspect of the queen's power was underlined by the use of the word 'queen' to express superiority. Bower described sacred history, for example, as the 'queen and mistress' of all histories and Jerusalem as 'the queen of cities'.[41] These descriptions did not imply relationships of power and authority – Jerusalem was the greatest of cities rather than the ruler of all cities – and the title of queen similarly did not confer authority upon its holder.

The power of the queen, as consort or dowager, was clearly inferior to, derived from, and to be channelled through, the authority of her husband or son. This association of the queen's power with her influence over the king carried with it the unacceptable prospect of her misuse of this influence. It was for this reason that late medieval writers emphasised the acceptable uses and limits of the queen's power as well as its subordinate status. Bower's glowing eulogy for Queen Annabella conforms to the ideal of the late medieval queen. With the assistance of the bishop of St Andrews, Bower's Annabella maintained harmony amongst the nobility, hosted visiting dignitaries, and symbolised the honour and dignity of the Scottish court.[42] She was a hostess, peacemaker and moral guide, roles arising from her status as wife and mother, rather than a political actor. Bower's censure of the actions of one of Annabella's predecessors effectively highlights the unacceptable uses of a consort's power. Margaret Drummond used her status as wife to persuade David II to arrest his heir before disrupting the kingdom by travelling to Avignon to appeal against her divorce. Bower speculated that the king had married Margaret 'not so much for the excellence of her character as a woman as for the pleasure he took in her desirable appearance'. Her beauty prevented the king from acting rationally either in his selection of a bride or in the treatment of his heir.

41 *Scotichronicon*, i, 207, v, 105.
42 *Scotichronicon*, viii, 37.

With the divorce and the removal of Margaret's negative influence, the king released his prisoners.[43] Margaret, in contrast to Annabella, caused dissent amongst the nobility, 'disturbed the whole kingdom by her legal action', and was not noted for the 'excellence of her character as a woman'. A good consort, according to Bower, was by definition a good woman. She did not attempt to direct or disrupt public life but enhanced it with her virtue.

The epitome of queenly virtue in medieval Scotland was St Margaret. By the fifteenth century, her cult had developed to such an extent that she was represented in chronicles as Malcolm's partner rather than his subordinate and, on some occasions, assumed greater importance than the king. Wyntoun referred to the greatness of the line descended from 'Malcolm oure kynge and Sancte Mergret', but also wrote about the time of 'Malcom the spousse of Sancte Mergret'.[44] Bower made reference to 'King Malcolm the husband of Saint Margaret' and the 'husband of blessed Queen Margaret'. He described David as 'son of St Margaret the queen' but at other times stressed the co-founding by divine will of the dynasty by Malcolm and Margaret.[45] Bower's ambivalence about Margaret's role and importance is further revealed in two of his allegories about the saint. The first describes a miracle which occurred during the translation of the body of St Margaret in 1250. The bishops and abbots carried the remains 'as far as the chancel door just opposite the body of Margaret's husband, King Malcolm ... when all at once the arms of the bearers became paralyzed, and because of the great weight they were no longer able to move the shrine which held the remains'. More helpers came to share the load,

> but failed all the more feebly the more they tried to lift it. At last, as they were all marvelling one to another, and saying that they were not worthy to touch such a precious relic, they heard a voice coming from one of the bystanders, but as is believed divinely inspired, which loudly proclaimed that it was perhaps not God's will that the bones of the holy queen be translated before her husband's tomb had been opened, and his body raised and honoured in the same way.

When the king and his companions raised Malcolm's bones, the remains of the queen were raised easily and both coffins were carried together to the new tomb and reburied. Bower commented that 'God

43 *Scotichronicon*, vii, 333–59.
44 *Chron. Wyntoun*, iv, 311, 323, 355, 307.
45 *Scotichronicon*, i, 15; iii, 53, 171; vi, 63.

in his mercy has often worked all manner of miracles through the merits of that holy queen'.[46] While the queen was holy, she was also a wife and subject to the same divinely-ordained hierarchy as other wives: her temporal form could not take precedence over that of the king, and God himself intervened to ensure that temporal order was maintained.

Bower's second story, set in 1263, gives Margaret quite a different status. The chronicler records that a knight dreamed of a beautiful royal lady coming out of the church at Dunfermline, the burial place of Malcolm and Margaret. The lady was 'resplendent in full royal attire' and 'was leading on her right arm a distinguished-looking knight, clad in gleaming armour, girded with the sword of a knight, and wearing a helmet with a crown on it. Three noble knights, brisk and cheerful in appearance, followed them at a stately pace and in due order, all gleaming in similar armour.' The lady spoke to the dreaming knight:

> I am Margaret, formerly queen of Scots. The knight who has my arm is the lord king Malcolm my husband, and these knights who are following us are our sons, the most renowned kings of this realm while they lived. In company with them I am hurrying to defend our country at Largs, and to win a victory over the usurper who is unjustly trying to make my kingdom subject to his rule. For you must know that I received this kingdom from God, granted in trust to me and our heirs forever.

After the dream, the knight went to Dunfermline to pray at the saint's relics and was miraculously cured just before a messenger arrived to announce that victory had been won at Largs.[47] The queen's declaration that God had granted the kingdom to her is remarkable. Even if Margaret's speech is the result of a copying error – another manuscript uses the first person plural rather than singular – it is still significant that it was she who led the group and who spoke for it.[48] The queen is also 'resplendent in full royal attire', while the status of her husband and sons is only indicated by the addition of a crown to their helmets. Here Margaret takes precedence over the four kings in a physical sense: by her dress, by appearing first, by leading the kings forward, by

46 *Scotichronicon*, v, 297–9.
47 *Scotichronicon*, v, 336–41.
48 In the Coupar Angus MS Margaret announces 'Nam nobis ut scias hoc regnum a Deo accipimus commendatum et heredibus nostris imperpetuum' (*Scotichronicon*, v, 337–8).

introducing and claiming them as her husband and their sons, and by speaking for them. The different representation of the queen in these two stories – in the first the king takes precedence over Margaret and in the second Margaret is dominant – is not as problematic as it at first appears. Margaret was represented as a partner to the king and in some areas his superior, but in both cases the basis of her relationship to him was her lineage, motherhood and sanctity; she did not compete with the king in the political arena in which he was supreme. The silence and attire of the kings in the knight's dream before the battle of Largs is understandable because they were kings; their authority was automatic and needed nothing more than a crown. The queen, on the other hand, represented God's will that the Scots would win at Largs. She proclaimed their victory but her husband and sons would effect it. The Scots would fight for her and she would protect them.

Margaret's role in this story was easily understood by Bower's audience because the limits of her power were clearly represented elsewhere. Wyntoun's brief portrayal of Margaret listed her children, described her burial and the translation of her body at Dunfermline, and her special role in uniting Scottish and Saxon blood.[49] Bower and Fordun outlined the genealogies of both Malcolm and Margaret, wrote about their marriage and children, and described the queen's death and burial.[50] Bower's version of Margaret's life, based on those of Turgot and Fordun, describes her as a 'servant' and 'very sweet mother', devout in her prayers and attendance at mass, who fed the poor and acted as a foster mother to nine orphaned babies.[51] In this account, Margaret's behaviour was the model of medieval queenship and brought honour to her husband the king. Malcolm learned from Margaret's saintly behaviour and began to pray more devoutly, to perform good works, and to appreciate books, even though he was himself illiterate. Bower, following Fordun, wrote that the king and queen 'were both equal in charity', and that the king listened to Margaret's counsel, but also specified that after performing good works, 'the king would devote careful attention to temporal matters and the business of his kingdom, while the queen would go into the church'. The queen was thus remembered and honoured for her sanctity but because her influ-

49 *Chron. Wyntoun*, iv, 323, 345–55.
50 J. Fordun, *Chronica Gentis Scotorum*, ed. W.F. Skene (Edinburgh, 1871–2), i, 251–3; *Scotichronicon*, iii, 171–7.
51 *Scotichronicon*, iii, 53–5, 71–3, 77–9; v, 297–9. See also *Chronica Gentis Scotorum*, i, 216–7.

ence and deeds were largely confined to the spiritual sphere she did not threaten the king's temporal superiority. The queen's excellence as pious mother and her lack of involvement in the political arena complemented rather than threatened the king's majesty. Indeed, her sanctity and learning provided the king with a means of improving his own spiritual life, making him an even greater king than he had been before his marriage. While both Bower and Fordun relied on Turgot's biography of Margaret for their information, they did make alterations to his account. Most significantly, they omitted Turgot's description of Margaret's temporal role, such as his statement that 'All things which became the rule of a prudent Queen were done by her; by her advice the laws of the kingdom were administered; by her zeal the true religion was spread and the people rejoiced in the prosperity of their affairs'.[52] While Turgot admired the queen's devotion 'amid the distraction of law-suits, and the countless affairs of the Kingdom', Fordun and Bower recorded that the king attended to the kingdom's business and the queen retired to church after they had jointly performed good works.[53] Turgot's Margaret appointed the king's servants and played a dominant role in Church councils at which Malcolm, 'fully prepared to say and do whatever she in this matter might direct', was merely an 'assessor' and interpreter. Fordun and Bower ignored this aspect of Turgot's biography altogether.[54]

In addition to downplaying the queen's role in political and church affairs, Fordun emphasised the king's sanctity and noted his involvement in the acts of charity which Turgot had ascribed to the queen alone. Turgot, for example, described the queen washing the feet of the poor, but Fordun's account of the act describes the king joining the queen in her good work when he was not engaged in managing the kingdom. Bower used Fordun's rather than Turgot's account in this case, and also repeated Fordun's statement, not found in Turgot, that the king and queen were equals in charity.[55] The changes made by Fordun and Bower to Turgot's portrayal of Margaret were designed to exclude any reference to her temporal activities and to promote the king as her spiritual equal. This representation of Margaret, like

52 Turgot, 'The Life of S. Margaret, Queen of Scotland' in W. M. Metcalfe (ed.), *Ancient Lives of Scottish Saints* (Paisley, 1895), 301.

53 Turgot, 'Life of Margaret', 304, 314; *Chronica Gentis Scotorum*, i, 217; *Scotichronicon*, iii, 73, 217–8.

54 Turgot, 'Life of Margaret', 305, 307.

55 *Scotichronicon*, iii, pp.xix, 73, 217–8; *Chronica Gentis Scotorum*, i, 216–7; Turgot, 'Life of Margaret', 314.

Wyntoun's, effectively limited her roles to those of mother of a dynasty and protectress of the kingdom, roles of great symbolic importance and worthy of veneration, but of little or no authority.

Margaret's potential power as wife and mother should not be under-estimated. A manuscript of the *Scotichronicon* dating from the reign of James II includes a diagram tracing his connections to St Margaret through both his father and mother.[56] James I is described in the genealogy as the son of Robert III and descended from Margaret, while Joan Beaufort is described as wife of James and also descendant of the saint. Margaret is positioned at the apex of the table and is described as 'S. margarita Scotorum regina et sponsa Regis malcolum kennemor', a placement and description emphasising her status as mother of the dynasty. In effect this placement suggests that she is not only the mother but the sole origin of the dynasty; her husband, King Malcolm, does not occupy a place in the table and is mentioned only in relation to his queen. His role as fatherly king of the Scots is subordinated to his wife's role as mother and queen. Another manuscript, copied during the reign of James III, contains four texts relating to Margaret, including a copy of Turgot's biography, notes for a continuation of that work and a collection of forty-two miracles attributed to the saint.[57] The fourth text is a history of Margaret's predecessors and successors down to James III, again drawing an explicit and conscious connection between the saint and the Stewart dynasty.

These historical works enhanced the prestige of the Stewart dynasty and while there is no evidence that the works were sponsored by the Stewarts directly, it is clear that they and their royal predecessors were aware of the potential value of such connections. The name 'Margaret' was not used until the second generation of the MacMalcolm dynasty: Earl Henry named his second daughter Margaret, and two of the earl's sons, William the Lion and Earl David, named their eldest daughters Margaret. The increasing use of the name coincided with the devel-opment of a campaign for Margaret's canonisation, which was finally achieved in 1250. Alexander II named his illegitimate daughter Marjorie, but his successor Alexander III named his daughter Margaret and she, in turn, gave the name to her daughter, Margaret, Maid of Norway. All of the five kings between 1292 and 1488 who had daughters named one of them Margaret: the eldest daughter in the cases of Robert II, Robert III and James I and the second in the cases of Robert I and

56 London BL, Royal MS. 13.E.x., f.26v.
57 *Scotichronicon*, iii, pp.xvii–xviii.

James II. The appearance of the name in every royal generation of women indicates that it was not simply a more popular name than its nearest rivals: Marjorie, Isabella and Mary. The consistent use of the name linked each female generation with its saintly predecessor and acted as a reminder to successive royal women of the role Margaret played as a woman of power.

It is difficult to ascertain how individual queens responded to the cult of Margaret. The only surviving evidence of such a response is Mary of Guelders' request for the saint's shirt to be sent to her for the impending birth of the princess Mary in July 1451. Mary's request may have been the result of increasing anxiety as her labour approached, particularly following the birth of a premature child in May 1450 who only lived a few hours.[58] It is noteworthy that this sole example of a fifteenth-century Scottish queen's appeal to Margaret emphasises the famous queen's status as mother and saint rather than as queen. Margaret as protector, intercessor, perfect mother and mother of kings was called upon to protect the royal mother as well as the hoped-for son. On this occasion the Scottish saint may also have been associated with another, Margaret of Antioch, the traditional protector of women in childbirth. Before her death 'she asked in especial that whenever a woman in labour should call upon her name, the child might be brought forth without harm'.[59] There is no surviving evidence that Margaret was remembered for her abilities as queen only.

Turgot's praise for Margaret was to be expected: he was her confessor and dedicated his biography to Margaret's daughter, 'the honourable and excellent Matilda, Queen of the English'.[60] Matilda was a pious and active queen, and her daughter, the Empress Matilda, was the sole surviving heir of Henry I. For the two Matildas, Margaret's biography was a model for ruling queens as well as a dynastic work designed to promote their lineage and secure the succession. Bower and Fordun, however, focused on the importance of the royal lineage and dynasty at the expense of Margaret's queenship. While Margaret's involvement in government was quite acceptable at the end of the eleventh century, such involvement was regarded as inappropriate in the later period. This change in attitude towards female roles was consistent with European trends. The power of the queen in Capetian France was at its greatest

58 *ER*, v, 447, 512; 'Auch. Chron.', 172.
59 *The Golden Legend of Jacobus de Voragine*, ed. and trans. G. Ryan and H. Ripperger, Reprint Edition (Salem, 1987), 354.
60 Turgot, 'Life of Margaret', 297.

in the early twelfth century while only a century later the queen had virtually 'vanished from the political arena'.[61] Similarly, the English queen's participation in government declined in the twelfth century but her importance to the developing rituals celebrating monarchy increased from the thirteenth century onwards.[62] This change in the queen's public role was caused by the expansion of royal bureaucracy and government in the twelfth century and the development of increasingly separate households for the king and queen. In the smaller courts of previous centuries, the queen was present and involved in royal decisions and acts, but the growth of more specialised courts removed her from the political centre. As her involvement in government decreased over time, so too did the expectation that the queen ought to play a role in the political arena. The growth of royal government and the increasing importance of education which affected the public lives of queens also restricted the opportunities available to noblewomen in general, the impacts of which were compounded by a decline in their economic power following changes in patterns of inheritance, dowry and dower.[63] The effects of these changes were balanced by the development of the queen's own household, which provided her with the opportunity to exercise power through influence and patronage. The substantial growth and diversification of the French queen's household throughout the fifteenth century indicates that individual queens made full use of their new opportunities.[64] In addition, the changes in familial economic behaviour were also indicative of the increasing importance of marriage and family to royalty and the nobility. It was as a wife and mother that the late medieval queen acquired prestige and exerted influence.[65] The queen's power did not necessarily diminish over time, but it did need to be exercised differently.

61 Facinger, M., 'A Study of Medieval Queenship: Capetian France, 987–1237', *Studies in Medieval and Renaissance History*, 5 (1968), 4.

62 Parsons, J.C., 'The Queen's Intercession in Thirteenth-Century England' in J. Carpenter and S. B. MacLean (eds), *Power of the Weak. Studies on Medieval Women* (Urbana, 1995), 149–150.

63 Facinger, 'A Study of Medieval Queenship', 4, 27–40; Parsons, J.C., 'Introduction: Family, Sex, and Power: The Rhythms of Medieval Queenship' in Parsons, *Medieval Queenship*, 2–3; McNamara, J. and Wemple, S.F., 'Sanctity and Power: the Dual Pursuit of Medieval Women' in Morewedge, *The Role of Woman in the Middle Ages*, 112–4; McNamara, J. and Wemple, S., 'The Power of Women Through the Family in Medieval Europe, 500–1100' in Erler and Kowaleski, *Women and Power*, 83–101.

64 Mooney, 'Queenship in Fifteenth-Century France', 261–3, 330–5.

65 McCracken, P., *The Romance of Adultery: Queenship and Sexual Transgression in Old French Literature* (Philadelphia, 1998), 6–9.

Fifteenth-century ideas about female power asserted that women could not possess authority but tended to be less precise about what they could do. The range of acceptable duties for a princess was not prescribed, suggesting that the duties were irrelevant as long as they were not undertaken independently. As a result, an able princess under favourable circumstances could do virtually anything, including the specifically masculine task of leading an army, as long as she did so in the name of her husband or son. Medieval writers often overlooked or downplayed the broad nature of the queen's role, however, and suggested that her power and its attendant responsibilities could only be channelled through the female roles of wife, mother and intercessor. In doing so, they highlighted the limits of the queen's power rather than its potential. Fordun and Bower recognised Margaret's greatness but adapted Turgot's account of her life to make that greatness conform to contemporary ideas about the queen's role; she became a perfect wife, mother and protectress rather than a powerful queen in her own right.

TWO

Scotland, England and France, c. 1423–36

'. . . blisse with hir that is my souirane'

Joan Beaufort and Mary of Guelders became queens by right of their marriages to kings. Their marriages, like those of their peers, were arranged in accordance with long-term national and dynastic policies and specific short-term goals.[1] In the cases of Joan and Mary, their marriages supported Scotland's relationships with England and Burgundy respectively, and illustrate the importance of marriage as an instrument of medieval foreign policy. An international marriage could support treaties of political and economic alliance and was recognised as a means of achieving peace between warring kingdoms. Henry VI's instructions to his ambassadors at Arras in 1435 stated that 'marriage is alweyes oon the principal thinges that nurisshethe and holdethe togideres rest and pees betwix princes, poeples and cuntrees that han stonde in longe difference...[2] Although foreign marriage alliances could not guarantee peace and friendship between kingdoms, they did create long-standing communication networks across borders. These networks were based on family relationships and continued to operate regardless of the success or otherwise of the political alliance they represented. The network established by the marital alliances of the Stewart family between 1424 and 1449 provides a striking example of the workings of the European marriage market and the potential of marriage as a political tool.

James I's marriage to Joan Beaufort in 1424 was the first European marriage contracted by Scottish royalty since that of David II and Joan Plantagenet in 1328. James had been captured at sea by English pirates in 1406 and remained a prisoner of the English king for 18 years. His

1 Crawford, A., 'The King's Burden? – the Consequences of Royal Marriage in Fifteenth-century England' in R. A. Griffiths (ed.), *Patronage. The Crown and The Provinces in later medieval England* (Stroud, 1981), 33–56.

2 Stevenson, J. (ed.), *Letters and Papers Illustrative of the Wars of the English in France during the Reign of Henry the Sixth* (London, 1861–4), ii, 433.

marriage to an English noblewoman was arranged to 'help to lous him furth' from his English captivity and was a key element in general plans for an Anglo-Scottish truce.[3] But James' marriage may also have been a love match. In *The Kingis Quair*, attributed to James I, a prisoner in a tower falls in love with a beautiful woman he sees in a garden. Fortune finally rewards the prisoner with his freedom and the woman, and he lives afterwards in 'blisse with hir that is my souirane.'[4] An English embassy acknowledged in 1423 that the Scottish king had come to know many noblewomen, including some of royal blood, and suggested that James, rather than the Scottish ambassadors, should discuss any proposed marriage alliance.[5] During his captivity in England, James had mixed with the royal family and nobility on occasions such as the coronation of Queen Katherine, the funeral of Henry V, and the Christmas festivities of 1423, which he spent at Hertford with Henry VI and Queen Katherine.[6] Joan Beaufort, related to the English king, was one of the many noblewomen known to James. It is probable, for example, that Joan was present at Queen Katherine's coronation in 1421; several members of her family were present at the feast and one source records the presence of 'My lady Ione Somersett', who may be Joan, daughter of the earl of Somerset.[7]

Despite its possible romance, the marriage of James and Joan Beaufort was fundamentally a political alliance. Joan's father, John Beaufort, earl of Somerset, was the illegitimate son of John of Gaunt and Katherine Swynford, and therefore half-brother to Henry IV. The pope declared John Beaufort and his siblings legitimate in 1396, and the king and parliament recognised their legitimacy in February 1397, allowing them to hold office and property but excluding them from any right of succession to the English throne. The Beauforts pursued an aggressive marital policy and, by 1424, had created links with several families of the upper nobility, including the Nevilles, Percys, Staffords, Yorks and Despensers.[8] The marriage of a Beaufort daughter to the Scottish king

3 'Auch. Chron.', 162.
4 *The Kingis Quair of James Stewart*, ed. M. P. McDiarmid, (London, 1973), stanzas 40, 179, 181.
5 *Foedera*, x, 295.
6 *The Brut or the Chronicles of England*, ed. F. W. D. Brie (EETS, 1906–8), 445, 493; *Chronicles of London*, ed. C. L. Kingsford (Oxford, 1905), 281.
7 *Queene Elizabethes Academy, A Booke of Precedence, The Ordering of a Funerall, etc.*, ed. F. J. Furnivall (EETS, extra series, 1869), 89.
8 Jones, M.K. and Underwood, M.G., *The King's Mother. Lady Margaret Beaufort, Countess of Richmond and Derby* (Cambridge, 1992), 20, 24; Harriss, G.L., *Cardinal Beaufort* (Oxford, 1988), 130.

was an added social coup for the family. The advantages of the marriage to the Beauforts and their possible engineering of the match did not go unnoticed by contemporaries. In 1440, Humphrey, duke of Gloucester, accused Joan's uncle, Henry Beaufort, of releasing James I 'to wedde his nece to the saide kyng' and of trying to defraud Henry VI financially. The accusations were not without foundation: the treaty of York, which settled James' marriage and liberation, allowed for the remission of 10,000 marks of his ransom at the instigation of another uncle, Thomas Beaufort, duke of Exeter.[9] These family connections were, however, of some value to the English government. Henry Beaufort played a significant role in the council ruling on behalf of the infant king Henry VI, and the council hoped that his relationship with the new Scottish queen could be used to represent English views north of the border. The royal wedding, which was celebrated in February 1424 by Henry Beaufort in his church of St. Mary Overy, highlighted the relationship between Joan and her uncle, then bishop of Winchester. In addition, the wedding feast 'was holden in the Bisshoppis Inne of Wynchestre.'[10]

The marriage of James I and Joan Beaufort was also part of a diplomatic arrangement between England and Scotland, and the marriage negotiations were expressed in those terms. James' release had been discussed at various times since 1406, culminating in Henry V's promise in May 1421 that he would be released within three months of the two kings' return from France.[11] The fourth earl of Douglas developed a scheme for James' temporary release in 1421, which proposed that the king return to negotiate an end to Scotland's support of France in exchange for Douglas' service for Henry V in France.[12] This plan, like others, came to nothing. James was a diplomatic asset in negotiations with Scotland, and an asset the English government did not intend to surrender easily. While he remained in England he could develop favourable attitudes towards the southern kingdom and its king which would be of benefit after his release. James was also useful in more direct ways. Henry V took him to France, for example, in an attempt

9 Stevenson, *Letters and Papers*, ii, 444; *Foedera*, x, 300; Balfour-Melville, E.W.M., 'James I at Windsor', *SHR* xxv (1928), 227.

10 *The Brut*, 440; *The Historical Collections of a Citizen of London in the fifteenth century*, ed. Gairdner, J. (Camden Society New Series, 1876), 157; *Chronicles of London*, 282.

11 *Foedera*, x, 125; Balfour-Melville, E.W.M., 'The Later Captivity and Release of James I', *SHR*, xxi (1924), 89–100.

12 Brown, *James I*, 23.

to dissuade Scottish soldiers from fighting for the French.[13] With James in custody and the treaty of Troyes sealed in 1420, it appeared that England had the upper hand over both its traditional enemies. Under such circumstances, England could continue to delay James' release. English fortunes changed in August 1422, following the death of Henry V and the accession of his infant son. The death of the French king Charles VI in October 1422 and succession of Charles VII, despite the fact he could not be crowned until 1430, ultimately strengthened France's position. In order to win Scotland away from her alliance with France, pacify the northern border and raise money to continue fighting the very expensive war, negotiations for James' release were intensified in 1423. The treaty of London, sealed on 4 December, required that the Scots pay a ransom of £40,000 to cover the expenses of James' captivity, a sum which was to contribute to the costs of the English war effort. In addition, twenty-one Scottish nobles were to stay in England at their own expense as security for the ransom and to secure James' good faith after his release. The arrangements were realised at Durham on 28 March 1424 when James swore to pay his ransom and delivered the Scottish hostages into English hands. On the same day, England and Scotland sealed a seven-year truce on land and sea which included a clause stating that Scotland would not aid France in her wars with England.[14]

The council's goals of securing a truce and raising revenue had apparently been met, but the plan was flawed. As a prisoner, James had to accept unfavourable terms; as a free man, he could not be forced to uphold these terms. If the king chose to stop paying the ransom and to renew the French alliance there was no way to prevent him from doing so. The English council hoped to rely on James' goodwill, a goodwill that had been carefully nurtured during his long years of captivity. James' inclusion in English court life was designed to establish relationships between the Scottish king and the English royal family and nobility, perhaps through marriage, that could be of use in the future. The uncertainty of such a policy and its reliance upon individual will is illustrated by the requirement that James swear an oath to uphold the agreed terms, and by the fact that in July 1424 he

13 Griffiths, R.A., *The Reign of King Henry VI. The exercise of royal authority 1422–1461* (London, 1981), 155; *Scotichronicon*, viii, 122; *The Brut*, 563. See also Bradley, P.J., 'Henry V's Scottish policy: a study in realpolitik', *Documenting the past. Essays in medieval history presented to George Peddy Cuttino*, ed. J. S. Hamilton and P. J. Bradley, (Woodbridge/Wolfeboro, 1989), 177–195; Brown, *James I*, 21–4.
14 *Foedera*, x, 300, 303–7, 326–31, 406; *Rot. Scot.*, ii, 241–3; *PPC*, iii, 242–3, 302–4.

had still not given his oath.[15] The king's marriage to an English bride, on the other hand, created a link between the two kingdoms that would continue to exist after James' release.

The council raised the possibility of an English marriage for the Scottish king in 1423 as part of their discussions regarding a truce and James' release. Instructions issued to the English ambassadors in July suggested that in order to nourish and maintain the great friendship between the two allies, the Scottish king might wish to marry an English noblewoman. The order of the instructions – the truce was to be discussed first – and the relative brevity of the items relating to marriage are indicative of the role of the marriage alliance as a security or safeguard measure in the overall plan. Marriage was again treated as a secondary item in the treaty of York, sealed in October, but its role in generating mutual love and friendship between the allies was more strongly stated than in the July instructions. The bride was identified in the treaty only as a high-born English lady. She was named for the first time in instructions issued on 5 February 1424, which approved the remission of 10,000 marks of James' ransom as a consequence of his forthcoming marriage to Joan, daughter of the earl of Somerset.[16] James and Joan were married in the same month and set out for Scotland, stopping at Durham to seal the seven-year truce on land and sea between England and Scotland. The marriage was thus preceded and succeeded by discussions for a truce, and constituted a way in which to cement it.

The dependence of the English policy upon individual cooperation was not its only flaw. The policy makers also underestimated Scotland's desire to maintain the French alliance. Scotland had provided considerable military assistance to the French in the latter years of James' captivity, supplying more than 16,000 Scottish soldiers in the space of four years.[17] After the assassination of the duke of Burgundy in September 1419, in which the dauphin was implicated, Burgundy's heir and other French princes allied with the English forces against the dauphin. The Scots were allied only with the dauphin, not the French princes, and were regarded as particularly reliable. The immediate

15 Griffiths, *Henry VI*, 172 n.12.
16 *Foedera*, x, 295, 300, 323.
17 Chevalier, B., 'Les Ecossais dans les armées de Charles VII jusqu'à la bataille de Verneuil', *Jeanne d'Arc. Une époque, un rayonnement* (Paris, 1982), 88; Contamine, P., 'Scottish soldiers in France in the second half of the fifteenth century: mercenaries, immigrants or Frenchmen in the making?' in Simpson, G.G. (ed.), *The Scottish Soldier Abroad, 1247–1967* (Edinburgh, 1992), 26 n.3.

threat to the French of the potential withdrawal of Scottish military assistance following the Anglo-Scottish truce at Durham of March 1424 was offset by the truce negotiated by the duke of Savoy between France and Burgundy in September 1424, and the change in the Breton alliance in favour of France in March 1425. These conditions did not last long. Charles VII's continuing military problems, plus Brittany's alliance with England in September 1427, inspired him to commission an embassy on 12 April 1428 to meet with James in order to renew the Franco-Scottish alliance and discuss the possibility of a marriage between the two kingdoms.[18]

The suggested marriage alliance with France was recognised as 'a most honourable proposal for Scotland' as it would marry a Scottish princess to 'no nondescript fellow, but the eldest child of the Most Christian king'. According to Bower, the inclusion of the archbishop of Rheims in the French embassy indicated the importance of the marriage and helped to win James' favour.[19] The presence in the same embassy of John Stewart of Darnley, constable of France, reveals that the ambassadors had martial as well as marital goals. Another ambassador, the poet Alain Chartier, utilised his skills to praise Scots fidelity and emphasise the military character of the Franco-Scottish alliance.[20] The 1428 mission was well-timed. Despite the various treaties and truces of 1423–4, problems had developed between England and Scotland over the payment of James' ransom and breaches of the truce. A meeting regarding breaches of the truce was held at Berwick as early as 15 August 1425, and another English embassy, which included Thomas, duke of Exeter (an uncle of the Scottish queen) was appointed to deal with the same problem in May 1426. Complaints about James' non-payment of his ransom were made throughout 1427, although receipts for 10,000 marks were ordered on 8 July 1428, suggesting that the English government still believed that a payment would be made. James' ransom was needed to maintain English military activities: to pay the wages of English soldiers in France and on the northern border, and fund the repair of Berwick Castle.[21] It was difficult to force James to pay without pushing him closer to France, and withholding the ransom was one means by which James could assert some independence with

18 Perroy, E., *The Hundred Years War* (London, 1965), 273; Edinburgh NAS, SP7/7–8.
19 *Scotichronicon*, viii, 247–9.
20 Paris BN, MS. Latin 8757, f.50v.–51r.; L. Barbé, *Margaret of Scotland and the Dauphin Louis* (London, 1917), 18.
21 *Foedera*, x, 347, 358, 406; *PPC*, iii, 242–3, 259–65, 302–4.

regard to England while implicitly supporting the French alliance. The French proposals must have seemed like an excellent opportunity to enhance his position further. In his letters to the French king, James left the way open for higher terms to be offered, and instructed his ambassadors to demand such terms, indicating that he was aware of his strong bargaining position.[22]

The French embassy carried two letters from Charles VII issued on 12 April 1428. The letters praised the faithful Scots and proposed a marriage between the houses of France and Scotland as well as an alliance intended to foster the friendship and affection between the two kingdoms. This alliance was to be the basis for James to provide an army to assist Charles against the English.[23] James accepted the offers in four letters dated 17 July. The first letter accepted the proposal on behalf of his eldest daughter, Margaret, and authorised three ambassadors to go to France to negotiate the terms of the marriage. The second authorised them to negotiate regarding the army to be sent to France with Margaret. The third letter promised to renew the Franco-Scottish alliance, while the fourth stated that the king, his queen, and the General Council would observe the terms agreed upon by the ambassadors. A further letter dated 19 July 1428 stated that Margaret and 6000 soldiers were to be sent to France before 2 February 1430.[24] The importance of a marriage alliance between the two families is indicated in the additions made by Charles to James' terms on 30 October at Chinon. If Louis died before consummating the marriage, Charles' second son would marry Margaret in his brother's stead, and if he too died before consummation, the third son. Similarly, if Margaret died before consummation, one of her sisters was to take her place, as long as the age difference between husband and wife did not exceed seven years. In November, Charles offered further incentives to the Scottish king in the form of the county of Saintonge and other territorial concessions with the promise of further and more significant grants from the lands he expected to recover with James' assistance.[25]

Margaret (represented by James' ambassador, Patrick Ogilvy, sheriff of Angus) and Louis were betrothed in December 1428.[26] The joining of hands at the betrothal symbolised the renewal of the alliance between Scotland and France, formalised in a treaty sealed by James

22 Paris AN, J678/25; *APS*, ii, 28.
23 Edinburgh NAS, SP7/7, 8.
24 Paris AN, J678/21–5. No. 25 is printed in *APS*, ii, 26–8.
25 Paris AN, J678/26–7.
26 Edinburgh NAS, SP7/9.

in Edinburgh on 4 March 1429.[27] James agreed to supply men and money to the French, to create a diversion by fighting England, and not to seek a peace with England without the consent of France. No further action was taken upon the treaty at the time. It seems that, despite renewing the French alliance in contravention of the 1424 Durham truce, James did not intend to sever his ties with England entirely. The French alliance was a useful lever in negotiations with England and the betrothal was prestigious, but neither the alliance nor the marriage could be viewed as secure while Charles VII's ability to retain the throne was in doubt, as it was in 1428.

By 1429, however, the emergence of Joan of Arc, the relief of Orléans in May and the coronation of Charles VII in July made the Scottish assistance, and therefore the alliance, temporarily unnecessary, vindicating James' policy of negotiating with both England and France simultaneously. A safe-conduct was issued on 1 December 1428 – before his daughter's betrothal and the sealing of the Franco-Scottish treaty – for James to visit England to meet with his wife's uncle, Henry Beaufort, cardinal of St Eusebius. On the following day receipts for 1500 marks from James were drawn up, suggesting that he was still promising to make his ransom payments. The strength of James' position was demonstrated when Beaufort, who required peace in the north in order to realise his crusading ambitions, arranged to travel to Scotland or the Marches rather than have James travel to England as originally planned.[28] Cardinal Beaufort was issued with instructions on 10 February 1429 to meet 'personelment' with the Scottish king to discuss matters relating to the Church and the English king's realms of England and France. On 15 February, five English ambassadors were commissioned to meet with James to discuss payment of his ransom, hostages and a continuation of the truce. The meeting between James and his wife's uncle reminded James of his personal links with England, and renewed those links to pave the way for more general talks.[29] It is likely that the Cardinal raised some of the issues of the later embassy in an informal way with James and capitalised on the family connections more directly. Not content with relying upon the personal touch, the English Privy Council acted to prevent the Franco–Scottish marriage from taking place, and on 17 April 1429 ordered a fleet to be fitted out to capture Margaret and the army of 6000.[30]

27 Paris AN, J680/69.
28 *Foedera*, x, 408–9, 419–23.
29 *PPC*, iii, 318–9; *Foedera*, x, 410; *ER*, iv, 466.
30 *PPC*, iii, 324.

Scottish and English commissioners met in July 1429 to discuss
breaches of the truce on the Marches, and additional commissioners
were appointed in October for further talks.[31] A meeting between
Scottish and English commissioners was arranged for the winter of
1429–30. On 16 February 1430, instructions were issued to English
ambassadors to address non-payment of the ransom, matters relating
to hostages, a truce and a marriage between Henry VI and a daughter
of James I.[32] Peace was to be negotiated first 'for it ne were in any wise
covenable the K[ing] to stande in mortal ennemytee and werre with
him whos doughter he had receyved and taken to wyf and maad him
as by that meene his fader'. The government was in no doubt that a
marriage represented, rather than created, a peace. The instructions
also stated that although James' daughter would be a worthy bride and
English kings had allied with Scottish kings through marriage previously, it would not have been 'accordyng to the seuretee of the K[ing's]
persone' to marry a woman whose father was his 'mortel adversarie and
ennemye'. The emphasis here was on the need for peace, and the possibility of a marriage was politely postponed. The instructions noted
that the king's marriage was 'the grettest mariage that can be thought
this day of any Prince', and that such an alliance was sought by many;
without a clearer idea of what the Scottish king could offer, the ambassadors could not discuss the matter further. Like Scotland, England was
searching for the most advantageous and prestigious match. If James'
eldest daughter had already been promised to the heir to the French
throne, the English king could not have accepted a younger daughter
unless the terms were very favourable indeed.

The instructions stated that the issue of marriage was 'originelly
moeved by the said K[ing] of Scottis' and that the 'matier of pees hath
dyvers tymes be moeved to the Kingis counsail by Maister Th Roulle
on the K[ing] of Scottis behalf'. James' efforts to maintain positive
relationships with both England and France at the same time enabled
him to negotiate better terms with each party. The king's policy was
also indicative of the need to keep his options open in view of the
French successes and the Franco-Burgundian truce of August 1429,
and the consequent diminishing need for Scottish help. James sought
to achieve his objectives through the marriages of his daughters and
to establish family connections with powers of great significance to

31 *PPC*, iii, 324; *Foedera*, x, 417, 428–31, 435.
32 *PPC*, iv, 19–27; Balfour-Melville, E.W.M., *James I, King of Scots: 1406-1437*
     (London, 1936), 182–3.

Scotland. The instructions also contain a statement, subsequently crossed through, that 'this matier of pees was mooved by the K[ing] of Scottis' during his communications with 'the Cardinal'. It appears that James' plans had previously been discussed with his wife's uncle, Henry Beaufort, cardinal of St. Eusebius. The policy of marrying James to an English noblewoman to establish goodwill and communication between Scotland and England, and of capitalising upon family connections to maintain that communication, was working.

The emphasis on peace in the English instructions stemmed partly from the fact that the seven-year truce agreed at Durham in 1424 was due to expire on 1 May 1431. England wanted the truce to continue, especially in light of recent French successes. The council's instructions to Lord Scrope – the ambassador to Scotland – stated that monthly truces should be sought in the Marches rather than allow the English king to 'stande in werre with the reaume of Scotland him being in his seid werres in France'.[33] Negotiations for a more general peace were not proceeding well, as James refused to discuss a truce by land and sea, or to prevent Scots fighting for the French. Despite their fear of a war in the north, the English felt that war between England and Scotland would be preferable to a truce 'suffring the king of Scottes at his fredam to sende poeple unto the Reaume of France in help of the kinges adversaire'. Although the council thought that France was a greater threat than Scotland, it did not underestimate the Scottish king. It recognised that James was a powerful man in his own kingdom, as an ally of the French, and as a potential English enemy. The council stated that 'the King of Scottis is now at hoom in his land a fel a fer seyng man', who 'conceyveth nought nor holdeth that he is or was bounden by eny writing contened in hem to abstene him fro sendyng of his poeple into the reaume of Fraunce ...' The council's instructions indicate that a marriage alliance with Scotland was a secondary aim of English diplomacy. The primary objective was to secure peace with Scotland and neutralise the Franco–Scottish alliance. This objective was achieved to some extent when James sealed a five-year truce on 15 December 1430 and took no immediate action on the treaties of 1428.[34]

Diplomatic activities resumed in 1433 following breaches of the Anglo–Scottish truce. Edmund Beaufort, count of Mortain and

33 *PPC*, iv, 73–5; Macrae, C.T., 'The English Council and Scotland in 1430', *EHR*, 54 (1939), 422–3.
34 *Foedera*, x, 482.

brother of the Scottish queen, was despatched to Scotland in August
1433. As was the case following Cardinal Beaufort's talks with James
I in February 1429, this initial approach by a family member was
followed by discussion of a possible marriage between Henry VI and
one of James' daughters. The instructions to the English ambassador,
Dr Stephen Wilton, of February 1434 stated that the possibility of
securing 'pees namely by the mene of mariage … hath ofte be greetly
comuned'. The instructions also announced the convening of a great
council to discuss the matter, and requested that James set a date for
the meeting of commissioners to discuss the truce. The order of the
items indicates that the council was convened to encourage James to
renew peace discussions rather than solely to discuss marriage. The
issue of further instructions to English commissioners on the same
day – to discuss breaches of the Durham truce and the financial losses
incurred as a result of the disruptions – also demonstrates that the
truce was the primary concern of the English government.[35]

The Anglo–Scottish discussions of 1434 were largely inconclu-
sive, but encouraged Charles VII to commission another embassy in
September to sail to Scotland and demand the implementation of the
1428 treaty. He had apparently already written to James in late 1433
to protest about the delay in sending Margaret to France. That letter
does not survive, unlike a copy of James' response, dated 8 January
1434.[36] In it, the Scottish king promised to send an army at any time,
but declared that Margaret could not be sent to France immediately
because of her young age and the perils of winter travel. James also
declared that, contrary to the rumours that Charles had heard, he had
not treated with the English to the prejudice of the French alliance
or the marriage. He explained that the English ambassadors had been
discussing the exchange of hostages, not peace or marriage, but in view
of English reports of the talks, it seems that James was dissembling in
order to placate Charles. He then accused the French king of creating
and extending the delay in negotiations. This may be partly true in
view of the lack of evidence of any French attempts to enforce the

35 *PPC*, iv, 178, 191, 193–6.
36 Paris BN, MS. Fr.17330, f.119r.–120r. The copies of the correspondence relating
    to the 1434–5 negotiations are found in a sixteenth-century copy of the account
    of the mission made by a French ambassador, Regnault Girard. The manuscript is
    60 pages long but is incomplete, and begins part of the way into James' letter. The
    letter itself has probably been translated, either by Girard or a copyist. Much of
    Girard's account has been printed by Barbé in his footnotes to *Margaret of Scotland*,
    but as he only refers to the manuscript and not the specific folio, all my references
    are to the original.

1428 treaty before 1433, but accusing Charles of causing the delay also allowed James to justify his parallel discussions with England. The rather imperious tone of the accusations and the vagueness regarding Margaret's departure, combined with James' denial of the purposes of the English talks and his role in continuing them, suggest that he was still unprepared to commit himself fully to an alliance with either France or England. This unwillingness was partly responsible for the length of the 1434–5 negotiations.

Charles delayed matters further. James' letter was written in January, but Charles waited until September 1434 to appoint ambassadors to Scotland. The second embassy was quite different from that of 1428. It consisted of Regnault Girard, lord of Bazoges, Master of the King's Household, and Hugh Kennedy, who had travelled from Scotland to France with the earl of Buchan to fight for the dauphin.[37] Charles apologised for the embassy's lack of prestige and the fact that it did not contain a prince of the blood with the explanation that he had few in his service willing to risk the journey.[38] The apology and explanation were necessary to avoid giving James the wrong impression: the personnel and behaviour of an embassy represented the honour of both its sender and receiver. The lack of prestige and the knowledge that an impressive English party had just visited the Scottish court encouraged Hugh Kennedy to provide an escort of at least 60 men gathered from his family's lands for the entry into Edinburgh on 25 January 1435.[39] An imposing entry was necessary not just to maintain the honour of the French king, but also to impress James and encourage him to accept the French proposals. Bower's emphasis on the distinction of the 1428 French embassy recognised the honour it had bestowed on Scotland. The lack of prestige of the 1434 mission, and the long delay between the two embassies, indicate that circumstances had changed in the intervening period.

In instructions to his ambassadors dated 4 October 1434, Charles blamed this delay on the expenses of resisting the English, common enemies of Scotland and France, and their allies, the Burgundians.[40]

---

37 Paris BN, MS. Fr.17330, f.121r.; Barbé, *Margaret of Scotland*, 38–9; Barbé, L.A., 'A Scots Soldier of Fortune', in Barbé, L.A., *Sidelights on the History, Industries and Social Life of Scotland* (London, 1919), 61–7.

38 Paris BN, MS. Fr.17330, ff.122r.-v.

39 Paris BN, MS. Fr.17330, ff.128r.-v; Queller, D.E., *The Office of Ambassador in the Middle Ages* (Princeton, 1967), 83, 100–1, 156, 185; Boyer, M.N., 'Status and Travel Stipends in Fourteenth Century France', *Speculum*, xxxix (1964), 45–52.

40 Paris BN, MS. Fr.17330, f.121v.-125v., 126r.-v.

He also claimed that the pressures of war meant that he was unable to provide an armed escort for Margaret's travel. While he could acquire an escort from Spain, it was probable that the English would discover the plan and attempt to capture Margaret, as they had intended to do in 1429. The ambassadors were instructed to ask James how Margaret might travel to France, presumably in the hope that he would offer to provide the necessary escort. Charles did not suggest outright that James should pay but, as the next item began 'if the king of Scots is not happy about paying for the crossing' and suggested the kings split the cost, this was clearly his intention. In view of the arrangements Charles had made with John Pymor a month previously to provide ships, the French king does not seem to have had much expectation that James would pay all of his daughter's travel costs. These arrangements also suggest that the expense of war was not the primary reason for the delay in sending the embassy. Charles had enough money to bribe members of the Burgundian council in July 1435 to win their support at the council of Arras, indicating that he could afford diplomatic expenses if the cause was sufficiently important.[41]

Moreover, it would seem likely that the pressure of war would have encouraged Charles to expedite rather than delay negotiations with Scotland in the hope of acquiring the assistance stipulated in the 1428 treaty. On the contrary, Charles explained in his letter that he no longer required the previously agreed army of 6000 men. He gave two reasons for this change – primarily that he could not afford to transport the troops and support them while in France, but also that the need for the army had diminished following French successes. Rather than have a Scottish army come to France, Charles proposed that James begin a war with the English 'on the border or elsewhere'. Such a plan would have provided military assistance for France at no cost other than the marriage of Margaret and the dauphin, and would have the added benefit of ending Anglo–Scottish discussions. As the need for military assistance had diminished, the offer of Saintonge as an incentive to James to provide such assistance became unnecessary. If James raised the issue, the French ambassadors were to explain that the county had been specifically promised in 1428 in exchange for the army of 6000, and that if Charles ever requested such an army, he would cede Saintonge to the Scottish king. The agreements of 1435–6, however, had specified an army of 2000 men, and most of these were to return to Scotland following the marriage of Margaret and the dauphin. As a

41 Vaughan, R., *Philip the Good* (London, 1970), 100.

result, Charles was not obliged to cede the county.[42]

James responded to Charles' letter in February 1435, offering to send Margaret, escorted by an army of 2000 men, by the end of May. He would pay the army until it reached France, and supply meat, fish, butter and cheese for the army and fleet, while Charles was to provide ships and bread, beverages, salt and all other victuals. The issue of whether the army of 2000 would fight in France or simply provide an escort for Margaret to France and then return was left unresolved. Before the army could be despatched, Charles was to reach a final decision as to its purpose and to determine how it would be supported should it remain in France. James added that he was prepared to pay the expenses of the army's return and ignored the issue of a possible diversion on the English border entirely.[43] In a letter dated 28 May 1435, Charles agreed to the division of expenses and stated that a fleet would leave La Rochelle before 15 July.[44] He explained that by the time Margaret and the army arrived in France, fighting would have ceased until the following summer, rendering the army unnecessary and free to return to Scotland. Charles added that the meeting to be held at Arras in July raised the possibility that military assistance would not be required at all. In 1428 Charles had proposed the marriage of his son and Margaret Stewart and offered a territorial incentive in exchange for a Scottish army. By the middle of 1435, he no longer required the army and was in a position to dictate terms on the marriage.

Charles' responses to James' demands in 1434–5 are indicative of his strong bargaining position. In February 1435, James had expressed concern that Margaret might be captured by the English and asked for the extra protection of an armed galley to accompany the fleet, to be provided partly at his expense. Charles replied that negotiations were proceeding with Spain for the provision of an armed galley and, if they were successful, the galley and ships for the transport of only 1600 men would leave La Rochelle by 15 July 1435. The French king also refused James' demands regarding where Margaret would live before her marriage and the number of Scots she could retain in her entourage following her arrival in France. In addition, Charles reminded the Scottish king in July 1435 of the recent French successes in war and his hopes for a successful conclusion to the discussions taking place at

42 Paris BN, MS. Fr.17330, ff.146v.-147r.; Barbé, L.A.,'A Scottish Claim to a French Province', in Barbé, *Sidelights on the History*, 69–75.
43 Paris BN, MS. Fr.17330, f.130r.
44 Paris BN, MS. Fr.17330, ff.133v-134r.

Arras. Charles suggested that these improvements in his position and that of his kingdom made an alliance with France more prestigious than it had been in 1428, and urged James to send his daughter to France without delay. James was not convinced. Charles' letter reached Scotland in September, but the Scottish king claimed that it was too dangerous for his daughter to sail until March. Girard records that the king was grief-stricken when she finally departed and it is possible that he was genuinely reluctant to part with his daughter.[45]

Regardless of his paternal feelings, James needed to delay in order to determine the outcome of the simultaneous Anglo–Scottish negotiations. The Anglo–Scottish truce agreed in December 1430 was due to expire on 1 May 1436. On 20 July 1435, an English embassy was commissioned to discuss issues relating to the ransom, hostages and infractions of the current truce, and to open discussions with the Scots to renew it.[46] The battle at Piperden on 10 September, and the preceding raids, threatened the success of these negotiations. The timing of the battle also affected French talks: Piperden occurred two days before the French fleet docked in Scotland carrying Hugh Kennedy with letters from Charles.[47] Rather than agreeing immediately to Charles' requests, James sent letters to Henry VI on 29 September offering to make 'redres of ony thyng yit done by onny of his ligis ageyn the trewes' and declaring his willingness to continue or renew the truce between the two kingdoms.[48] By the time this letter reached England, the talks at Arras had broken down, leaving the French and Burgundian parties reconciled to England's disadvantage. The death in September of the duke of Bedford, Henry VI's representative in France and co-ordinator of the English war effort, added to English problems.

The truce with Scotland was now even more important for England and on 8 November, Henry wrote that he wished it to continue. He asked James to appoint a time and place for further talks before 14 February. On 5 February he appointed an embassy to treat for peace with Scotland and instructed its members to consent to a five year truce if the Scots 'entende to repaire that is mys doon'. If they did not, Henry would have to 'sette hande of his proteccion tuicion & defense in the best wise he can for his subgittis ayenst such oppressours & misdoers the which it semeth in that cas desire rather werr

45 Paris BN, MS. Fr.17330, ff.131r.-139v., 140r., 143v.
46 *Foedera*, x, 482, 620–1.
47 *Scotichronicon*, viii, 292; Paris BN, MS. Fr.17330, f.135r.
48 *PPC*, iv, 309–10.

than pees'.[49] Under such circumstances, a truce for only twelve months could be offered to the Scots. The apparent English impatience seems to have been intended to force James to make a commitment to either England or France. By the time such views reached him, he had already done so. The French ambassadors in Scotland had reminded James in early February that March was fast approaching and asked him for his final decisions about Margaret's departure. Their visit coincided with that of Aeneas Sylvius, secretary to the Cardinal of Sante Croce, papal legate to France, who may have persuaded the Scottish king of papal support for the French cause.[50] James made the arrangements quickly, and the French ambassadors left Perth on 15 February 1436, thirteen months after arriving in Edinburgh. Margaret left Scotland on 27 March and arrived in France on 17 April. Charles VII confirmed the marriage contract of Margaret and Louis on 3 June 1436 and the marriage took place on 25 June.[51]

It may appear that being courted by both England and France placed James in an enviable position, but his power of decision was not as great as it may seem. A royal marriage was not something that could be negotiated by the king alone but, like other acts of government or policy, was arranged following consultation between king and council. One of the letters to Charles VII regarding Margaret's marriage declared that not only the king but the queen, the bishops, the earls of Athol, Douglas, March, Mar, Crawford, Moray and Orkney, and other members of the General Council agreed to observe the Franco–Scottish alliance. In September 1435, James informed the French ambassadors that he wished to show one of Charles' letters to the queen and council.[52] The council's involvement both monitored personal control of foreign policy and limited the king's plans. Although he managed to entertain competing offers of marriage and alliance from both England and France for eight years, James was not allowed to abandon the French alliance of 1428 for an English one. Bower records that when an English embassy suggested peace in 1433, James called a General Council at which it was suggested that he was 'not free to negotiate on the subject of peace with the king of England on account of his alliance

49 *PPC*, iv, 311–4.
50 Paris BN, MS. Fr.17330, f.141r; du Fresne de Beaucourt, G. *Histoire de Charles VII* (Paris, 1881–91), iii, 318–9; Dunlop, A.I., *The Life and Times of James Kennedy, Bishop of St. Andrews* (Edinburgh, 1950), 16; Hume Brown, P. (ed.), *Early Travellers in Scotland* (Reprint: Edinburgh, 1978), 24–9.
51 Paris BN, MS. Fr.17330, ff.141v., 143v.-144r.; Edinburgh NAS, SP7/10.
52 Paris AN, J678/24; Paris BN, MS. Fr. 17330, ff.140v.

with the king of France'.[53] The Council debated the matter and came to the conclusion that the English offer was intended to create division and should be rejected. The General Council's interest in the French alliance reflects the opportunities afforded by such an alliance, particularly the monetary and territorial rewards offered in exchange for military service.[54]

James' freedom of action was further limited by external factors. His position in choosing between England and France was a fortunate one in terms of advancing Scottish power and prestige in Europe, but it also presented a situation beyond his control. In 1428, James may have been able to 'exploit' the French need to renew the alliance but, as this need waned, so did his power to exploit it.[55] He was able to keep his options open and maintain relations with both England and France between 1424 and 1436 despite not honouring his promises to either kingdom. This was a well-handled and far-sighted policy, but its success was assisted by the fact that neither England nor France forced James to decide one way or the other. Neither kingdom could apply significant pressure on the Scottish king without one first asserting superiority over the other. When external circumstances changed, James could equivocate no longer. While he was trying to maximise the advantages of his position in 1435, the conference of Arras was reconciling the French factions in their battle against England, rendering James' previous policy unworkable.

Not only did Arras and papal support make the French offer more attractive, they also created a situation in which France could have become so powerful that she was no longer interested in courting Scotland. In 1436 it was Charles who dictated terms, who refused the assistance of a Scottish army, and who concluded the Scottish alliance by means of a relatively cheap marriage, secured with prestige rather than territorial concessions. Under such circumstances, James needed to decide quickly and take the French offer with its attendant prestige and power before it disappeared, or before a similar offer was made to England, thus nullifying James' bargaining position altogether. The English decision on 20 May 1436 to send ambassadors to Charles VII to discuss a truce and a marriage between Henry VI and one of Charles' daughters illustrates that such a scenario was more than a possibility.[56]

53 *Scotichronicon*, viii, 289.
54 Contamine, 'Scottish soldiers in France', 16–30.
55 Brown, *James I*, 110; Grant, A., *Independence and Nationhood: Scotland, 1306–1469* (London, 1984), 49.
56 *Foedera*, x, 642–3.

The change in the balance of power and France's diplomatic strength made James' decision to ally with France rather than England almost inevitable. The marriage of his daughter in June and the worsening of Anglo-Scottish relations, beginning with the expiry of the truce on 1 May 1436 and culminating in the siege of Roxburgh in August, firmly committed James to France.

The renewal of the Franco–Scottish alliance only four years after sealing a seven-year Anglo–Scottish truce demonstrates that an international marriage alliance could not actually guarantee peace or prevent a war. But, in one sense, the original purpose of the marriage between James I and Joan Beaufort was fulfilled. As queen, Joan did not lose contact with her family in England. Her uncles and brother travelled to Scotland on several occasions to meet with James in advance of formal embassies, and the possibility of a second Anglo-Scottish marriage, this time between Henry VI and a Stewart princess, was often discussed. James' marriage to an English noblewoman had indeed facilitated communication across the border. His decision to renew the French alliance at the expense of his English one was not entirely unexpected and, more importantly, was made over the course of eight years during which the possibility of a closer relationship with England was never out of the question. This careful balancing of diplomatic interests ended with Margaret's French marriage and James' death. In the 1440s, Scottish marital diplomacy focused not on England and France, but on the continent generally.

THREE

The Stewart princesses and the European marriage market, 1437–48

'Pour vous javoie la mer passee'

The 1436 French alliance raised Scotland's profile in Europe – a matter of considerable significance for the marriage prospects of Margaret's five younger sisters. As sisters-in-law of the dauphin, the Stewart princesses were now more valuable on the marriage market than they had been simply as daughters of James I. Jean V, duke of Brittany, who had provided some of the ships necessary for Margaret's transport to France in 1436, was one of the first to recognise the new potential of a Scottish alliance.[1] The duke sent an embassy to Scotland in 1437 to discuss the marriage of one of his sons and a Stewart princess. His eldest son, Francis, had married Yolande of Anjou in 1431, and his middle son, Pierre, had been betrothed in September 1436, leaving the youngest, Giles, as a candidate for a Scottish match.[2] Five years before, Giles had been sent to England to be brought up 'circa personam regis' at the English court, home of his grandmother Joan of Navarre, widow of Henry IV.[3] The grant of an annuity of 250 marks to Giles in November 1433 suggests that he was intended to remain in England for more than two years, but he was granted permission at his father's request to return to his family in 1434.

The proposed marriage between Giles, sometime companion of Henry VI, and a Stewart princess, cousin of Henry and sister-in-law of the heir to the French throne, was typical of Brittany's often complex foreign policy. The duke's allegiance had changed several times in the course of the Hundred Years War. In the 1430s the duke maintained communications with England, Burgundy and France and made several

---

1 Paris BN, MS. Fr.17330, f.143r.
2 Barbé, L.A., 'A Stuart Duchess of Brittany' in Barbé, *Sidelights on the History*, 1–10; *Lettres et mandements de Jean V, duc de Bretagne*, ed. Blanchard, R., 8 vols (Nantes, 1889–95), vii, 139.
3 *PPC*, iv, 121–2, 128, 137–8, 181, 278.

attempts to negotiate peace between them. Breton embassies were sent to both Burgundy and England in 1434 to discuss a general peace and to urge Henry VI to make peace with Charles VII. The duke also offered to act as mediator between the kings of England and France in May 1437, the same year in which he suggested a marriage alliance between Brittany and Scotland. Such a marriage would have established indirect links with both France and England and had the further benefit of adding Scotland to his wide list of international allies. The duke had not confined his foreign policy to France, Burgundy and England, but maintained political and commercial alliances with Spain, in treaties of 1430 and 1435, and with Yolande, queen of Jerusalem and Sicily, through the marriage of his eldest son to her daughter, Yolande of Anjou, in 1431.[4]

The 1437 proposals were unsuccessful. International marriage alliances were probably not high on the Scottish political agenda following the murder of James I on 21 February 1437. It is also possible that following the marriage of Margaret and the dauphin, the Scots were hoping for a better match for a Stewart princess than the youngest son of the duke of Brittany. Brittany approached Scotland again following the death in 1440 of Francis' wife, Yolande of Anjou. On 12 April 1441, the duke issued a letter nominating ambassadors to treat for a marriage between his eldest son and a sister of James II. He issued another letter on the same day repeating his promise made a month earlier to assist in concluding a peace between England and France.[5] Brittany, and the dukes of Orléans and Burgundy, had been asked by Charles VII to mediate between the two kingdoms. Brittany was a logical choice, given his frequent communication with the English government – in particular with the duke of York throughout 1441 – but it is unclear whether or not the French king was involved in, or approved, the parallel negotiations for the Scottish marriage alliance. The inclusion of William Monypenny (who may have been in French service from 1439) in the Scottish embassy to Brittany could indicate some French involvement in the marriage plan.[6] If Charles was involved, it is likely that his role was limited to supporting an alliance which he hoped would create closer ties with the independent-minded duke.

---

4 Vaughan, *Philip the Good*, 10; *Lettres et mandements*, vi, 164–5, 275–7, 295–8; vii, 17–20, 118–20; Barbé, *Margaret of Scotland*, 38; *IACOB*, v, 198–9; *PPC*, iv, 254–9; v, 52–5.
5 Nantes ADLA, E12/2; *Lettres et mandements*, viii, 5–6, 11–12.
6 Beaucourt, *Charles VII*, iii, 202; Nantes ADLA, E12/3; McGladdery, *James II*, 97.

The second Breton embassy met with a favourable response from the Scots. Letters were issued on 19 July 1441 nominating George Crichton, William Foulis and William Monypenny as ambassadors for the negotiations, and the marriage contract was sealed on 29 September.[7] Isabella was to receive 100,000 gold marks as her dowry and 6000 livres as dower from the revenues of the castle of Succinio. Her marriage also made her the duchess of Brittany: Jean V had died and her future husband, Francis I, had succeeded to the duchy by the time the marriage took place in October 1442. The new duke of Brittany, like his father, was unwilling to commit himself to France formally and, in December of the same year, he sealed a treaty of alliance with the duke of Burgundy. He also maintained his English links by sending his brother, Giles, to England as a Breton ambassador in August 1443, an appointment capitalising on the experiences and contacts Giles had made in 1432–4. Over time, he seems to have reconsidered his position and performed homage to Charles VII for Brittany in 1446.[8]

The marriage in 1444 of Mary Stewart to Wolfaert van Borselen, son of the lord of Veere, admiral to Philip, duke of Burgundy, broadened Scotland's diplomatic options. Not only did the alliance consolidate Scotland's trading position in the Low Countries, it also secured contacts with Burgundy.[9] The French alliance had been renewed in 1428 and was secured by Margaret's marriage, but the growing likelihood of an Anglo-French peace threatened to neutralise any diplomatic advantage Scotland had acquired. Charles VII had already reassured the Scots in May 1442 that no long truce or final peace would be concluded without Scottish consent, and the king of Scots was included as a French ally in the Anglo-French truce of 1444 in fulfilment of this promise.[10] The conclusion of a ten-year Anglo-Scottish truce in May 1444 left Scotland free to explore new alliances.[11] A Burgundian alliance was the obvious choice given Scottish trading interests, the relationship of Burgundy to both England and France, and the importance of the Franco-Burgundian relationship to contemporary European diplomacy. It is possible

---

7 Nantes ADLA, E12/3, E12/1; *ER*, v, 118; *Lettres et mandements*, viii, 27–9.
8 *IACOB*, v, 204; Beaucourt, *Charles VII*, iii, 261–2, 266–9, iv, 182–3; *PPC*, vi, 3–7.
9 Dunlop, *James Kennedy*, 66–7; Stevenson, A.W.K. , 'Trade Between Scotland and the Low Countries in the Later Middle Ages' (unpublished PhD thesis, University of Aberdeen, 1982), 75–7, 280–1; Ditchburn, D., 'The Place of Guelders in Scottish Foreign Policy, c.1449–c.1542' in G. G. Simpson (ed.), *Scotland and the Low Countries, 1124–1994* (East Linton, 1996), 63–4.
10 Beaucourt, *Charles VII*, iii, 278, 324.
11 *Foedera*, xi, 58.

that the purpose of Bishop Kennedy's visit to the Low Countries in 1444 was to seek an alliance and negotiate a suitable marriage. The Veere accounts recorded a payment made in June 1444 'To the Lord of Veere, because he should give further to Mr. Donaet for the use of the Bishop of St. Andrews, £6gr.'. Kennedy also received a payment from the customs of North Berwick in the preceding months.[12]

While the marriage alliance was specifically concluded with Veere, it is likely that the duke of Burgundy, a noted marriage broker, was involved in some capacity. Wolfaert van Borselen was awarded the title of the earl of Buchan, perhaps in lieu of dowry, and his family shared in the prestige of a royal marriage, but the choice of a Scottish marriage was nevertheless unusual.[13] The van Borselen family, like other noble families in Burgundian territories, tended to marry bastards of the ducal house.[14] The chronicler d'Escouchy implies that the unusual choice of marriage partner was made at Burgundy's direction. D'Escouchy noted that Veere was chosen by Burgundy to escort Mary of Guelders to Scotland in 1449 partly because his daughter-in-law was Mary Stewart. He then goes on to state that all of these alliances were 'made by the said duke of Burgundy, and in large part at his expense.'[15] D'Escouchy's claim supports other signs of Burgundy's interest in arranging a Scottish marriage alliance. The duke had been alerted to the diplomatic potential of Scottish support by Hue de Lannoy, governor of Holland, in November 1435. His contacts with France and Brittany ensured that he knew of the marriages of Margaret and Isabella, and probably of the existence of their four unmarried sisters even before Bishop Kennedy's visit. Furthermore, the Anglo–Scottish truce meant that a Scottish alliance would not interfere with his English plans. The nomination of the count of Charollais, the duke of Burgundy's son, as godfather to Mary and Wolfaert's first child in 1451 is further evidence of the long-term Burgundian interest in the Veere match.[16]

Mary's marriage marked the start of a year of intense marital diplomacy regarding the remaining unmarried Stewart princesses. By the

12 From the (no longer extant) Veere accounts, quoted in Dunlop, *James Kennedy*, 66 n.4; *ER*, v, 143–4.
13 Watson, G.W., 'Wolfart van Borssele, Earl of Buchan', *The Genealogist*, new series, xiv, 10–11 and new series, xvi, 136; Dunlop, *James Kennedy*, 66.
14 Armstrong, C.A.J., 'La politique matrimoniale des ducs de Bourgogne de la maison de Valois' in C. A. J. Armstrong, *England, France and Burgundy in the Fifteenth Century* (London, 1983), 251.
15 D'Escouchy, M., *Chronique*, ed. G. du Fresne Beaucourt (Paris, 1863–4), i, 176.
16 Vaughan, *Philip the Good*, 101–2; Dunlop, *James Kennedy*, 66 n.3.

end of July 1445, Joanna, Eleanor and Annabella had followed their
sisters to the continent in search of husbands. All three undertook their
journeys with the support of Charles VII, the dauphin and the duke
of Burgundy, all of whom already had some form of marital alliance
with the Stewart family. The complexities of European politics and
the growing power of these three men in 1444–5 created a situation
in which the Scottish princesses were particularly attractive. By 1444,
strains were being placed on the Franco–Burgundian rapprochement
reached at the conference of Arras in 1435. French power was strengthened in 1444–5. The Anglo–French truce and the proposed marriage
of Henry VI and Margaret of Anjou enabled Charles VII to turn his
attention to the east, where he secured alliances with rulers such as
Frederick III, king of the Romans and others that were designed to
oppose Burgundian rule in Luxembourg and Liège. A French army of
Ecorcheurs, led by the dauphin on behalf of Frederick III and the duke
of Austria, crossed Burgundian lands and, following success against the
Swiss, moved to Alsace in September 1444. Not only did the expedition
extend French power and enhance the attractiveness of a French alliance,
it highlighted the growing power and independence of the dauphin.
Savoy made territorial concessions in order to secure an alliance, and
Genoa and Milan sent embassies to the dauphin. Burgundy responded
by seeking to build his power in the Low Countries and the east, and
by maintaining his links with England and other French princes such
as Bourbon and Orléans.[17] This political environment encouraged
smaller powers to maintain links with both France and Burgundy and
provided Charles VII, the dauphin and the duke of Burgundy with the
opportunity to negotiate marriages that would secure those links.

   The betrothal of Annabella Stewart to Louis, count of Geneva, in
December 1444 provides an example of the way in which a Scottish
marriage suited the needs of the Franco–Burgundian marriage brokers
and their clients. Like Brittany, the duke of Savoy was interested in a
Scottish marriage as part of his broader foreign policy, which aimed
at maintaining relationships with both France and Burgundy.[18] The
duke's father, Amadeus VIII, favoured the French alliance towards the
end of his reign, and betrothed his son to a daughter of the French

17 Vaughan, *Philip the Good*, 98–126; Griffiths, *Henry VI*, 443–90. On the Swiss expe-
    dition, see Beaucourt, *Charles VII*, iv, 7–46 and Kendall, P.M., *Louis XI* (London,
    1971), 55–61.
18 Downie, F., "'La voie quelle menace tenir": Annabella Stewart, Scotland and the
    European Marriage Market, 1445–1455', *SHR*, lxxviii (1999), 170–191; Vaughan,
    Philip the Good, 163.

king in 1436. The betrothal was accompanied by a military treaty and an act recognising the duke's right to collect revenues in Mâcon and Lyon in exchange for a financial gift.[19] Duke Louis' accession in 1440, following Amadeus' elevation to the papacy, saw the re-adoption of a more ambivalent foreign policy in the 1440s. Louis sealed a treaty of alliance with the duke of Burgundy in July 1443, a month before sending an embassy to the French court on unspecified business. The duke also agreed to the marriage of his sister Margaret to the Elector Palatine Louis IV in October 1444, only seventeen days after the Elector had sealed a treaty of alliance with the duke of Burgundy. In November of the same year, Savoy sealed an alliance with the dauphin.[20] The duchy of Savoy lay between France, the Burgundian and Swiss territories, and the Italian states. It was essential that Savoy negotiate alliances with Charles VII, the duke of Burgundy and the dauphin, all of whom had ambitions in the Italian peninsula. The decision to send an embassy to Scotland in July 1444 to secure a Scottish marriage – a match which would maintain the balance of these continental alliances – was another part of this general diplomatic activity.

In view of Savoy's geographic and strategic significance in the political climate of the 1440s, it is unlikely that the proposed Scottish alliance was solely designed to secure support for the duke's father, the antipope Felix V.[21] In 1441 the Scottish Estates had barred Scots from attending the Council of Basel and from obeying its judgements, including the election of Felix V as pope. Felix V did, however, make ecclesiastical provisions in Scotland in April and May 1441, all of which were overturned by a council of the Scottish church in July 1442. Scottish support for Felix was weakened further with the decision of the General Council of November 1443 in favour of Eugenius IV.[22] While the duke of Savoy may have hoped to secure Scottish support for his father by means of a marriage alliance, it is doubtful whether such support was sufficient incentive to justify such a strong deviation from established Savoyard marital policy. The dukes of Savoy consistently

19 Paris AN, J409/60, 61; Turin AS(2), Inv. 102 Mazzo 12/1; I. Jori, *Genealogia Sabauda* (Bologna, 1942), 63–4; Beaucourt, *Charles VII*, iii, 325–6.
20 Turin AS(2), Inv.118 Paquet 9/1; Inv.92 Mazzo 1/12; Beaucourt, *Charles VII*, iv, 67, 70; *IACOB*, v, 208; Turin AS(2), Inv.118 Paquet 9/2.
21 Dunlop, *James Kennedy*, 61 n.4.
22 Burns, J.H., *Scottish Churchmen and the Council of Basle* (Glasgow, 1962), 68–82; Watt, D.E.R., 'The Papacy and Scotland in the Fifteenth Century' in R. B. Dobson (ed.), *The Church, Politics and Patronage in the Fifteenth Century* (Gloucester, 1984), 118–19.

sought marriage alliances with the ruling families of neighbouring states in order to protect and expand the duchy. As both duke and pope, Amadeus/Felix sought the maintenance and expansion of Savoyard power on the continent.[23] A Scottish marriage might have won him some personal support but was of limited benefit in the longer term.

Several Franco-Burgundian princes, however, saw considerable benefit in a marriage alliance between Scotland and Savoy. The marriage contract states that James II had received letters in favour of the match from his 'beloved brothers' the king of France and the dauphin, and from other 'illustrious' but unnamed dukes and princes.[24] The French king and dauphin did not simply write letters in support of the match but offered territorial concessions to Savoy as incentives to conclude it, granting the barony of Faussigny to Annabella's betrothed. At the time the contract was sealed, the duke of Savoy performed homage to the dauphin for the barony, but in April 1445 the French king ratified his son's decision to relieve the duke of Savoy of his homage obligation.[25] The dauphin's influence can also be seen in the role played by his ambassador, William Monypenny, who escorted the Savoyard embassy through Scotland before accompanying Annabella to the Low Countries.[26] Charles VII and the dauphin promoted the marriage largely because it suited their ambitions in the Italian peninsula. As a frontier state between France and the peninsula, Savoy was of enormous strategic significance to these ambitions. The king and dauphin used their support of the marriage as part of an attempt to increase their influence in Savoy and ensure that the duchy's marital plans did not interfere with their larger goals. It was unlikely that Scotland would wish, or be able, to hinder French plans.[27]

The dukes of Brittany and Burgundy were among the unnamed dukes and princes who sent letters of support for the Savoy alliance to James II. The duke of Brittany was named in the marriage contract as James II's heir after the dauphin, a position he had acquired as a result of his marriage to James' second sister. Brittany's inclusion is also indicative of the relationship between the two duchies before the Scottish marriage alliances. Brittany and Savoy had previously worked together to negotiate peace between France and Burgundy and had

23 Downie, 'Scotland and the European Marriage Market', 179.
24 Turin AS(2), Inv.102 Mazzo 12/3.
25 Turin AS(2), Inv.118 Paquet 9/4.
26 Turin AS(1), Inv.16 Reg.93, ff.372v–373v, 384v–391r.
27 Downie, 'Scotland and the European Marriage Market', 182–3.

discussed marriage alliances. Brittany was also a supporter of Amadeus VIII following his election as the anti-pope Felix V in 1439.[28] Burgundy also supported the match. A member of the Savoy embassy, Lancelot Luriati, and William Monypenny, who escorted the embassy through Scotland, were in the service of the duchess of Burgundy in April 1445. The accounts for the Savoy embassy provide considerable evidence of Burgundian involvement in the mission. The ambassadors left Savoy in August 1444 for the Low Countries, visiting various towns including Middelburg and Bruges before going to Veere to organise ships to transport them to Scotland. One of the ambassadors returned to the Low Countries in April 1445 to make arrangements for Annabella's journey to the continent later in the same year. Annabella and her party spent a fortnight in Veere's household, home of her sister Mary, before continuing to Bruges in the company of knights and ladies of the households of the duke and duchess of Burgundy. Annabella remained in Bruges with the duchess of Burgundy for five days and it was there that she received the news of the deaths of her mother and her sister, Margaret. Mourning clothes were purchased for the young princess by the duchess on August 29. The party left Bruges on 7 September and travelled through Rheims, Troyes, and Dijon before reaching Savoy in October.[29]

Charles VII, the dauphin and the duke of Burgundy also co-operated to invite Annabella's elder sister, Eleanor, to France for marriage in 1445. The duchess of Burgundy, at the instigation of the dauphin and his wife, Margaret Stewart, wrote to James II on 20 April 1445 inviting Eleanor to France to secure a marriage.[30] As part of her invitation, the duchess appointed knights to accompany Eleanor and provided the group with a safe-conduct to travel through Burgundian territory. The two knights selected for the mission were William Monypenny and Lancelot Luriati, both of whom were in Scotland negotiating Annabella's betrothal, the former as a servant of the dauphin, and the latter as a representative of Savoy. Eleanor arrived in France in August 1445, just after her sister's death, and remained at the French court for three years before marrying Sigismund, duke of Austria-Tyrol in September 1448. Another sister, Joanna, accompanied Eleanor to France and resided at the French court for over twelve years before returning to Scotland to

28 *Lettres et mandements*, vi, 134–6, 164–5, 295–8; *IACOB*, v, 198–9; Jori, *Genealogia Sabauda*, 55, 57; Vaughan, *Philip the Good*, 212.
29 Edinburgh NAS, SP9/2; Turin AS(1), Inv.16 Reg.93, ff.371v.–383v.
30 Edinburgh NAS, SP9/2.

marry James Douglas, earl of Morton.[31] Joanna had not been included in the Burgundian invitation, and does not seem to have been called to France at all, but the willingness of the French king to support her over such a long period is indicative of her potential value as a marriage candidate.

The decision to send Joanna to France uninvited is also an indication of Scottish initiative in regard to foreign marriage negotiations. It is difficult to ascertain who directed Scottish negotiations for the marriages of Margaret Stewart's younger sisters, particularly before late 1444. Joan Beaufort had been forced to surrender custody of her children and the pension granted for their care to Alexander Livingston and his allies in September 1439. The Livingstons exercised considerable direct influence on the Stewart princesses by virtue of the number and importance of the offices held by the family, in particular those positions involving care or custody of the royal children. They could not, however, arrange their marriages. But while 1444–5 was characterised by intense marital diplomacy, it also saw the growing power and influence of the eighth earl of Douglas.[32] The earl's rise began with his accession in March 1443 and was boosted by his rapprochement with the Livingston family later in the same year. By the end of 1444 war had broken out between the Douglas–Livingston faction on one side and the queen, Kennedy, Crichton, Angus and their supporters on the other. If Kennedy did play a role in securing the Veere marriage, he must have done so before his split with Douglas in late 1444.

The accounts of the Savoyard embassy provide a rare, if oblique, record of those in power in Scotland in the autumn and winter of 1444. During their time in Scotland the ambassadors met with James II, the earls of Douglas, Crawford, Orkney and Angus and Bishop Kennedy. Kennedy met with the embassy on 1 October but had allied with the queen against the Douglas–Livingston faction by mid-November. Angus only met the ambassadors once and the queen is not mentioned at all. The failed attempt of the queen, Kennedy, and their supporters to raise resistance to 'tha persownis that nw has the kyng in gouernance' in November would further suggest that they had little input to the final draft of Annabella's marriage contract, sealed at Stirling on 14 December.[33] Similarly, it is unlikely that they played any significant part in the deci-

---

31 Stevenson, *Letters and Papers*, i, 352–7; Dunlop, *James Kennedy*, 182.
32 *APS*, ii, 54–5; *ER*, v, 116, 176; Brown, M.H., *The Black Douglases* (East Linton, 1998), 272.
33 Turin AS(1), Inv.16 Reg.93, ff.372v.–373v; *Extracts from the Council Register of the Burgh of Aberdeen, 1398-1570*, ed. Stuart, J. (Spalding Club, 1844), i, 399.

sion to send Eleanor and Joanna to France in the company of James Livingston in July 1445.[34] The queen had taken refuge in Dunbar while Crichton was besieged in Edinburgh Castle in June. The Douglas-dominated parliament of June-July contemplated an attack on Kennedy and the third earl of Angus, betrothed to Joanna Stewart in October 1440, was threatened with forfeiture.[35] While parliament sat, Joanna was sent to France with her sister. Unlike Eleanor, Joanna had not been invited to the French court; the decision to send her to France uninvited was a Douglas initiative, intended to prevent her marriage to Angus.

The high level of continental interest in the Stewart princesses in 1444–5 provided an opportunity for Douglas to prevent any domestic marriage alliances, such as the betrothal of Joanna and Angus, which might erode his power and influence in the future. Royal alliances with the nobility could be of enormous long-term significance, particularly as the sons of these marriages could become regents and rivals for power in the event of a king's minority or incapacity. Margaret and Mary Stewart, sisters of James I, married the fourth earl of Douglas and the earl of Angus respectively, and their sons played leading political roles following the king's assassination. Mary's third son by her second husband was James Kennedy who, as the bishop of St Andrews, was a leading figure during the minority of James III. The long-term success of the Douglas faction's strategy to claim and consolidate power depended, in part, upon the prevention of marriages between its rivals and the Stewart princesses. Fortunately for Douglas, he did not need to seek alternative marriage alliances for the princesses but was provided with a variety of highly prestigious options at virtually no cost to Scotland. The cost of keeping the princesses and of providing dowries and negotiating marriages for Eleanor and Joanna was simply transferred to European princes.

More importantly, the marriages of the princesses secured new alliances for Scotland or strengthened existing links with France. Douglas was not unaware of the advantages that could be derived from an involvement in prestigious marriage negotiations. International marriages reflected well on the kingdom and its leaders, including the earl, the leader of a family with European as well as national fame and aspirations. The Douglas claim to the French duchy of Touraine had lapsed with the failure of the direct male line following the death of the sixth earl. The eighth earl entrusted William Crichton, a member

34 *ER*, v, 116, 225.
35 Edinburgh NAS, GD 52/1042; *APS*, ii, 59–60.

of the 1448 Scottish embassy sent to the continent to negotiate the marriages of James II and Eleanor, with the mission of representing the earl's claim to part of the duchy to the French king.[36] The claim was unsuccessful but, even without lands on the continent, the Douglas family were recognised as nobility of European stature. The Burgundian knight, Jacques de Lalain, is reported to have heard of a talented Scottish knight and came to Scotland to joust with him. James Douglas, the earl's brother, and his two companions jousted with the two Lalain brothers and their squire in February 1449.[37] The earl and several of his followers, like many other members of the European nobility such as the lord of Veere and the duke of Guelders, made a pilgrimage to Rome in 1450 for the papal jubilee. In October, en route to Rome, he and his company were entertained to a banquet held by the duke of Burgundy in Lille, and may also have visited the French court. The earl spent time with the English king before returning to Scotland, and his brother James was 'with the kyng of yngland lang tyme and was meikle maid of' later in the same year.[38] James II himself recognised the earl's international fame by writing to Charles VII to announce Douglas' death in 1452.[39]

While all of the Stewart princesses had departed for the continent by the end of July 1445, three of them remained unmarried nearly three years later. The lack of Scottish protests at continental delays in celebrating Annabella's marriage and in securing marriages for Eleanor and Joanna indicates that the main concern of the Douglas faction was to send the Stewart princesses abroad relatively quickly rather than to pursue specific marriage strategies. The design and implementation of such strategies was left to European marriage brokers such as Charles VII and the duke of Burgundy. In 1445 the duchess of Burgundy had suggested that Eleanor marry Frederick III, king of the Romans. This plan was eventually abandoned and replaced with another which saw Eleanor marry Frederick's nephew, Sigismund, duke of Austria-Tyrol, in 1448. This new marriage plan was the result of changes in the complex diplomatic relationship between the empire, Burgundy and France in the 1440s. Frederick III was opposed to attempts to extend Burgundian power into the empire, particularly in Luxembourg, but he

---

36 Stevenson, *Letters and Papers*, i, 20–1.
37 Hume-Brown, *Early Travellers*, 30–8; d'Escouchy, *Chronique*, i, 148–53; 'Auch. Chron.', 164.
38 Dunlop, *James Kennedy*, 118 n. 1, 3, 124; *IADNB*, viii, 23; Vaughan, *Philip the Good*, 112; *ER*, v, lxxxv; 'Auch. Chron.', 164.
39 Stevenson, *Letters and Papers*, i, 315–16.

entered negotiations with the duke of Burgundy in the early 1440s in an attempt to reach an agreement over the disputed lands. Burgundy, however, seized Luxembourg in 1443, though the duke of Saxony continued to use the title duke of Luxembourg and twice attempted to reclaim the duchy in 1445 and 1447. Nevertheless, negotiations over Luxembourg and Burgundy's title in the imperial territories of Brabant and Holland continued before grinding to a halt in August 1448. The various marriage alliances between the houses of Burgundy and Habsburg which had been proposed over the years were also abandoned, including the match suggested in 1446 between Albert, duke of Austria, and Burgundy's great-niece, Mary of Guelders.[40] Burgundy's promotion of Frederick III as a husband for Eleanor in 1445 may have been intended as yet another attempt to create links with the empire. If it was, the cooling of Burgundian-Habsburg relations allowed the initiative in determining Eleanor's marriage to pass to Charles VII, at whose court Eleanor had been resident since 1445.

Plans for a Habsburg marriage were not, however, abandoned. Charles VII had long held an interest in Austrian affairs through the betrothal of his daughter Radegonde to Frederick III's nephew and ward, Sigismund, duke of Austria-Tyrol, in 1430. The betrothal had constituted one element of a French–Austrian alliance against Burgundy, an alliance which was soon superceded by a six-year treaty between Austria and Burgundy sealed in May 1432.[41] The diplomatic competition of 1430–2 for an Austrian alliance seemed about to be repeated a decade later. Sigismund wrote to the French king in August 1443 supporting the request of his uncle, Frederick III, for assistance against the Swiss, a request that had previously been rejected by the duke of Burgundy, and which justified the French campaign in Switzerland of 1444. However, Frederick's reluctance both to allow his sixteen year-old nephew to rule Tyrol and to fulfil his own promises to the French following the dauphin's Swiss campaign led to a cooling of his relationship with Charles VII. The duchess of Burgundy's letter inviting Eleanor to France and proposing her marriage to Frederick III was dated 20 April 1445. Sigismund entered his capital of Innsbruck and began his independent reign as duke of Austria-Tyrol three days later.[42] It may be that Charles supported the suggested marriage in response to the softening of Frederick's attitude with regard to his nephew. The match

40 Beaucourt, *Charles VII*, iv, 333–58; Vaughan, *Philip the Good*, 274–88.
41 Vaughan, *Philip the Good*, 64–5.
42 Beaucourt, *Charles VII*, iv, 10–11, 40–76.

would also have created indirect ties between France and Austria to replace those broken by Radegonde's death in March 1445.

The possibility of marrying Eleanor to Sigismund was apparently not suggested until June 1447. It is not clear whether other suggestions had been made in the course of Eleanor's residence at the French court, but James II claimed in May 1447 to have heard a rumour that his sister might marry the dauphin, a match of which he approved.[43] The letter also authorised Charles to arrange Eleanor's marriage on his behalf, and it was on this basis that the French king received an embassy from Sigismund in June 1447 which proposed that the duke marry the princess. The Saxon ambassador at the French court reported that Charles did not at first favour the plan: Charles had responded that he would have to refer the matter to James II and await his answer. At this juncture, the king was already engaged in secret talks about his Italian ambitions with the duke of Savoy, and the French king's apparent lack of interest in an alliance which would further these plans is curious.[44] The Saxon ambassador's letter indicated why the French king was so vague about a matter in which he subsequently took such an interest. While the Austrian embassy was at court negotiating Eleanor's marriage, Charles had indicated that he favoured a match between James II and Annette, daughter of the elector Frederick, duke of Saxony. Frederick's younger brother, William, was at that time leading an army in support of the archbishop of Cologne against the duke of Cleves and, if the campaign were successful, intended to use the army to press the Saxon claim to Luxembourg. The campaign did not, however, succeed. The war was over in July, and its brevity may partially account for the short-lived nature of the plan for the Saxon marriage.[45]

Although both Frederick and William of Saxony had allied with Charles VII in February 1445, as had the archbishop of Cologne, the timing of the Saxon marriage proposal emphasised the French support of William's claim to Luxembourg and constituted an attack on Burgundy. The duke of Burgundy had sealed a treaty of alliance with Albert, duke of Austria in May, only six weeks before William of Saxony, with the knowledge and implicit support of Frederick III, began his campaign against Cleves. Burgundy and Austria then sought Sigismund's consent to their treaty – which he gave with reservations in

43 Paris BN, MS. Latin 10187, f.8.
44 Beaucourt, *Charles VII*, iv, 362–3. Beaucourt quotes from a letter dated 15 June 1445 which was held in the Dresden archives.
45 Vaughan, *Philip the Good*, 282–3; Beaucourt, *Charles VII*, iv, 364–5.

September – three months after his embassy had proposed his marriage to Eleanor at Charles VII's court.[46] Charles was not opposed to the Austrian match as the Saxon ambassador had assumed, but was awaiting the outcome of William of Saxony's campaign and searching for the best means of preventing a Burgundian-Habsburg rapprochement. The failure of Saxony's campaign made Sigismund's offer more useful to French foreign policy. James II gave his consent to the marriage on 1 September 1447.[47] The match was not the French one for which he had expressed a preference in May, but it had French connections and was approved by Charles. In accepting the offer, James referred to the perpetual and indissoluble alliance between Scotland and France and thanked the French king for his efforts on Eleanor's behalf, indicating that he regarded the Austrian match as part of that alliance.

Succeeding negotiations for the Austrian marriage further emphasise that it was but one part of a larger complex of political and marital alliances. On 9 January 1448, James wrote to Charles VII informing him that he was about to send an embassy to France to discuss matters relating to his marriage and those of his sisters. Another letter of 6 May 1448 referred to the ancient alliance between France and Scotland, appointed ambassadors, and awarded them full powers to continue that alliance and to select a bride for James II.[48] On the same day, James sent similar letters announcing the same embassy to the dukes of Burgundy and Austria.[49] The two Burgundian letters indicated that the ambassadors were in search of a wife for James, while the Austrian letter stated that the embassy was seeking husbands for Eleanor and Joanna from the families of the dukes of Burgundy and Austria and the count of Armagnac. Jean V, count of Armagnac, was brother-in-law to the duke of Brittany and an ally of the duke of Savoy. James' letter to Austria suggests that the embassy was seeking a husband for Joanna while negotiating the details of Eleanor's marriage, or perhaps that James was keeping his options open until the contract for Eleanor's marriage was sealed. Two further undated letters from James in 1448 stated that Joanna and Eleanor were of an age to marry and that husbands were sought in the house of Austria.[50]

While the official correspondence was non-committal, the undated

46 Beaucourt, *Charles VII*, iv, 68, 352.
47 Paris BN, MS. Latin 10187, ff.9–10; Stevenson, *Letters and Papers*, i, 194–6.
48 Paris BN, MS. Latin 10187, ff.11–2; Stevenson, *Letters and Papers*, i, 197–8.
49 Lille ADN, B427/15853bis, 15853; Vienna HHSA, Fam.Urk. 604.
50 Vienna HHSA, Familien-Akten 18/II/4, ff.49, 52.

instructions issued to Thomas Spens informed him of discussions with the French and Austrian ambassadors and directed him specifically to negotiate on matters relating to the marriage of Eleanor and Sigismund.[51] The non-committal nature of the correspondence reflects the delays that occurred from December 1447, initially requested by Sigismund, and then caused by Charles VII's efforts to secure James' consent and to inform the dukes of Brittany and Savoy of proceedings.[52] The marriage was not the only point at issue. Hostilities had broken out between the duke of Savoy and the inhabitants of Fribourg in late 1447 and, in the following May, Sigismund wrote to Charles VII requesting his intervention on behalf of Fribourg. French and Burgundian ambassadors, including William Monypenny, arrived in Fribourg on 26 May and a settlement was reached by the middle of July. Sigismund issued a letter on 1 June nominating his ambassadors to negotiate his marriage to Eleanor, but matters proceeded slowly until the treaty of marriage was sealed on 7 September 1448. On the same day, treaties of alliance were sealed between Charles VII and Sigismund, and between James II and Sigismund. The marriage was celebrated on 8 September but the Scottish embassy does not seem to have reached the French court until the end of the month, indicating that Scottish involvement in the final negotiations was limited.[53] At the same time, Eleanor's meeting with her younger sister Annabella in Savoy en route to Austria underlined the role of the Stewart family in maintaining a broader network of continental alliances.[54]

Regardless of James' intentions, which were represented by the same Scottish ambassadors at each of the three courts involved in negotiations in the course of 1448, the marriage plans for Eleanor were dictated by diplomatic competition between the three continental powers of France, Burgundy and Austria. While his direct involvement in the Austrian marriage was limited following the failure of his marital policy in the empire, the duke of Burgundy continued to take an interest after the proxy ceremony had taken place on 8 September. He wrote a letter of congratulation and safe-conduct to Sigismund on 22 September in which he described Eleanor as his 'consanguineam' and offered her

51 Vienna HHSA, Familien-Akten 18/II/4, f.50.
52 Vienna HHSA, Fam.Urk. 603; Innsbruck TLA, Sigm. IVa 9/9, f.14; Paris BN, MS. Latin 5414A, f.79v.; Beaucourt, *Charles VII*, iv, 366–7.
53 Vienna HHSA, Fam.Urk. 604e, 607; Beaucourt, *Charles VII*, iv, 367–70; Paris BN, MS. Latin 10187, f.13; Stevenson, *Letters and Papers*, i, 221–2.
54 Turin AS(1), Inv.16 Reg.96, f.456r.

every assistance on her journey.[55] Charles VII's role in organising the marriage was far greater, and both he and his wife were present at the wedding by proxy at Belmont in September, which his counsellor and chamberlain, William Monypenny, had done so much to arrange.[56] Charles VII also noted the consent of the dukes of Brittany and Savoy to the marriage in an undated letter to Sigismund, an indication that like the Savoy betrothal, the alliance was a matter of general political importance outwith Scotland.[57] The duke of Savoy's hostility to Frederick III in 1446, for example, may have contributed to the change in Eleanor's marriage plans by 1447.[58] The consent and involvement of all these powers underscored Charles' success in creating a wide complex of continental alliances at Burgundian expense, a network that also influenced James' marriage plans.

55 Vienna HHSA, Familien-Akten 18/II/4, f.42.
56 Vienna HHSA, Fam.Urk. 608, Familien-Akten 18/II/4, f.63.
57 Innsbruck TLA, Sigm. IVa 9/9, f.14.
58 Beaucourt, *Charles VII*, iv, 349.

FOUR

The Marriage of Mary of Guelders and James II, 1446–9

'And all thire war bundyn'

James II notified Charles VII in January 1448 that he was about to send an embassy to the continent in search of a suitable consort. The French king had already begun to plan possible matches for James and briefly considered Annette of Saxony in 1447. James, however, had begun his own search even earlier. The Scottish interest in a Burgundian, and specifically Gueldrian, marriage alliance had been indicated as early as 1446. The visits of embassies to Bruges in March and to Arnhem in June of that year may have been inspired by the marriage of Mary Stewart to the son of the lord of Veere two years earlier. The journey of a Scottish herald accompanied by a Burgundian messenger to the court of Guelders to see the 'maiden of Guelders' in July 1446 was almost certainly not connected with the Veere marriage.[1] It is likely that Scottish ambassadors visited many courts to view potential marriage candidates, but the final decision to seek a Burgundian bride was made by the end of 1447 at the latest. Bishop Kennedy's departure for the continent in the winter of 1447–8 and his visit to Veere may also be connected with negotations for James' marriage. The bishop wrote an undated letter to the lord of Veere to inform him of his imminent arrival and to request his assistance in negotiations with Burgundy. Veere's involvement in the marriage plans may also be inferred from the visits of the duke of Guelders and 'Sir Henry the Young of Veere' to the court of Charles VII at Paris in 1447. The lord of Veere also escorted Mary of Guelders to Scotland for her marriage in 1449.[2]

In July 1447, a year after the Scottish herald saw the 'maiden of Guelders', her father, Duke Arnold, convened the Estates to discuss a potential marriage.[3] It is by no means clear, however, that the Estates

---

1 Ditchburn, 'The Place of Guelders', 62; Beaucourt, *Charles VII*, iv, 365.
2 Dunlop, *James Kennedy*, 95 n.5, 96 n.1; d'Escouchy, *Chronique*, i, 176.
3 Ditchburn, 'The Place of Guelders', 62.

discussed a Scottish marriage alliance. All of the correspondence in the Archives du Nord relating to the marriage has been catalogued and described under the erroneous assumption that Mary was always the intended candidate for the Scottish marriage.[4] Mary was only identified as James' prospective bride for the first time in the marriage contract, sealed in 1449. In fact, while the Scots may have sought a marriage alliance with Guelders in 1446–7, the first official record of an agreed marriage alliance between Scotland and Guelders (dated 6 September 1448) names Margaret of Guelders, not Mary, as James II's intended bride.[5] Margaret (born 1436) was the second of the three daughters of the duke of Guelders and Catherine of Cleves. The eldest, Mary, was born in January 1433 and the youngest, Catherine, around 1439.[6] The 'maiden of Guelders' in whom the Scots showed an interest in 1446 was presumably Mary, who would have been thirteen at the time, rather than her younger sisters, particularly if James was hoping to assert his majority and authority through the early birth of an heir. It is unlikely that the king of Scots would settle for a younger daughter, regardless of her Burgundian connections, especially in view of his sisters' European marriages. The dukes of Burgundy and Guelders, on the other hand, had different plans in mind for Mary.

Burgundian marriage policy was designed to secure international alliances and advance Burgundian interests. This advancement was achieved by means of two basic strategies. The first aimed to maintain links with the French royal family and princes of the blood, while the second sought marriages that would promote Burgundian territorial interests. Mary of Burgundy, for example, married Adolf, duke of Cleves, in 1406. Their daughter, Mary, was married to a prince of the blood, Charles, duke of Orléans, in 1440, and two sons were married within the Burgundian family circle. Five daughters were married into families whose lands were of interest to Burgundy or to Cleves. The most important of these marriages was that of Catherine and Arnold, duke of Guelders, in 1430.[7] The marital potential of Guelders' three daughters was of particular interest to the duke of Burgundy who lacked legitimate daughters of his own to offer in marriage. Charles VII had already attempted to arrange a marriage between Mary of Guelders

---

4 See for example, Baxter, J.H., 'The Marriage of James II', *SHR* 25(1928), 69–72.
5 Lille ADN, B427/15859.
6 Van Schilfgaarde, A.P., *Zegels en Genealogische Gegevens van de Graven en Hertogen van Gelre, Graven van Zulphen* (Arnhem, 1967).
7 Armstrong, 'La politique matrimoniale', 237–342; Vaughan, *Philip the Good*, 290–1.

and Charles of Anjou in 1441, a match of which Burgundy had disapproved. The following year, Mary went to the Burgundian court at Brussels, and later became a full-time resident of the court at the duke's expense.[8] Her presence at court allowed the duke to oversee, if not arrange, her marriage to Burgundian advantage. His generosity was also intended to secure greater influence within the duchy of Guelders itself. Guelders had remained outwith Burgundy's influence at a time when his control over the rest of the Low Countries was growing. Matters were not improved by the outbreak of war between the duke of Guelders and Philip's ally, the duke of Berg, in 1444. Burgundy later took advantage of the growing hostility between Guelders and his subjects to gain a foothold in the state and, in October 1448, during negotiations for the Scottish marriage, Arnold's subjects tried to force him to ally with the duke.[9]

Mary of Guelders' residence in the household of the duchess of Burgundy, meanwhile, significantly enhanced her value as a candidate for marriage. Fifteenth-century Burgundian noblewomen were educated and trained to exercise their power and to act as their husbands' lieutenants. Isabel of Portugal, duchess of Burgundy during Mary's residence, was more than capable of fulfilling her responsibilities. The duchess negotiated on her husband's behalf in matters of domestic unrest, raised and organised the payment of the army in Luxembourg in 1443 and occasionally acted as regent during the duke's absences. She represented her husband at several peace conferences, including Arras in 1435, Gravelines in 1438–9 and Châlons in 1445. She also participated in the negotiations leading to an Anglo–Flemish truce in 1442–3 and the liberation of the duke of Orléans in 1440, and in discussions with the emperor at Besançon in 1442.[10] At Gravelines, the duchess and Cardinal Beaufort – as promoters of the peace – were to decide when talks would begin, who was to attend and whether or not the participants would be allowed to carry arms. In addition to her duties of mediation, the duchess took an active part in the discussions.

8 Beaucourt, *Charles VII*, iii, 211–24; Lille ADN, B3340, Premier compte, f.5r; Nijsten, G., *In the Shadow of Burgundy. The Court of Guelders in the Late Middle Ages* (Cambridge, 2004), 135 n.90. See also Lille ADN, B3409–B3414.
9 Ditchburn, 'The Place of Guelders', 66–7.
10 *Foedera*, x, 787, 791; xi, 24, 125–6, 129, 137, 169–71, 220; *PPC*, v, 169, 176, 212, 334–407; vi, 69–73, 76–85, 100, 253; Looten, C., 'Isabelle de Portugal, duchesse de Bourgogne et comtesse de Flandre (1397–1471)', *Revue de Littérature Comparée*, xviii (1938), 5–22; Willard, C.C., 'The Patronage of Isabel of Portugal' in McCash, *The Cultural Patronage of Medieval Women*, 306–20; Vaughan, *Philip the Good*, 107–9, 116–20, 167–8, 171–2; Beaucourt, *Charles VII*, iii, 148–9, 174–5.

Her political activities were so wide-ranging that some contemporaries outside the Burgundian court believed that it covered all facets of administration and that she even ruled the duke.[11]

The duchess also pursued her own policies, as at Arras when Charles VII recognised her efforts to restore peace by giving her an annual rent of £4000. She was a diligent administrator of her own estates and affairs and a noted patron. She was also conscious of the importance of creating and maintaining networks through which she could exercise her influence. Before meeting the French queen and the dauphiness at Châlons, Isabel researched French court etiquette in order to be aware of its variations from Portuguese practices. Her efforts were indicative not only of the Burgundian obsession with etiquette, but also of the professionalism with which the duchess undertook her duties. Her contacts with the French king and her careful maintenance of them, including the establishment of supporting relationships with the French queen and dauphiness, were particularly important to Burgundy given that the duke never met his nephew himself.[12] As a woman of power, the duchess was aware of the potential of her role and the need to train the ladies of her household for similar positions. She endorsed Christine de Pizan's views on female power by sending copies of the work to several of her female relatives and, perhaps more importantly, ensured that the ladies of her court witnessed her work in fulfilling her tasks and responsibilities. At Gravelines, for example, discussions took place in a tent owned by the duchess, and were attended by the ambassadors and by eleven ladies from the duchess' household, including her niece, the daughter of the duke of Cleves.[13] Mary of Guelders spent several years in the company of the duchess, observing her behaviour and learning how to exercise female power.

Mary's value as a prospective bride did not go unnoticed. Charles VII had proposed in 1441 that she marry Charles of Anjou, and when the Scots first showed an interest in her in 1446, she had been put forward as a possible bride for Albert, duke of Austria.[14] An Austrian embassy in February 1447 secured approval for the match from Mary's great-uncle, the duke of Burgundy, but had to wait for the consent of the duke and duchess of Guelders who, at that time, were engaged

11 Vaughan, *Philip the Good*, 167–8.
12 Vaughan, *Philip the Good*, 100–1, 120, 168, 213, 215, 234; Willard, 'The Patronage of Isabel of Portugal', 306–20; Vale, *Charles VII*, 230; Beaucourt, *Charles VII*, iv, 96.
13 *PPC*, v, 336–42.
14 Vale, *Charles VII*, 84–5.

in talks with the king of Denmark. The proposed marriage between Albert of Austria and Mary of Guelders accorded with Burgundian plans to create political and marital links with the empire. The treaty of alliance sealed in 1447 by the dukes of Burgundy and Austria was to be supported by the marriage of Burgundy's son, Charles, and Elizabeth, sister of Ladislas, king of Hungary. Ladislas, whose claim to Luxembourg was recognised by the king of the Romans, was to be married to a niece of the duchess of Burgundy.[15] These marriages and the proposed match between Albert and Mary were designed to create links with the Habsburgs and extend Burgundy's power over Luxembourg and in the imperial territories of Hainault, Holland and Zeeland.

Much of the French diplomatic activity from the middle of 1447 was concerned with preventing the proposed Burgundian–Habsburg alliance. This activity included the suggestion of possible marriages between James II and Annette of Saxony to support Saxony's claims in Luxembourg, and between Eleanor Stewart and the duke of Austria-Tyrol to strengthen the French–Austrian alliance. French efforts hindered Burgundian plans but did not stop Burgundy and Albert of Austria from negotiating either the marriages or the alliance. Burgundy's mishandling of negotiations and Ladislas' refusal to renounce his claim to Luxembourg in favour of his sister, proposed bride of Burgundy's son, led to the breakdown of negotiations in the summer of 1448. On 17 August, Duke Albert informed the duke of Burgundy that he could not and would not agree to the creation of a kingdom from Burgundy's imperial territories, and a final statement explaining the reasons for this refusal was issued on 6 September.[16] The failure of the political settlement also meant the failure of the various proposed marriages intended to support it. Charles VII succeeded in creating an Austrian alliance where Burgundy had failed: Eleanor Stewart married the duke of Austria-Tyrol by proxy on 8 September 1448 in the presence of the king and queen of France.

The proposal that Mary of Guelders marry Albert of Austria did not necessarily preclude the conclusion of a parallel alliance between Guelders and Scotland, and it is clear that James II and his ambassadors still hoped to secure such an alliance. On 6 May 1448 James appointed an embassy and gave it the power to seek the assistance of Charles VII in securing a marriage and to negotiate the renewal of the Franco–Scottish alliance. Another letter issued on the same day

15 Beaucourt, *Charles VII*, iv, 350–1, 353.
16 Beaucourt, *Charles VII*, iv, 356–8.

gave the ambassadors power to choose a consort from the houses of Burgundy, Guelders or Cleves and to negotiate the details of the marriage.[17] The inclusion of Guelders and Cleves in James' specifications acknowledged the fact that the duke of Burgundy lacked legitimate daughters of his own but was able to provide the daughters of his sisters and nieces as potential brides, including those from the houses of Guelders and Cleves. It also permitted the embassy to continue their discussions regarding the favoured alliance with Guelders. The duke of Burgundy entertained the Scottish ambassadors at two lavish banquets on 26 August and 12 September 1448, soon after Albert of Austria had withdrawn from the proposed Austro–Burgundian alliance and its accompanying marriage. The banquets were attended by, among others, the duchess, Charles, count of Charollais, and the 'damoiselles destampes de bourbon et de guelres'.[18]

The duke of Guelders, however, still assumed that Mary was to marry the duke of Austria when he formally granted the duke of Burgundy the power to negotiate his daughters' marriages on 6 September 1448. The grant awarded Burgundy the power to arrange the marriages of Mary to Albert, duke of Austria, and of Margaret to James II.[19] It is unlikely that Arnold confused his daughters in his letter, particularly as the letter was issued from Hesdin, the location of the Burgundian court at the time and venue for the banquets for the Scottish ambassadors on 26 August and 12 September. It is possible that Guelders did not realise that the plans had been changed. Although the duke of Austria had refused Burgundy's demands on 17 August, the reasons for this refusal were not formally stated until 6 September, when Guelders still believed that Mary was to marry Albert. Guelders' political difficulties may also have delayed communication of the changes in marital negotiations. Arnold's subjects tried to force him to ally with Burgundy on 8 October, only a month after Arnold had surrendered the power to negotiate his daughters' marriages to the duke. The grant was presumably given grudgingly, and the duke of Guelders does not appear in the

17 Lille ADN, B427/15853.
18 Lille ADN, B3340, Premier compte, f.27v., f.29v; Compte second, f. 12r; Sommé, M., 'La jeunesse de Charles le Téméraire d'après les comptes de la cour de Bourgogne', *Revue du Nord*, 64 (1982), 731–50.
19 Lille ADN, B427/15859. This document has been incorrectly described in the inventory as 'Lettres d'Arnould, duc de Gueldre, donnant pleins pouvoirs au duc de Bourgogne pour traiter des mariages de sa fille Marie avec le roi d'Ecosse et de sa fille Margeurite avec Albert, duc d'Autriche' (*IADNB*, i, 297), an error repeated by Baxter in his article 'The Marriage of James II' (71) and by Armstrong in 'La politique matrimoniale' (253).

Burgundian accounts, not even at the time of his daughter's marriage and departure for Scotland. The duchess of Guelders, Burgundy's niece, stayed in her uncle's household with her daughter from 28 May to 4 June 1449, the week prior to Mary's departure.[20] Guelders' absence from the Burgundian court is perhaps evidence of the hostility between the two dukes, but may also suggest that the duke did not favour his daughter's marriage. The duke was not opposed to a Scottish marriage – he had authorised Burgundy to negotiate Margaret's marriage to James II – but may have preferred another option for his eldest daughter. His approval of Mary's proposed marriage to Albert of Austria indicates that he regarded a continental alliance as more beneficial to Guelders than a Scottish one.

While discussions between Burgundy, Guelders and the Scottish ambassadors continued in late summer 1448, James II again raised the possibility of a French marriage. In a letter he received on 29 September, Charles VII was reminded of the importance of the Franco–Scottish alliance and the 1436 marriage between Margaret Stewart and the dauphin, and asked if there were a daughter of the French house whom James could marry.[21] A French marriage may have seemed more attractive following Charles' success in negotiating Eleanor's marriage and his diplomatic victories over Burgundy in the summer of 1448. However, as James knew, Charles did not have a daughter of eligible age to marry but was prepared to marry a daughter of one of his allies to James, as he indicated by his approval of the proposed match between James and Annette of Saxony in 1447. The Burgundian marriage plans were well-developed by September, and it may be that James suggested a French marriage, which he knew to be unlikely, in order to maintain good relations in the event of success in the negotiations with Burgundy. As it happened, James II's marriage was achieved with the approval and assistance of Charles VII. The French king was kept informed of the progress of negotiations with Burgundy, and two of his ambassadors were present when the marriage treaty was sealed.[22] The treaty made explicit reference to the Franco–Scottish alliance, which had been successfully renewed on 31 December 1448.

James empowered his ambassadors on 5 November 1448 to conclude the marriage between himself and the house of Guelders, discuss the matter of dowry and secure an alliance with Burgundy and Guelders.[23]

20 Lille ADN, B3414/116178, 116179, 116180, 116182, 116184.
21 Paris BN, MS. Latin 10187, f.13; Stevenson, *Letters and Papers*, i, 221–3.
22 Paris AN, J678/28; Stevenson, *Letters and Papers*, i, 239–40.
23 Lille ADN, B427/15859bis.

The terms of the marriage and accompanying alliance were negotiated through the winter of 1448–9 and finally set out in the treaty of
Brussels, sealed on 1 April 1449. James endorsed his embassy's negotiations in four letters issued on 25 June 1449. One of the letters ratified
the treaty of Brussels; another two renounced the king's claim to the
Gueldrian succession and promised to return Mary's dowry should
she die childless within a year and a day of the consummation of the
marriage. The fourth letter confirmed the arrangements made by the
Scottish ambassadors for Mary's dower, the value of which had been
set at 10,000 gold crowns a year. This income was provided in the
form of the earldoms of Strathearn and Atholl, the castle and lands of
Methven, and the palace, lands and customs of Linlithgow.[24] This was
an enormous dower in Scottish terms, well in excess of that offered to
Mary's predecessor, Joan Beaufort. The size of the dower may have
been intended to persuade Burgundy and Guelders that the king of
Scots was a worthy husband for Guelders' eldest daughter and that she
would be well-provided for as queen of Scotland.

The marriage of James and Mary was secondary to the broader
alliance outlined in the treaty of Brussels.[25] The treaty was agreed
between Scotland and Burgundy rather than between James and his
future father-in-law. The family links between Scotland and Burgundy,
though indirect, were recognised by the inclusion of Guelders as a
minor party in the treaty. Guelders' inclusion occurs in item seven, and
is something of a formality. Burgundy's arrangement of the marriage
and provision of the dowry had eroded Arnold's role as father of the
bride, a role he had formally renounced in his letter of September
1448. The clause referring to Guelders follows that incorporating the
duke of Brittany in the alliance, further emphasising Arnold's lesser
role and his growing subjection to Burgundy. Brittany's inclusion in
the alliance despite his lack of direct involvement in the marriage is in
part indicative of the broader political and military objectives of the
treaty. Duke Francis I of Brittany had sworn homage to Charles VII
in 1446 and was in need of military support following the increase in
English strength on the Breton-Norman border in 1448. Brittany was
also included in the treaty as 'parens affinis et amicus'. The duke had

---

24 Lille ADN, B308/15876, B427/15877, 15877bis, 15877ter.
25 The treaty survives in a number of copies, including Lille ADN, B308/15876;
    Vienna HHSA, Nied.Urk. 1449, IV 1; Edinburgh NAS, SP7/14; London BL, MS.
    Harl. 4637 III, ff.12-6; Göttingen SA, Cod. Ms. hist.657, xvi, ff.316–21. See also
    Stevenson, 'Trade Between Scotland and the Low Countries', 79–82, 281–2.

entered an alliance with Burgundy in 1442 and was a Scottish ally by virtue of Isabella Stewart's marriage and the Scottish–Breton pact of 22 October 1448.[26] The pact declared that Isabella, James' eldest surviving sister, and her husband were his heirs and specified that Brittany be included in any Scottish alliance. The treaty of Brussels also contained a clause exempting the Scottish king from any action undertaken in the name of the treaty that would be contrary to his alliance with France, renewed in December 1448.

The treaty represented a complex and carefully-constructed network of alliances and is indicative of a desire to widen Scotland's diplomatic options. Charles VII had written to James II early in 1447 to inform him of progress in the recent Anglo-French talks, the success of which would have neutralised Scottish foreign policy as it had done in 1444.[27] The developing unrest on the Anglo–Scottish border in 1448 acted as a further incentive to secure new alliances, and the benefits of securing the treaty were indicated by the renewal of Anglo–Scottish talks after 1 April.[28] But the Burgundian alliance also built on a series of diplomatic relationships secured by the betrothals and marriages of the Stewart princesses. James II's marriage to Mary of Guelders extended and strengthened a broad European network of alliances: it was arranged 'with the counsall of the king of fraunce The duke of sawoy The duke of ostrich the duke of bertane the duke of burgunze and all thire war bundyn'.[29]

The marital successes of the Stewarts between 1424 and 1449 contributed to a growing awareness of Scotland as a European power. It has been easy to assume that these successes are indicative of Scotland's, and the Stewarts', growing power and prestige in the early fifteenth century.[30] It seems, however, that Scotland's attractions included the minority of its king, which allowed European princes to capitalise on domestic power changes and dominate Scottish matrimonial policy. The Stewarts were known and available, and their marriages could be used to further French and Burgundian interests on the continent. Charles VII and Burgundy negotiated James II's marriage and that of his sister Eleanor as part of a competition for an imperial alliance rather than to protect or advance Scottish interests. Scotland's relative

26 Ditchburn, 'The Place of Guelders', 65; Edinburgh NAS, SP7/13.
27 Paris BN, MS. Latin 5414A, f.77.
28 Nicholson, R., *Scotland: The Later Middle Ages* (Edinburgh, 1974), 345–6; Dunlop, *James Kennedy*, 104.
29 'Auch. Chron.', 171.
30 McGladdery, *James II*, 42; Dunlop, *James Kennedy*, 85; Brown, *James I*, 111.

geographic isolation was a further attraction. Charles VII and the duke of Burgundy could create ties with other European states through Scottish marriages without establishing or strengthening a continental alliance. Furthermore, the complex network of Stewart marriages ensured that any new alliance was mutually acceptable to France and Burgundy.

But the significance of these marriages is not confined to their roles as indicators of Scotland's status within Europe. These marriages were the foundation of a complex and active network of family relationships. Annabella's betrothal was approved, and promoted by, Charles VII, the dauphin and the duke of Burgundy. Her brother-in-law, the duke of Brittany, was included in the marriage contract, and Annabella stayed in the household of her Veere in-laws en route to Savoy in 1445. Eleanor was invited to France at the instigation of Margaret Stewart, and visited another sister, Annabella, en route to Austria. The negotiations leading to Eleanor's marriage took over six months and needed the agreement of James II and her in-laws, the dukes of Brittany and Savoy. The marriage by proxy took place in the presence of its engineer, Charles VII, and his wife, Marie of Anjou. The involvement of the Stewart in-laws in the negotiation of additional Scottish matches is indicative of the broader significance of international marriage alliances. These marriages were each arranged in accordance with long-term policies and short-term requirements and, regardless of their initial purpose, linked to create a broader family network. This network facilitated both formal and informal communication and took a long-term interest in its members.   Furthermore, it was the women who created the links in this network by leaving their birth family to join another. They had little control over their eventual marriages, but because of their importance to the successful operation of the network they were prepared as much as possible for the upheavals they faced. Prospective brides were constantly reminded from an early age of the power and status they would acquire as a result of their marriages. Bower relates an improbable tale of Margaret Stewart's response to her betrothal to the dauphin in 1428. Margaret is reported to have said 'in admiration: "Why is this happening to me, that the throne of France is falling to me?"'[31] It is highly unlikely that the four-year-old Margaret uttered these words, but it is certain that she was well-versed in the greatness of her future from the time of her betrothal. James I and Joan Beaufort reminded their eldest daughter as she embarked

31 Bower, *Scotichronicon*, viii, 247.

on her journey to France of 'the honour the king of France was doing them and the honour of the prince to whom she would be married'. They then advised her to do well and wept with her.[32] The grief of separation could not be allowed to prevent an advantageous marriage. A book of hours owned by Isabella Stewart contains verses describing Margaret's farewell to the dauphin, saying 'Pour vous javoie la mer passee ou jay prins moult de grans plaisirs Si avoit tretouz mon lignage de france et descoce aussi car javoie este mariee au plus noble des fleurs delis...'[33] The use of Margaret's voice suggests that her role in uniting the Scottish and French royal houses was accepted by the young princess and that the honour of the French match more than justified her journey to France for marriage to a stranger at the age of eleven. The verses were similarly appropriate for Isabella, who also left her home and family for a foreign marriage, albeit at a slightly greater age. The transcription of these verses into Isabella's book of hours provides another example of the way in which women were educated about their role and behaviour.

Daughters were continually exhorted to be virtuous and obedient in order to be prepared for marriage. Another book of hours owned by Isabella Stewart includes 'advice for young girls and others' which reminds girls always to be aware of and to love their creator, and to avoid sin and sinful thoughts.[34] The instructions advise that when at table, girls only desire enough food for sustenance and then leave the table to thank God for what they have received or to beg his pardon if they have taken more than required. They also suggest that girls be on their guard when speaking to men and to ensure that any conversation is honourable and brief. There is a great deal of advice about behaviour, particularly about speech, including the reminder to 'contemplate your sins and faults' rather than talk in church. The advice is followed by a prayer in another hand beginning 'Hail Queen...pray for us' which is in turn followed by the plea to God to 'pray for the soul of Isabella, daughter of the King of Scots'.[35] The advice for girls may have been included in the original work and is indicative of the way in which clerical ideology was translated into lay terms. The prayers were later additions to the book, and it would seem that they were copied at Isabella's direction, indicating that she was using the book and was aware of its contents.

32 Paris BN, MS. Fr.17330, f.141v.
33 Paris BN, MS. Latin 1369, ff.447–8.
34 Paris BN, MS. n.a.Latin 588, ff.206r.-213r.
35 Paris BN, MS. n.a.Latin 588, f.213v.

Young girls of royal or noble houses were expected to marry, and the importance of virtuous behaviour to their ability to contract a good marriage was also emphasised in saints' lives. The most popular collection of such stories was the thirteenth-century *Golden Legend* which combined medieval social values with Christian virtues. Saint Margaret, for example, was 'fair, rich and noble' and 'was guarded by her parents with zealous care and taught to live virtuously; and so great were her probity and modesty that she refused to appear before the eyes of men'.[36] Margaret, like several other virgin martyrs, rejected the marriage arranged for her in favour of devoting her life to God, but her chastity and humility compensated for her disobedience to her parents' wishes. Other female saints such as Mary and Anne were able to remain virtuous despite marriage and motherhood. Anne married three times and bore three daughters, all named Mary. Her popularity was greatest in the fifteenth century and it has been argued that the growth of her cult was associated with the late medieval emphasis on marriage and the family.[37] Because Anne married by divine command rather than for love or lust she represented the virtue of obedience; young royal and noble girls were similarly expected to be obedient to marital decisions made for them by their parents. Anne's story and those of other saints were familiar to both the literate and non-literate laity. *The Golden Legend* was translated into English twice in the fifteenth century and used as a source for Scottish writers preparing their own vernacular *Legends of the Saints* around 1400.[38] These stories were read aloud in churches and formed the basis of popular feast days and pageants. The feast of the Purification of the Virgin, or Candlemas, commemorated Mary's purification following the birth of Christ and her status as virgin mother. The Aberdeen Candlemas pageant of 1442 featured Mary and Saints Bridget and Helena, virgin and mother saints respectively, and thus publicly displayed and celebrated the virtues of chastity and maternity.[39]

The fifteenth-century emphasis on the future glory and honour of marriage was in a sense a validation and celebration of female power

36 *Golden Legend*, 613.
37 Brandenbarg, T., 'St Anne and her family. The veneration of St Anne in connection with concepts of marriage and the family in the early-modern period' in L. Dresen-Coenders (ed.), *Saints and She-Devils: Images of Women in the 15th and 16th Centuries* (London, 1987), 102.
38 *Legends of the Saints in the Scottish Dialect of the Fourteenth Century*, ed. Metcalfe, W.M. (Edinburgh, 1896).
39 Mill, A.J., *Medieval Plays in Scotland* (London, 1927), 116.

through marriage. The protest of Margaret's youngest sister, Annabella, at the dissolution of her betrothal to the count of Geneva provides a rare example of a personal reaction to the vicissitudes of international marriage policy. Annabella did not necessarily question the right of her brother and his allies to arrange her marriage but objected to being asked to return to Scotland after ten years at the court of Savoy. Annabella was expected to abandon a decade of expectation that she would one day be the countess of Geneva, of training for the role, of developing networks of support for future use, and to start again in her early twenties.[40] This was a potentially greater sacrifice for Annabella than leaving her family and home as a child.

The huge effort, expense and public celebration of international marriage alliances provided a potent reminder to young brides of their potential. The steps on the path to marriage for young royal and noble brides were major life events, and were clearly marked and acknowledged as such. Mary of Guelders left her home and family at a young age to take up residence in the household of the duchess of Burgundy in preparation for marriage. During her residence in Burgundy, several marital alliances were discussed, potential suitors such as the king of Scots sent representatives to see her, and the duke hosted banquets for foreign embassies negotiating marriage alliances. The young noblewoman would have been keenly aware of the significance of her marriage. Soon after her marriage to the king of Scots was finalised in the treaty of Brussels, a proxy betrothal ceremony would have been held to celebrate the match before the Burgundian court. Her new status had immediate impact: Mary ceased to be referred to as the lady of Guelders in the Burgundian accounts and was styled 'la Royne descosse' in April. On 1 June, Mary joined her mother, the duchess of Guelders, in the duke's household. A week later, Mary left the Burgundian court to commence her journey to Scotland.[41] D'Escouchy reported that her departure for Scotland drove the duchess of Burgundy, her son and many other lords and ladies to tears.[42]

The lord of Veere, the duke's illegitimate sister and her husband, Isabel de Lalain and other gentlemen and women, accompanied Mary on her journey.[43] They stopped at the Isle of May, where Mary

---

40 Downie, 'Scotland and the European Marriage Market', 188–91.
41 Lille ADN, B3340, Compte second, f.19r.; B3414/116178, 116179, 116180, 116182, 116184, 116186.
42 D'Escouchy, *Chronique*, i, 176–7; Sommé, 'La jeunesse de Charles le Téméraire', 735.
43 The following account is from d'Escouchy, *Chronique*, i, 175–81.

disembarked to pray at the chapel of St Andrew, before finishing their journey in Leith on 18 June. The party was met by Scottish lords and escorted into Edinburgh where a large crowd had gathered to see the king's bride and pay their respects. An unnamed bishop and the chancellor took Mary and senior members of her entourage to meet her betrothed. Mary kneeled before the king, who lifted her to her feet, a signal for the onlookers to greet each other warmly and begin nearly three hours of festivities. The following day, several 'grandes dames du pays' visited Mary, including the countess of Orkney, the daughter of the earl of March and the king's aunt, Margaret, countess of Douglas. Mary received the ladies, who paid 'grant honneur et reverence à la Royne' and offered her their service. A week passed, in which the king ratified the formal contracts and provisions of the marriage and Mary met the great lords and ladies of Scotland and familiarised herself with her new home. Finally, on 2 July, the king sent his chancellor to inform her that they would be married the following day.

The marriage and Mary's coronation were formally celebrated at Holyrood on 3 July, 'le jour de la feste du Roy et de la Royne', with a mass attended by the Scottish court and its foreign visitors. After the wedding, Mary was taken into a chapel where she changed out of her gown, probably one of those purchased for her by the duchess of Burgundy, into a violet gown trimmed with ermine.[44] James II also replaced the gown trimmed with white cloth he had worn for the wedding ceremony with a gown of violet and ermine. The similarity of their clothing after the wedding underlined the partnership of king and queen created by the marriage, and emphasised the way in which her marriage to the king naturalised the foreign bride and qualified her for coronation as queen of Scotland. Marriage was a necessary condition for Mary's implicit adoption into the kingdom and for her coronation. Mary's hair was rearranged to lie loose on her shoulders, and she was then led back into the hall for her coronation. European queens, even those who became mothers before the coronation ceremony, were usually crowned with their hair loose to signify purity and virginity.[45] After several days of feasting and celebration, the Burgundian wedding party began its return journey, leaving only Isabel de Lalain and a few servants with the queen. Mary, then aged about sixteen, shed tears at

44 Lille ADN, B2004, f.335r.
45 Parsons, J.C., 'Ritual and Symbol in the English Medieval Queenship to 1500' in Fradenburg, *Women and Sovereignty*, 62; Scott, M., 'A Burgundian Visit to Scotland in 1449', *Costume*, xxi (1987), 17.

yet another separation, the culmination of a series of departures and new beginnings signifying her transformation from the daughter of the duke of Guelders to the queen of Scotland. The celebrations in Edinburgh marked the commencement of a career for which she had long been prepared.

FIVE

The public face of the Scottish queen consort

'. . . at the Request of the qwene'

The ceremonies of marriage and coronation marked the commencement of the careers of Joan Beaufort and Mary of Guelders as queens of Scotland. As such, these ceremonies did not simply celebrate the partnership created between two individuals but made larger statements about the nature of authority and the relationship between the king and his kingdom. They publicly displayed the queen's power and her access to royal authority, and symbolised the unity and prosperity of the kingdom and the king's duty to his subjects. Most importantly, they clearly demonstrated that the king and queen, or the king and kingdom, were two complementary parts of one whole. Neither the king nor the queen, the king or his kingdom, were regarded as self-sufficient. The way in which this 'gendered complementarity in royal roles' was displayed to, and understood by, the political community is basic to an appreciation of the role and power of the queen consort in fifteenth-century Scotland.[1] The ceremonies of marriage, coronation and intercession both acknowledged the queen's power and clearly defined its limits. In doing so, they also provided her with a means to cultivate and utilise her influence to greatest effect.

The royal marriage ceremony made few explicit statements about the role of queen consort and relied on contemporary perceptions of marriage and the relationship of husband and wife to define it. The theoretical equality of bride and groom was emphasised in canon law: each party had an equal right to give or withhold their consent to marriage, and marriage signified that each had surrendered power over their bodies to the other. However, while canon law stressed the equality of both parties, even in the right to request the dissolution of

---

1 Parsons, 'The Queen's Intercession', 161–2; see also Parsons, J.C., 'The Pregnant Queen as Counsellor and the Medieval Construction of Motherhood' in Parsons and Wheeler, *Medieval Mothering*, 53.

a marriage, it also assumed that in practice the wife was the weaker of the two.[2] This weakness was stressed in secular legal codes. A wife did not exercise her own legal rights, but required her husband's consent for her acts, even with regard to her own property, unless her husband was unable to give it. Lack of legal rights and the consequent lack of economic independence meant that any equality a wife had in theory did not exist in practice.

Literary representations of marriage also reveal that the wife was the inferior partner in a marital relationship.[3] Much of this literature was based on the work of a Greek scholar, Theophrastus, who argued that one could not be a scholar and have a wife because the wife consumed the time, money and energy that the scholar should be spending on his studies. Theophrastus identified the garrulousness and continual complaining of wives as particular problems, and these characteristics continued to be emphasised in later works. His views were elaborated by Jerome and influenced writers such as Abelard, John of Salisbury and Walter Map. Theophrastus was sufficiently well-known to be referred to by name in the *Roman de la Rose*, *The Canterbury Tales*, and by Boccaccio, Eustache Deschamps and Christine de Pizan. Widespread familiarity with his ideas was also ensured by the popularity of a late fourteenth-century French translation of a twelfth-century anti-marriage work, the *Lamentations of Matheolus*.[4] Walter Bower knew of Theophrastus' name from the work of Walter Map, and displayed a close knowledge of the anti-marriage tradition in his description of good and bad wives, an account which relies particularly heavily on the works of Map and Jerome.[5]

Many late medieval literary representations of marriage elaborated on the difficulties caused by a disruptive or disobedient wife. Problems arose, for example, when the wife was bossy or disobedient, when she controlled her husband through her sexuality, or when she wasted the

---

2 Hay, W., *Lectures on Marriage*, ed. and trans. J. C. Barry (Stair Society, 1967), 16, 65, 91–2; Scanlan, J.D., 'Husband and Wife. Pre-Reformation canon law of marriage of the officials' courts' in G.C.H.Paton (ed.), *An Introduction to Scottish Legal History* (Stair Society, 1958), 69–81.

3 For a survey of this literature, see Dow, B.H., *The Varying Attitude toward Women in French Literature of the Fifteenth Century: The Opening Years* (New York, 1936), 48–127 and Rogers, K.M., *The Troublesome Helpmate: A History of Misogyny in Literature* (Seattle, 1966), 72–99.

4 Schmitt, C.B., 'Theophrastus in the Middle Ages', *Viator*, 2 (1971), 255, 262–5; Bloch, *Medieval Misogyny*, 14–5, 54–5; McLoughlin, 'Equality of Souls', 231; Blumenfeld-Kosinski, R, 'Christine de Pizan and the Misogynistic Tradition', *Romanic Review*, 81 (1990), 284, 290; Dow, *Varying Attitude*, 104–12.

5 *Scotichronicon*, vii, 333–59.

family's economic resources.[6] A good wife was someone who knew her place and who maintained the family honour and wealth. These duties were also emphasised in didactic literature. A fifteenth-century Scottish poem, *Ratis Raving*, included specific advice on selecting a wife, suggesting that she be 'of gud lynag and gud renown' and that attention be paid to her mother: if the mother was a good wife, the daughter was likely to be also. The poem also advises the husband to 'leid hir wysely with fauore gyf thow wyll haf ess and honore' and to 'wyrk alan with that wnskill that scho has chosin of hir wyll', recognising the wife's essential weakness and the husband's duty to oversee her behaviour.[7] The dangers of covetousness and pride are described in another poem, *Documenta Matris ad Filiam*, which states that a wife's excessive interest in clothes ensured that her husband's wealth 'Sall scant be worth his viffis class' and that men would presume that she 'dois it for paramour'. Modesty and avoidance of excess were the key virtues of a wife, who was expected to make everything run smoothly without drawing attention to herself.[8] The parallels between the roles of queen consort (in the kingdom) and wife (in the household) were noted by Christine de Pizan in *The Treasure of the City of Ladies*. Several chapters of the work describe the ways in which a good princess should conduct herself towards her husband and his family and friends amongst the more general advice on morality, finance and court management.[9] The implications of the queen's mismanagement of her role were, however, greater than those of the average wife in that her potential influence over her husband and her preference for her own family could interfere with the government of the kingdom, while her extravagance could affect crown finances.

Bower described in detail the potential damage a 'bad' queen consort could inflict upon the kingdom. The chronicler wrote that before their divorce in 1369, Margaret Drummond had persuaded her husband, David II, to arrest and imprison Robert the Steward and three of his sons. Following the divorce, Margaret travelled to Avignon to appeal against the divorce, an action which 'disturbed the whole kingdom'.[10]

---

6 Jeay, M., 'Sexuality and Family in Fifteenth-Century France: Are Literary Sources a Mask or a Mirror?', *Journal of Family History*, 4 (1979), 329, 323–3, 341–2; Jordan, *Renaissance Feminism*, 87.

7 *Ratis Raving and Other Early Scots Poems on Morals*, ed. Girvan, R. (Scottish Text Society, 1939), 27.

8 *Ratis Raving*, 83, 88–9.

9 *Treasure*, 62–6.

10 *Scotichronicon*, vii, 359.

The order of Bower's account implies that Margaret's meddling in Avignon was typical of her misuse of power as queen and evidence of her determination to retain that power. His account makes it clear that the level of the queen's influence over the king was unacceptable, but in stating that the king released his prisoners and restored them to favour after the divorce, he explicitly linked that influence to marriage. One manuscript of the chronicle goes further by stating that the king had acquiesced to the queen's suggestion because he was 'boiling with passion', equating Margaret's political power as a queen with her sexual power as a woman. This equation is significant. It was unacceptable for anyone to exercise undue influence over the king, but the queen's influence was differentiated from that of other royal favourites and treated in a gender-specific manner.

The broader context surrounding Bower's account of the marriage of David II and Margaret Drummond provides further illustration of the chronicler's gendered representation of her queenship. He introduced the subject of the marriage by asserting that the king was attracted to Margaret's beauty rather than her character.[11] Bower used the king's decision as an example of the importance of giving careful consideration to the decision to marry and the choice of bride, implicitly suggesting that Margaret's desirability overpowered David's ability to think rationally. This implication in turn established a link between Margaret's influence and bad government: if this woman caused the king to act irrationally, his marriage to her would impede rational and effective government. The suggestion that Margaret was a bad influence was further emphasised in Bower's list of four issues to be considered when choosing a bride. He explicitly rejected beauty and passion as bases for a sound marriage and gave advice on how to correct, guide and love a wife after marriage. Bower followed this advice with a long discourse on the subject of bad women and by a shorter section on the merits of good wives before returning to the subject of David II's marriage and divorce. The statement that Margaret was responsible for the arrest and imprisonment of Robert the Steward thus follows not only the account of her marriage and divorce but also six chapters of rhetoric on the subject of bad women and good wives. This structure emphasised that Margaret's political influence was acquired through sexual power and institutionalised by marriage. This personal relationship had political implications. Any individual's power over the king represented an erosion of the natural order and of royal authority, but

11 *Scotichronicon*, vii, 333. The following discussion is based on *ibid.*, vii, 333–59.

a wife's power over her husband completely inverted natural order. A king was expected to rule his kingdom as a husband ruled his wife, and the queen's undue influence over the king constituted a double challenge to that order. In allowing the queen to influence his government, the king was not only less of a king but less of a man.

Bower's account of the dangers represented by an unruly wife reflected the assumption that the relationship between the king and his wife was symbolic of that between the king and his kingdom. The metaphor of the king's marriage to his kingdom became increasingly popular in late medieval Italian political thought and spread through Europe in the fifteenth and sixteenth centuries. Henry II of France received a ring to symbolise this relationship at his coronation in 1547, and in 1604, James VI told the English parliament 'I am the husband, and all the whole Isle is my lawfull Wife'.[12] The metaphor drew on established Church practice, which represented nuns as brides of Christ and invested bishops with an episcopal ring at ordination to symbolise their marriage to their churches. These practices were in turn intended to represent the union between Christ and his Church. The precedents were clerical, but what made the metaphor of king as husband of his kingdom especially useful to late medieval political theorists were the multiple parallels between this relationship and that of husband and wife. Both king and husband were obliged to make vows to fulfill their duties of government and defence, but their spouses, despite their obligation to obey their husbands, were separate entities and partners in the relationship. In particular, the property provisions made for a wife at the time of marriage provided an analogy for the kind of power the king had over the financial resources of the crown.[13] A wife could use the lands bestowed on her as dower but she had no power to dispose of them, and they returned to her husband's family following her death.

Scottish understanding of the relationship between the king and his kingdom drew heavily on Celtic myth and ritual. In Irish mythology, the kingdom was represented as a goddess, and her true ruler was her husband, the king. Celtic king-making ceremonies emphasised the relationship between king/ruler and goddess/land in the form of the

---

12 Burns, J.H., *Lordship, Kingship, and Empire. The Idea of Monarchy 1400–1525* (Oxford, 1992), 52, 110; Enright, M.J., 'King James and his island: an archaic kingship belief?', *SHR*, 55 (1976), 29; Kantorowicz, E., *The King's Two Bodies: A Study in Medieval Political Theology* (Princeton, 1957), 218–23.

13 Hay, *Lectures on Marriage*, 18, 28; Kantorowicz, *The King's Two Bodies*, 212–18.

'wedding-feast of kingship' and rituals requiring the king to sit or stand on a sacred stone.[14] Versions of these myths were part of Scottish political vocabulary in the early fifteenth century and appear in the works of Fordun, Wyntoun and Bower. Bower, following Fordun, wrote that the Scottish people were descended from Gaythelos, the son of a Greek king, and Scota, the daughter and only child of a pharaoh. The two were married to reward Gaythelos for his services to the pharaoh, a match which gave the ambitious Greek a claim to succeed to the kingdom of Egypt. The figure of Scota parallels the goddess of Celtic myth: by marrying her, Gaythelos can claim rulership of the kingdom. More importantly, Scota became the mother of the Scottish people, and provided them and their kingdom with a name which, as Bower records, they were proud to use. Bower also related a story about an ancient stone given to Simon Brecc by the gods as a sign that he would become king. Like the sacred stone of Celtic king-making rituals, it was carried by the Scots from Spain to Ireland and finally to Scotland, to be used as a throne for all their kings.[15]

The belief in the personal relationship between king and kingdom embodied in mythology was represented in ritual and ceremony. In Scotland, while the king did not marry his kingdom at his coronation, he did swear to be a 'loving father to the people', a paternal metaphor echoed in the recitation of the king's genealogy at the ceremony.[16] At the inauguration of Alexander III in 1249, according to Bower, the king was seated on the royal stone while a highlander recited the genealogy of the king back to Gaythelos and Scota, illustrating the ways in which the old mythology could influence contemporary ritual and represent contemporary ideas.[17] In addition, after inauguration or coronation, the medieval Scottish king was known as 'rex scotorum' rather than 'rex scotiae'; he was the leader of his subjects rather than head of an abstract state. The belief in the close relationship between king and his people was also implicit in official sources. The language of marriage negotiations, for example, stressed that the personal bond between two individuals or two families created a bond between two political communities, a belief resting on the assumption that the individual symbolised the community, and that the two were to some degree interchangeable.

14 Enright, 'King James and his island', 32, 34–5.
15 *Scotichronicon*, i, 27–9, 31, 45, 65–7; *Chron. Wyntoun*, ii, 191, 199.
16 Lyall, R.J., 'The Medieval Scottish Coronation Service: some seventeenth-century evidence', *Innes Review*, xxviii, 1 (1977), 9, 18–9.
17 *Scotichronicon*, v, 295; *Chronica Gentis Scotorum*, i, 294–5.

The king's marriage therefore provided an opportunity to celebrate the peace and prosperity of the kingdom, and to anticipate the continuity of the monarchy and good government through the birth of the king's legitimate heirs. The king's bride was essential to the continuing prosperity of the kingdom but was otherwise of secondary importance in the marriage ceremony and ritual.

The queen was a secondary figure even at her own coronation. There is no evidence of any kind of coronation ceremony for Scottish queens taking place before 1331 when Joan Plantagenet was crowned at the same ceremony as her husband, David II, at Scone by the bishop of St Andrews on 24 November.[18] In some respects this is not surprising, as a woman became queen through marriage to a king rather than as the result of a coronation ritual or vow, but it is unusual in a European context. French and English queens, for example, had enjoyed coronation ceremonies for centuries despite the fact that the ritual was not essential to their changed status. It is possible that the Scottish queen's coronation was instituted in 1331 as part of the elaboration of the new ceremony for the king – David II's coronation was the first since the papal grant on 13 June 1329 of the right of Scottish kings to receive coronation and unction – and that it was used in some form for every queen thereafter.[19] If this is the case, it would seem that the 1329 bull admitted queens to what had previously been a masculine inauguration rite derived in part from Celtic practice. The installation of the Scottish king on the sacred stone and the recitation of his genealogy at the inauguration were features of Celtic ceremony that could not easily be adapted to include his wife. The desire of Scottish kings to receive the rites of coronation and unction was representative of their interest in achieving parity with other European monarchies, but also of the need to secure the Bruce, and later the Stewart, claim to the Scottish throne. The coronation of both David II and Joan at the same ceremony strengthened the king's claim to the throne in the face of the combined opposition of Joan's brother, Edward III, and Edward Balliol, the rival claimant. The rights of the children of the marriage, as the children of two crowned parents, to succeed to the throne would have been virtually beyond dispute, and the Bruce dynasty would have been securely established.

The coronations of Queens Euphemia and Annabella in the late fourteenth century supported the Stewart efforts to elevate the dynasty

---

18 *Scotichronicon*, vii, 71–3.
19 Lyall, 'Medieval Scottish Coronation Service', 3.

and to establish distance from the nobility from which it came. The Stewarts' intermarriage with European royal families and increasing identification with St Margaret in the fifteenth century further differentiated them from the rest of the Scottish nobility. This royal dynastic interest coincided with that of the political community itself which, it has been argued, supported the Stewart dynasty and accepted its excesses in order to safeguard the monarchy and the kingdom's independence. The parallel interests of the Stewarts and of the political community were also expressed in the popularity of the work of historians such as Fordun and Bower which promoted the Stewart dynasty and 'an ideology of patriotic conservatism' as opposed to the evils of succession crises, wars and national servitude.[20] The institution of a ceremony for the queen's coronation in the fourteenth century was therefore part of an overall domestic political interest in strengthening the institution of monarchy. The elevation in status of the Scottish queen through the ceremony of coronation set her apart as first lady in the kingdom which in turn emphasised the king's superior status and set apart their children as more royal.

The institution of a coronation ceremony for Scottish queens was intended to enhance the power and authority of the king rather than that of the queen. In this respect it was representative of another European trend that saw the symbolic and ceremonial role of queenship expanded at the expense of its overtly political features.[21] In countries such as France and England, for example, there are signs of change in the queen's coronation ceremonies in the later Middle Ages. The surviving accounts of the French queen's coronation – written in 1364, 1492 and 1504 – describe increasingly elaborate ceremonies which, it has been argued, reflected the increasing importance of the 'cult of rulership' and dynastic concerns.[22] A similar cult may also have inspired the composition of the *Liber Regalis*, the earliest detailed evidence of English coronation rituals for both king and queen, in the 1380s.[23] The later evidence of the Scottish medieval coronation

---

20 Mason, R., 'Kingship, Tyranny and the Right to Resist in Fifteenth Century Scotland', *SHR*, lxvi, 143–4, 146–7.
21 Strohm, P., 'Queens as Intercessors' in P. Strohm, *Hochon's Arrow. The Social Imagination of Fourteenth-Century Texts* (Princeton, 1992), 95; Facinger, 'Study of Medieval Queenship', 1–48; Parsons, 'The Queen's Intercession', 149–50; McCartney, E., 'Ceremonies and Privileges of Office: Queenship in Late Medieval France' in Carpenter and McLean, *Power of the Weak*, 178–219.
22 McCartney, 'Ceremonies and Privileges', 180–2.
23 Parsons, 'Ritual and Symbol', 62.

service indicates that it was 'firmly in the Western European tradition', suggesting that the late medieval elaboration of the service may also have had an impact on the queen's coronation ritual in Scotland.[24] Just as the institution of a coronation ritual for the Scottish queen was not intended to benefit her directly, the late medieval French and English evidence indicates that this elaboration of ceremony was not designed to promote the queen as a figure of authority but rather to emphasise her status as the king's wife.[25]

The act of coronation itself emphasised the queen's relationship with the king rather than with the political community. Like her European counterparts, the Scottish queen did not swear an oath at her coronation ceremony. Coronation oaths emphasised a king's moral responsibilities and his duties to defend the kingdom and uphold justice and order. They summarised the functions of kingship and publicly announced that a king derived his authority in part from, and was to some degree accountable to, the political community. The queen, however, was not accountable to the community but to her husband, and the community did not owe loyalty to her directly but to the king. The queen's power was acquired by marriage to the king and, as a wife, she was expected to be obedient and accountable to her husband. Her responsibilities and duties as wife were encapsulated in her marriage vows and needed no further elaboration. This in turn meant that the queen was represented as her husband's partner rather than as possessing a separate political persona, and that her responsibilities consisted of assisting the king in his duties. The queen acquired the power and status of royalty through coronation but not the authority of the king's majesty.

The queen's symbolically equal yet politically subordinate status was also illustrated by the timing of her coronation ceremony. The coincidence of Mary of Guelders' marriage and coronation ceremonies underlined the secondary and derivative nature of the queen's power: her acquisition of power explicitly depended upon her marriage to the source of that power. Similarly, Margaret Drummond was 'exalted ... in splendour as queen' following her marriage to David II.[26] Euphemia Ross and Annabella Drummond were crowned after their husbands despite the fact that their marriages took place before their husbands

---

24 Lyall, 'Medieval Scottish Coronation Service', 17; Mason, 'Kingship, Tyranny and the Right to Resist', 149 n.2.
25 McCartney, 'Ceremonies and Privileges', 178–84; Parsons, 'Ritual and Symbol', 61–6.
26 *Chronica Genta Scotorum*, i, 382; *Scotichronicon*, vii, 359.

succeeded to the throne. The deferral of their coronations illustrated that their status and power as queen were doubly derivative: acquired through marriage to men who later gained the authority of kingship. Neither Euphemia nor Annabella could be crowned until their husbands were kings in their own right. Annabella's coronation was performed at Scone on 15 August 1390, the day after that of her husband, Robert III.[27] Euphemia was crowned at Scone in 1372 by the bishop of Aberdeen while her husband, Robert II, was crowned at Scone on 26 March 1371 by the bishop of St Andrews. The lengthy delay in her coronation may have been due to succession politics: Euphemia, once crowned as queen, might have attempted to raise her sons higher in the order of succession than their step-brothers. There is some doubt over the exact date of the ceremony, but it occurred between 6 December 1372 and 24 March 1373, before the passing on 4 April of the entail determining the order of succession and probably while the matter was under debate. With the succession under discussion, any risk Euphemia's coronation may have posed was considerably diminished.[28]

Joan Beaufort married an uncrowned king but, unlike Euphemia and Annabella, was crowned on the same day (21 May 1424) and by the same bishop (St Andrews) as her husband. This dual coronation did not, however, suggest that Joan's power was equal to that of the king. James I had succeeded to the throne in 1406 and possessed the royal title for 18 years before his coronation. In his case, the coronation ceremony was a formal celebration of his succession nearly two decades before rather than a confirmation of a recent elevation in station or authority. His queen could be crowned on the same day because her husband was, in effect, already the king. The different significance of the two coronations is revealed in Bower's description of the event. He records that the king was installed upon the royal seat by the earl of Fife as custom demanded, and that six days later, the king opened a parliament at Perth at which 'he put forward many matters for the future welfare of the kingdom'.[29] The king's coronation was therefore explicitly linked to ancient and national traditions as well as to the authority and functions of kingship. The queen's coronation, on the other hand, was an adjunct to, and confirmation of, the king's own, and underlined her role as subordinate partner to the king.

27 *Scotichronicon*, vii, 367, 375; viii, 3.
28 *Scotichronicon*, vii, 508 n.5.
29 *Scotichronicon*, viii, 221, 241.

The nature of the royal relationship and the queen's influence over the king were most clearly displayed in acts of intercession. The assumption behind requesting the queen's intercession with the king was that she could use her influence as wife to persuade her husband to grant her wishes. The belief in the queen's power to change the king's will was so common it was utilised in a fourteenth-century Franciscan exemplum to explain the power of Mary, as Queen of Heaven, to intercede with Christ: 'We ought to imitate the man who has incurred the King's anger. What does he do? He goes secretly to the Queen and promises a present.'[30] Several powerful men requested the assistance of Joan Beaufort and Mary of Guelders in persuading their husbands, James I and James II, to see the reason of the petitioners' arguments. Pope Eugenius IV sent three letters to Scotland in July 1436 in support of his nuncio, the bishop of Urbino. One letter was addressed to James I directly, while the other two sought the support of the queen and the clergy and nobility in securing the king's assistance. The letter to Joan Beaufort asked her 'to exhort the king', her husband, to assist his nuncio.[31] Joan's support as a wife rather than as a queen or political figure was sought by the pope and her efforts were to take the form of wifely persuasion rather than direct action.

Similarly, Charles VII wrote to Mary of Guelders in 1450 to request her assistance in persuading James II to support the French. The French king sent an embassy to Scotland before mid-April requesting Scottish military aid and wrote a letter to Bishop Turnbull to solicit his support for the scheme. Mary's letter to Charles dated 1 July was written in response to a similar request which she had received. The queen began her letter by assuring Charles that she was well, perhaps referring to the premature birth and death of her first child in May, then offered her services to the French cause.[32] While these letters illustrate a basic belief in the queen's influence, the fact that the petitioners sent similar letters requesting the assistance of other influential figures in Scottish political life indicates that these European potentates did not write to Scottish queens in the belief that they were the true powers behind the throne. Petitioners wrote to the king directly to persuade him of the justice of their cause and to other figures who might assist in that persuasion. The queen was particularly useful in this context. She could use her influence as a woman and wife over her husband and,

---

30 Quoted in Parsons, 'The Queen's Intercession', 157.
31 *CPR. Papal Letters*, viii, 229–30.
32 Stevenson, *Letters and Papers*, i, 299–306.

as in the case of Charles VII writing to Mary of Guelders, could be in debt to the petitioners for earlier support or share family connections with them.

This dual persona of public weakness and private power was institutionalised in the acts of intercession performed by queens in public settings. English evidence, much fuller than Scottish, suggests that while queens often added their support to petitions before forwarding them, public acts of intercession by queens were relatively rare. Furthermore, it has been argued that the rarity of those occasions and the way in which they were conducted indicates that they were 'undoubtedly devised in advance'.[33] An examination of the acts of intercession performed by Joan Beaufort and Mary of Guelders, who each performed such acts at least twice, reveals that the acts share common features and utilise the same basic symbolism, suggesting that they too were staged events. Joan Beaufort's first recorded act of intercession took place in August 1429 and was performed on behalf of Alexander, Lord of the Isles. Bower records that Alexander had attempted to make peace with James I but that 'the king was in no way prepared to negotiate, [and so] Alexander surrendered himself absolutely to the king's mercy'. The ceremony of submission was intended to emphasise the lord's complete abjection before the king through his state of undress, his kneeling posture before the king and his offering of a sword, symbol of his power as knight but also the weapon of noble execution, to the king. While Alexander was offering the sword, 'the queen and the more important lords of the kingdom' interceded for him and the king 'admitted him to his grace' before sending him to Tantallon Castle while he debated what to do with him.[34] The act of intercession was thus the mechanism by which the king could move from a position of intractability to one of conciliation while maintaining an appearance of strong and decisive kingship. Given the contemporary awareness of the process and meaning of intercession and the need for a resolution to the dispute, it is likely that the court would have been aware of the potential of staging such a ceremony. The fact that it was the queen and the important lords who interceded for Alexander is also significant: the only way to ensure such coordinated activity would have been to choreograph the event beforehand. James I was especially cognisant

33 Parsons, 'The Pregnant Queen as Counsellor', 47.
34 *Scotichronicon*, viii, 263; *Liber Pluscardensis*, ed. Skene, F.J.H. (Edinburgh, 1877–80), i, 376; Neilson, G., 'The Submission of the Lord of the Isles to James I: its Feudal Symbolism', *The Scottish Antiquary*, xv (1901), 118.

of the benefits of public intercession as he had been the beneficiary of such an act at the coronation of Katherine of Valois in 1422 when she pleaded with Henry V for James' release.[35] Joan's involvement in the 1429 ceremony was but one element of a larger ritual designed to clarify the relationship between the king and his subjects and to portray the king as merciful and all-powerful. The ceremony recognised the existence of the queen's influence but was not primarily intended to make statements about her power as intercessor. Her influence was not unique but was explicitly linked with that of the leading nobles and, more importantly, the outcome of the ceremony had been decided before the ritual took place.

Joan Beaufort interceded a second time for the Lord of the Isles and for the earl of Douglas in 1431. Douglas had been arrested earlier in the year and imprisoned in Loch Leven Castle before being released on 29 September, while Alexander had remained in captivity following his submission to the king in 1429. At parliament in October 1431 the king pardoned the two earls 'at the urging of the queen, bishops and prelates, earls and barons' but, as in 1429, the outcome was most likely determined by the king before intercession was performed. Douglas was released at Michaelmas in order to win the support of the political community in the forthcoming parliament. The reluctance of that parliament to continue funding the king's northern campaign meant that James was obliged not only to confirm Douglas' pardon but also to pardon the Lord of the Isles and abandon his military campaign.[36] Once again, the only way to pardon Alexander without losing authority was to stage an act of intercession. This ceremony displayed the king's willingness to listen to his subjects and to be merciful while simultaneously acting as a reminder of his power, unique in the kingdom, to punish and to pardon his subjects. The queen's role was analogous to that she played in 1429: her influence was not decisive but was simply part of the overall influence of the major political figures in the kingdom, an influence which itself was not decisive but staged in order to achieve a predetermined objective.

A similar ceremony occurred in the parliament of June 1451 at which Mary of Guelders and the Estates interceded with James II for the earl of Douglas. The Auchinleck chronicler records that Douglas

35 Crawford, A. (ed.), *The Letters of the Queens of England 1100–1547* (Stroud, 1994), 118.
36 *Scotichronicon*, viii, 265; Brown, *James I*, 139–40.

put him body landis and gudis in the king's grace and the king resavit him till his grace at the Request of the qwene and the three estatis and grantit him all his lordshippis agane outtane the erldome of wigtoun … and gaf him and all his a fre Remission of all things bygane to the day forsaid. And all gud scottismen war rycht blyth of that accordance.[37]

On this occasion, Douglas seems to have chosen to perform formal submission to the king in order to gain time before making his next move. The king's interest in accepting the submission stemmed from his desire to humiliate the earl and to remind him of the extent of the king's authority. It was this authority that enabled the king to receive the earl's lands as well as to regrant them. At the same time, the earl's course of action forced the king to display mercy. The king could not refuse to accept the submission and his response of regranting the earl's lands minimised the earl's grounds for complaint at his treatment. It was therefore in the interests of both parties to arrange formal submission and intercession at parliament, and in the interests of parliament itself, 'rycht blyth' of the temporary resolution of the conflict, to mediate and ensure that resolution was reached. As in the previous two cases, the outcome of the formal act of intercession was predetermined and the queen only a bit player in the proceedings.

Mary of Guelders' first recorded act of intercession had been performed two days after the confirmation by parliament of her marriage settlement on 24 January 1450. Eight bishops had protested to parliament about the king's requisition of the personal estates of deceased bishops, and the queen and bishops exhorted the king to approve and seal a charter intended to redress the problem. The intercession was successful, but the fact that the king needed clerical support following the forfeiture and execution of the Livingstons suggests that it had been planned in order to secure that support.[38] While the queen's involvement in this matter was primarily of importance to the king, the fact that the queen's contribution was explicitly recognised suggests that she was also intended to benefit. Mary had been in Scotland for six months, but the sheer size of her dowry and the measures taken to pay it – the attack on the Livingstons – may have made her the focus of discontent. The Livingston executions took place on 21 January, Mary's dower was confirmed on 22 January and she interceded for the

---

37 'Auch. Chron.', 165; *APS*, ii , 67–71.
38 *APS*, ii, 37–8; *RMS*, ii, no. 307.

bishops two days later. The timing of the ceremony strongly suggests that it was intended in part to emphasise the queen's female weakness and subordination and to allay suspicions regarding the extent of her influence. The act of intercession served as a reminder that her political power was not her own but was derived from the king's authority, that her requests had to be approved by him before having the force of law. Perhaps more importantly, the ceremony's utilisation of assumptions about the marital relationship and the power of wifely influence illustrated that just as the king listened and acceded to his wife's plea, so he would also protect her from attack. The ceremony may also have secured the support of the bishops for the queen and provided her with further protection.

These four instances of the queen's intercession were formal occasions apparently staged in order to achieve a predetermined outcome. There was, however, one further act of intercession performed by Joan Beaufort which appears from Bower's description to have been spontaneous rather than pre-planned. Bower related that a noble relative of the king struck another man. Upon hearing the victim's complaint, the king ordered the victim to stab his attacker's hand. The 'queen with her ladies and the prelates with their clerics prostrated themselves on the floor' and pleaded with the king for an hour to pardon the culprit. The king finally relented, and punished the man by temporarily banning him from the court and the king's presence.[39] The event as described was spontaneous, but Bower's account must be treated carefully. It is used to illustrate the king's virtue of punishing evil before it was able to take root and spread and to demonstrate that the king could be merciful without losing sight of justice. The absence of dating for the incident and Bower's admission that he could not remember the occasion for the attacker's presence at court adds to the impression that the story is more of an example of good kingship than an account of a specific event. This vagueness contrasts with Bower's clarity about the basic elements of the story which illustrate the king's authority over his nobility. The weakness of the women and clergy, traditional intercessors and recipients of the king's protection, and their posture of prostration is juxtaposed with the strength and authority of the king and serves to emphasise those qualities. The queen's intercession is not the focus of the account and is only necessary as the mechanism by which the king's authority and mercy can be revealed. Furthermore, the queen's intervention is represented as the culprit's last chance, and

39 *Scotichronicon*, viii, 321.

its association with clerical intercession underlines the almost divine nature of her intervention. The queen and her associates are implicitly removed from normal procedures of government and justice. Bower in this account presented his readers with an idealised king and an idealised queen, just as publicly performed acts of intercession displayed those idealised roles to the political community.

Scottish evidence of the queen's intercession in the fifteenth century is similar to that of French and English examples in its promotion of basic ideals and themes about kingship and queenship. The queen's intercession enabled her to reveal a potential failing in the king and provided him with the opportunity to correct it. It was also a mechanism for the king to change his mind. Finally, the emphasis on the queen's femininity, often highlighted by pregnancy, in accounts of intercession emphasised the king's masculinity.[40] These stereotypes of royal roles were representative of wider perceptions of the queen's power. Petitioners directed requests for redress to the queen who then forwarded them, with her support, to the appropriate recipient. Only two examples of petitions to Mary of Guelders survive. In May 1451, a barber named Aitkyne was made a burgess of Edinburgh following the intervention of Mary of Guelders on his behalf.[41] In April the following year, Mary interceded with the Teutonic Order for an Edinburgh merchant, James Lauder.[42] On both occasions Mary was in the later stages of pregnancy: she interceded for Aitkyne before the birth of her daughter, Mary (before July 1451), and for Lauder while pregnant with the future James III (born before June 1452). The figure of the pregnant queen was a central motif in many accounts of intercession and was used to draw attention to the queen's femininity and similarity to Mary, holy mother and intercessor. It is likely that both Aitkyne and Lauder deliberately chose to appeal to Mary of Guelders during her pregnancies, and that they were not alone in doing so. The volume of such activity in the English records suggests that the perceptions of the queen as more approachable than the king and possessed of considerable powers of persuasion were widespread.[43] The reaction of the

40 Strohm, 'Queens as Intercessors', 102–5. See also Parsons, 'The Pregnant Queen as Counsellor', 39–61.
41 *Extracts from the Records of the Burgh of Edinburgh, AD 1403–1528* (Scottish Burgh Records Society, 1869), 12.
42 Mary of Guelders' letter is held in the Berlin archives (Geheimes Staatarchiv, OBA, 9485) and is mentioned in a subsequent letter by Lauder, printed in Stein, W. (ed.), *Hansisches Urkundenbuch*, 8 (Halle, 1899), no.172.
43 Parsons, 'Queen's Intercession', 147–77.

citizens of London to the new queen, Anne of Bohemia, in January 1382 provides a striking example of this belief. The citizens requested the queen's assistance in preserving the liberties of the city either on the day of her London reception or of her marriage to Richard II.[44] The citizens' lack of experience of Anne's queenship was irrelevant on this occasion. They were reacting to an ideal rather than a particular queen, and the wording of the request clearly stated that they were calling upon her to act as mediator just as her predecessors had done.

The ubiquity of the representation of the queen as intercessor has a further implication for an examination of queenship. In the preceding examples, the queen has appeared as a passive figure defined by the symbols and imagery of others rather than as an active figure capable of utilising the same imagery to define and maximise her own power. Queens could not alter the basic structure of the proceedings of intercession, but they could attempt to gain some advantage from the existing processes. Christine de Pizan advocated just such behaviour when she exhorted the princess to *play* a passive role, to achieve objectives discreetly while maintaining a facade of delicate propriety and femininity. In this sense, it is important to note that while the king and political community could choreograph acts of intercession in order to achieve certain objectives and to illustrate qualities important to them, they could not actually control how these acts were understood. Ceremonies of intercession relied upon the femininity of the queen and her lack of authority for their effect. They publicly demonstrated that her influence required the king's approval to become law. But in doing so they clearly displayed to everyone present that the queen possessed, and was capable of using, influence over her husband. They revealed that her femininity could be a source of strength rather than a weakness. It was in the queen's interest to foster the belief in her power as intercessor. The more influence she was seen to wield, the more people would be drawn to her in an attempt to seek her goodwill, a process which further expanded her influence.

Furthermore, staged acts of intercession clearly identified the queen as a political figure. In all of the accounts of the intercession performed by Joan Beaufort and Mary of Guelders the queen was explicitly associated with one or more of the estates of the realm. Representing the queen as wife functioned as a reminder of the limits within which she had to act and of the appearances she had to maintain while doing so. It also demonstrated that as wife of the king she had a political role to

44 Strohm, 'Queens as Intercessors', 105–6.

play. While she lacked the authority to govern alone, she was nonethe-less associated with government. Modern studies of intercession, based largely on English sources, emphasise the queen's marginality in the political arena and the way in which she moved suddenly to the centre of that arena to perform intercession spontaneously and alone. Her centrality as intercessor effectively underlined her exclusion from the official processes of government.[45] The intercession performed by Joan Beaufort and Mary of Guelders does not fit this pattern but rather provides a highly visible demonstration of the partnership of king and queen in fifteenth-century Scotland.

45 Strohm, 'Queens as Intercessors', 96, 101; Parsons, 'Queen's Intercession', 154, 160–1.

SIX

The Scottish queen consort, 1424–60

'Rex cum consensu et assensu consortis sue'

The Scottish queen consort's involvement in political life was only rarely transformed into something approaching official power. In summer 1428, James I was preparing to travel north to deal with the Lord of the Isles and faced opposition to his plans in the July General Council. The king, with the advice and consent of his council, ordered noble heirs and the newly-installed bishops to swear an oath to the queen, as well as to him, as they received their inheritances and benefices.[1] This act effectively and explicitly established the queen's status as the king's partner in government. Like other wives, the queen was regarded as one person with, and obedient to, her husband, and did not require a separate relationship with the political community. The oath of 1428 thus had major political implications: it endowed Joan with a separate identity and, in effect, a quasi-official role in government. At the same General Council, the queen was included with the king and his seven bishops and eight earls in the oath to uphold the alliance with France. Her inclusion in the oath and the discussions of her daughter's marriage further demonstrated the king's trust in the queen and associated her with the leaders of the kingdom.[2] The queen then travelled north to Inverness with her husband, presumably because the king valued her company and her counsel, but also to endow the journey with the appearance of a stately procession rather than a military expedition.[3] In August of the following year, she interceded with the king on behalf of the Lord of the Isles. The queen's status as a political figure was therefore highlighted during a period of political tension. She supported her husband and, by participating in a General Council, a northern expedition and a staged act of interces-

1 *APS*, ii, 17.
2 Paris AN, J678/24.
3 *ER*, iv, 473; Brown, *James I*, 97.

sion, enabled the king to secure a desirable and workable solution to a pressing political problem.

The Estates were also asked to give their letters of fidelity to the queen in the parliament of January 1435.[4] The king's demand reflected the growing hostility in preceding years to his financial demands and to his intervention on behalf of his nephew, the earl of Angus, in Angus' dispute with the earl of March. More importantly, the oath recognised the extent of the queen's political influence and sanctioned that influence by effectively naming her as the king's choice as regent in the event of his death. It was made during the final phase of Franco–Scottish negotiations over Margaret's marriage, in which the queen participated, and during a period in which the queen's income and land-holdings were increasing, partly at Atholl's expense. It also recognised the queen's potential unpopularity should James decide to abandon the French marriage plans in favour of an English alliance. The possibility of an Anglo–Scottish truce and a marriage between Henry VI and one of James' daughters had been raised in February 1434. A General Council rejected the truce proposal in October on the basis that it had been suggested in order to create division within the Scottish kingdom.[5] Bower's description of the event suggests that there had been some initial support for the English proposals, but that this support had dissipated in the face of arguments suggesting that the proposals were a trick. Even if Bower's statement that 'these English indeed behaved like the artful wolf' was representative only of a minority opinion, it is evidence of some distrust of the English amongst the Scottish political community. Any such distrust was likely to extend to the English-born queen, who was clearly involved in royal marriage negotiations and whose brother had visited Scotland to renew Anglo–Scottish talks only months before the General Council discussed the English proposal.

The swearing of the two oaths in 1428 and 1435 does not indicate how acceptable this expansion of the queen's role was to the political community. The fact that the oaths were made during the negotiations for Margaret's marriage may have assisted in their acceptance: her daughter's marriage was an issue in which the queen, as concerned mother, could expect to play a role without overstepping the acceptable limits of female power. This explanation seems unlikely, however. The very acceptability of the queen's involvement in the marriage negotiations for her daughter rendered the oaths of loyalty unneces-

4 *APS*, ii, 23; Brown, *James I*, 148–52, 180.
5 *Scotichronicon*, viii, 286–90.

sary, and the implications of the oaths – in which loyalty was owed specifically to the queen as well as to the king – were too significant and wide-ranging to be accounted for by one specific issue. While Joan was not appointed regent in 1437, the fact that she was able to rally members of the political community and maintain some form of stability in the immediate aftermath of James' murder suggests that the community recognised her right to do so. More importantly, the fact that the assassins who killed James also attempted to kill the queen is indicative of an awareness of her political role and the possibility that should she survive, Joan rather than Atholl might have become regent for the young James II.[6] At the same time, however, the arrangements made for government following the murder of James I suggest that widespread support for the king's interpretation of his wife's political role was lacking. It was one thing for the king to rely upon his wife and order his subjects to swear loyalty to her, but quite another to enforce those oaths after his death. The political significance of the oaths rests more on their intention rather than on their usefulness to the queen in the public arena.

The private arena, however, was another matter entirely. James' requirement that the community swear loyalty to the queen is indicative of his faith in her abilities and of his political trust in his queen. This faith would suggest that his reliance upon Joan and her involvement in political life, at least in terms of her influence on the king, were not as limited as the evidence suggests. In this sense, the oaths of 1428 and 1435 represent attempts by the king to convert the queen's influence into a more official role in keeping with her status as his most trusted ally. The 1428 marriage treaty listed the queen and the king's nephews and uncle, the earls of Douglas, Angus and Atholl, separately from the rest of the nobility and prelates. Of these four key figures, only the queen and Angus remained in the king's favour throughout his reign. Even Angus, however, may have felt some resentment at the king's promotion of Atholl's inexperienced grandson to the position of constable of the army at Roxburgh in 1436. The army was divided by jealousy amongst the nobility, and one account of the failed siege of Roxburgh states that the queen arrived and led the king away from his army. There could be few more public displays of the importance of the queen's support and counsel to the king than her actions at

---

6 Brown, M.H.,' "That Old Serpent and Ancient of Evil Days": Walter, Earl of Atholl and the Death of James I', *SHR*, 71 (1992), 40–1.

Roxburgh.[7] Even if the account of the queen's role at Roxburgh was a later invention, it is indicative of public perceptions of her influence over the king: the queen led the king from the field and away from his subjects. James' reliance upon Joan was also a practical policy. Unlike the Scottish nobility, the queen was an outsider to Scottish political life and was, as a result, completely reliant upon her husband for political protection and support. She had no other competing alliances within the kingdom and no independent power base from which to challenge the will of the king. Of all the people he could trust in government and to protect his family in the event of his death, Joan Beaufort was the logical choice.

The oaths sworn to Joan Beaufort were exceptional, generated by unusual political and personal circumstances. They illustrate the enormous potential of the daily partnership between king and consort in fifteenth-century Scotland revealed in royal land policy and accounts. The establishment and maintenance of a consort had major financial implications for the kingdom, and her future wealth was the subject of lengthy discussions before, and often after, she became queen. The burden of meeting the vast expense of royal marriage lay heaviest on the crown, but it was also possible on occasion to ask the political community for assistance in covering costs. Bower recorded that the Estates were asked to contribute to the expenses of the 1433 embassy to France and funds were raised in 1435–6 for Margaret's wedding.[8] The burgh of Aberdeen made a contribution to the marriage of the 'kingis dochter Elizabeth, in Brettan' in 1442, and it is likely that the marriages of the other Stewart princesses incurred similar charges.[9] Such levies were very unpopular, as Bower noted in his description of the 1436 aid, indicating that the provision of the far larger sums required for a queen's dower created potential difficulties for the crown's financial resources. While the Scottish crown benefited from both the remission of 10,000 marks of James I's ransom in lieu of dowry for Joan Beaufort and from Mary of Guelders' dowry of 60,000 crowns, it was required to allocate lands and income to each queen as dower. The dower was unusual in marriage arrangements in that while it was offered as an incentive to secure the match, its actual provision really only benefited

7 Brown, *James I*, 164–5; *Liber Pluscardensis*, i, 380. A 1509 manuscript of the *Scoti-chronicon* includes additional information on the siege of Roxburgh and states that 'Ecce inopinate regina clam destine supervenit et regem secum ab exercitu manduxit' (*Scotichronicon*, viii, 378 n. l.24).

8 *Scotichronicon*, viii, 241, 250.

9 *Extracts from the Council Register of the Burgh of Aberdeen*, 7–8, 10.

the bride herself. In this sense, the dower recognised the sacrifices made by the royal bride in leaving her home and family to make a political marriage. The 1428 treaty of Chinon, for example, ordained that if Louis died without leaving a brother to marry Margaret in his stead and she remained in France, she was to receive 40,000 gold crowns in 'compensation for her work and burden'.[10] Marriage was a professional career for a medieval princess, and a career that deserved substantial remuneration.

The queen's dower often became a customary allocation from crown lands, with some estates set aside as dower lands. Joan Beaufort does not seem to have been allocated any dower at the time of her marriage, but it is possible that the evidence of any such provision has been lost. Her predecessors were allocated income from the customs of various burghs and Joan would have been similarly endowed. Annabella Drummond was allocated 2500 marks sterling from the great customs of Edinburgh, Linlithgow, Perth, Dundee, Montrose and Aberdeen at her husband's first parliament in 1390.[11] Euphemia Ross was allocated 3500 marks drawn from the customs of Edinburgh, Linlithgow, Haddington, Aberdeen, Dundee and Perth, and Margaret Drummond received income from Inverkeithing and Aberdeen.[12] The actual payments received by queens did not always match the sums allocated to them and were not always drawn from the burghs specified in the endowments. Annabella received income from Dunbar instead of Edinburgh in 1398–9 and from Stirling rather than Linlithgow in 1400–1, while payments for Euphemia's household were occasionally made by North Berwick, Montrose and Inverkeithing.[13] Evidence of dower land allocations to Joan's predecessors does not survive. Margaret Drummond held and granted land in Dull to John Logie in 1368, and given that Dull was later awarded to both Joan Beaufort and Mary of Guelders as dower land, it is possible that Margaret also held the lands as part of her endowment.[14] Joan Plantagenet was granted £2000 from unspecified lands as part of the terms of her marriage to the future David II.[15]

While there is no record of Joan Beaufort receiving any dower early

---

10 Paris AN, J678/26.
11 *APS*, i, 216; *ER*, iii, 152–3
12 *ER*, ii, pp.lxxx, 138, 143, 343, 345, 472, 475, 479.
13 *ER*, iii, 152–3, 466, 520.
14 *ER*, ii, 298.
15 Stones, E.L.G. (ed.), *Anglo-Scottish Relations, 1174–1328, Some Selected Documents* (London, 1965), 330–1.

in the reign, she did receive several grants of land and income between
1433 and 1435. In a charter issued at Perth by the queen on 20 April
1435 she stated that the king and Estates had granted her the lands
of the Appin of Dull as dower 'the qwilkis as ze [knaw] we haf takyn
nowther estat no sesing'.[16] The Appin of Dull had been held by the
earls of Fife, and it is possible that the queen was awarded other lands
in Perthshire, if not the earldom of Fife itself, before James' death.
This possibility is suggested by a charter referring to lands in Fife,
issued from Falkland by Joan in 1440, and by the awards of the Appin
of Dull and other lands in Fife, and eventually the earldom itself, to
Mary of Guelders in 1449 and 1451.[17] Joan was entitled to receive a
dower but the timing of this allocation suggests that she was awarded
the lands as a reward for her political involvement, acknowledged only
three months earlier in parliament by an oath of loyalty to the queen.
The king may have recognised that the queen required economic
independence as well as political loyalty in the event of his early death.
The queen was also awarded income from the customs of Aberdeen,
Edinburgh and Haddington between 1433 and 1435. Joan received
annuities of a hundred pounds from the customs of Aberdeen and of
two hundred pounds from the customs of Edinburgh before June 1434,
and of an unknown sum from the customs of Haddington before June
1435. Such grants may have formed part of the Scottish queen's traditional income – her two immediate predecessors received income from
Edinburgh and Aberdeen – but, like the allocation of her dower lands,
the timing of the grants made to Joan Beaufort seems significant.[18]

While grants of land and income to the queen were due her as dower
and could be augmented in recognition of her efforts, such allocations
were also dictated by the requirements of the king. In the case of Joan
Beaufort's award of lands in the Appin of Dull, the king's involvement
is made quite clear. David Menzies had been granted the lands by the
king a week earlier and asked to give seisin of the lands, apart from
the ones he personally held, to the queen four days after she issued
her charter on 20 April.[19] Menzies was described by the queen in her
charter as 'owr welbelufit David Menzeis' and was a loyal and trusted
servant of the king and queen. He had been with them at Melrose in
1431, arranging for prayers to be said for the couple at the abbey, and

16 *HMC*, vi, 691 no.20.
17 Edinburgh NAS, GD 20/301; *RMS*, ii, 462; Brown, M.,'"Vile Times": Walter
    Bower's Last Book and the Minority of James II', *SHR*, 79 (2000), 178.
18 *ER*, iv, 568, 575, 608, 623–4; v, 493, 552, 554, 557, 627; *RMS*, ii, 462; *APS*, ii, 66.
19 *HMC*, vi, 691, nos.19, 21.

he and his son received rewards from James II for their services. The lands continued to be administered by a trusted servant but, by placing them in the hands of the queen, James I removed them from the overall control of the earl of Atholl. This act constituted an attack on the earl's rights in the region and added to the growing estrangement between king and earl.[20] Joan issued her charter from Perth, indicating that she was well-placed to take an active interest in her lands and play a role in the region. The oath of loyalty to the queen taken by parliament a few months earlier had implicitly promoted the queen as a potential regent ahead of Atholl, and this enhancement of her power within a region generally under his control was irksome to the earl. The queen received the lands she was due, but the king chose the lands she was to receive on the basis of his own ambitions in the region. The queen was, however, involved in the allocation process. While the queen's charter was issued in the name of 'Jehan by ye grace of God Qwein of Scotland', it recognised that the king had appointed David Menzies as bailie in the lands and that the queen approved the appointment. The fact that the king's charters were issued from Stirling on 14 and 24 April and the queen's from Perth on 20 April suggests that the royal policy with regard to the lands had been carefully planned and was facilitated by regular communication between king and queen.

The allocation of Mary of Guelders' dower had far greater political and financial implications for the queen and the kingdom as a whole than did that of her predecessor. As part of the terms of her marriage, Mary was assigned an income of 10,000 gold crowns from the earldoms of Strathearn and Atholl, which had reverted to the crown following the earl's execution in 1437; the castle and lordship of Methven; and the palace, lordship and great customs of Linlithgow.[21] The dower, substituting Menteith for Methven and including the lands of 'apnedull' which had been in the possession of Joan Beaufort, was confirmed by the king with the consent of the Estates in parliament on 22 January 1450.[22] The difficulty in assigning the dower was apparent from the forfeiture of the Livingstons at the same parliament and the execution on 21 January of Robert Livingston, the comptroller, and Alexander Livingston, second son of the justiciar and captain of Methven castle. The record of charges against the family does not survive, but a statute regarding 'crimes committit agaynis the king or again his derrest

---

20 Brown, *James I*, 178–80; *HMC*, vi, 691–2, nos. 22–4.
21 Lille ADN, B427/15877ter.
22 Lille ADN, B427/15882; *RMS*, ii, no. 306; *APS*, ii, 61.

modir of gud mynde' was enacted in the same parliament.[23] These
'crimes' referred to the imprisonment of Joan Beaufort by the justiciar, Alexander Livingston, and his son James, and their subsequent
domination of government offices and the person of the king during
the minority. The king took further action against the Livingstons
in subsequent months. In March he awarded lands in Filde to the
new comptroller, Alexander Napier, for his services to Joan Beaufort
during her imprisonment. The lands had been forfeited by the younger
Alexander Livingston, later expelled from Scotland as a punishment
for rebellious activities, for his father's role in the 'incarceration of the
queen'.[24]

The two members of the family executed on 21 January were not,
however, responsible for Joan Beaufort's imprisonment. It is also clear
from the subsequent return to favour of one of the culprits, James
Livingston, that the charge of treason was less important to the king at
that time than the need to access the Livingstons' wealth. In addition to
the office of comptroller, an office he may have been using to increase
his personal wealth at the crown's expense, Robert Livingston also held
the post of custumar of Linlithgow. His death enabled the transfer
of the customs to the queen.[25] Similarly, the execution of Alexander
Livingston, captain of Methven castle, would have facilitated the
transfer of the castle, promised to the queen in June 1449, but for some
reason Menteith was substituted for Methven in the final ratification of
the treaty. These awards still fell short of the required total of 10,000
crowns, but had to be made in order to reassure the duke of Burgundy
that the full sum would be allocated so that he would continue to send
instalments of Mary's dowry. The grants to the queen entailed a short-
term loss of income to the crown which would be offset by the eventual
return of the grants to the crown on the queen's death and by the lump
sum of cash promised by the duke of Burgundy. James II was suffering
from a cash shortage. He was apparently unable to repay a loan of £930
to Robert Livingston, a debt automatically cleared with Livingston's
death, and continued to borrow money. The accounts for August 1450
show a deficit of over £1300, yet the crown was expected to provide a
dower for Mary that would generate the equivalent of £5000 annually.[26]
The prospect of another instalment of Mary's dowry of 60,000 crowns,

23 *APS*, ii, 35.
24 *RMS*, ii, no.324; McGladdery, *James II*, 52.
25 Dunlop, *James Kennedy*, 109, 330–2.
26 Macdougall, *James III*, 15, 17.

the equivalent of £30,000, must have been very enticing indeed.

James had received only a third of the dowry before May 1450 and the balance was slow to follow: just over half of the dowry, 35,000 crowns, was still owed in January 1452.[27] It is possible that the duke of Burgundy was not prepared to pay the balance until Mary's dower had been fully allocated, but non-payment of dowry, at least from a Stewart perspective, was not unusual. In 1428 the proposed Scottish army of 6000 soldiers was substituted for Margaret's dowry, and Charles VII does not seem to have demanded any dowry when the army became unnecessary before the marriage took place. Isabella's marriage contract promised 100,000 saluts d'or as dowry, but she later claimed that this money had never been paid.[28] The details of Mary's marriage have not survived, but it seems that the marriage conferred the title of earl of Buchan on her husband, and it may be that this title formed at least part of her dowry. Annabella's dowry was set at 60,000 ducats but it was never paid as the marriage never took place. There is no record of Eleanor's dowry, and Joanna did not make a foreign match. Of even greater value to the crown was the fact that although unmarried, the daily living expenses of Annabella, Eleanor and Joanna were met by the duke of Savoy and the French king rather than by their own family from 1445. For the Scottish government at least, the promise of a dowry was a means of securing a foreign match and relieving the crown of the expense of supporting royal daughters. It was also a promise that could be neglected once the marriage was concluded. Burgundy, having achieved his objectives through Mary's marriage, may have been similarly neglecting his promises.

James may have hoped to remind the duke of his obligations by awarding further grants to the queen in July 1451.[29] The grants included the earldom of Fife, the manor of Falkland, lands in Fife which had been held by Atholl, Stirling castle, the lands of Methven, the lordship of Brechin, and the great customs of Cupar, Perth and Stirling, plus £100 from those of Aberdeen. Later in the same year she received further grants arising from the forfeiture of the Livingstons, including the barony and lordship of Callendar, and in April 1452 she received the lands of William Lauder of Hatton, a Douglas adherent forfeited in

27 Dunlop, *James Kennedy*, 135 n.3. In February 1450, the duke of Burgundy paid 5,000 crowns to James' ambassadors in part payment of the second instalment of the dowry and stated that he had previously paid a first instalment of 10,000 crowns (Lille ADN, B427/15882bis).
28 Nantes ADLA, E12/1; Paris AN, K1151/1, f.5r.
29 *RMS*, ii, no. 462; *APS*, ii, 66–7.

late 1451.[30] The queen was awarded Garioch in August 1452 following
the death of the countess of Orkney and received further awards in
May 1453, April 1459, March 1460 and October 1463.[31] Mary was also
in temporary possession of the earldom of Wigtown at the expense of
the earl of Douglas by August 1452. In January 1453 James promised
to restore Wigtown to Douglas and the grants of land in Edinburgh
in May 1453 and from the customs of Edinburgh sometime before
June 1453 may have been intended to persuade the queen to resign the
earldom.[32]

The queen was only one beneficiary of the reallocation of forfeited
estates, and while the necessity of providing her dower was one reason
for the king's forfeiture of several of his subjects, it was not the only one
nor the most important. The Livingston forfeiture marks the beginning
of James II's attempts both to exercise power following his marriage
and the end of his minority, and to increase the wealth of the crown.[33]
James II's successes were sanctioned in the parliament of August 1455
which passed an act permitting the permanent annexation of various
lordships and castles, many of them previously held by the earl of
Atholl and by the Douglases, to the crown.[34] In this context, the grants
of land to the queen not only fulfilled the king's obligation to provide
her dower, but also ensured that his hard-won annexations remained
in the hands of the crown. The queen's rights in those estates granted
to her as dower and declared to be crown lands in the act of annexation
– including Stirling Castle, the earldoms of Fife and Strathearn and
the lordship of Brechin – were explicitly recognised in the act. The act
concluded with the statement that 'the annexacione of the lordschippis
and castellis to the crown mak na preiudice to our souerane lady the
quenys infeftment that now is anent the lordschippis and castellys
assignit till hir dowry be our souerane lord with the consent of the thre
estatis'. This act of annexation was followed by an act of revocation
made by James II on 16 October 1455, revoking grants of land made
during the minority and judged to have been against crown interests.[35]
Grants made within the royal family were not regarded as alienation
of crown lands, and lands granted to the king's son, Alexander, and to

30 *RMS*, ii, nos. 508, 544.
31 Edinburgh NLS, MS. Adv. 20.3.4, ff.203–4; *RMS*, ii, nos. 592, 693, 694, 746, 762.
32 Tytler, P.F., *The History of Scotland from the Accession of Alexander III to the Union*
    (Edinburgh, 1864), ii, 386–7; *ER*, v, 552; Dunlop, *James Kennedy*, 142.
33 'Auch. Chron.', 166; McGladdery, *James II*, 55–8, 64–6, 69–70, 78, 87–8.
34 *APS*, ii, 42–4.
35 Edinburgh NAS, GD 25/1/65.

the queen were exempted from the act of revocation. The earldoms of March, Mar and Moray were granted to the king's sons Alexander, John and David, and the earldom of Atholl was awarded to his step-brother, Sir John Stewart. Mary was thus the beneficiary not only of the generous promises made in her marriage contract but also of James II's policies regarding land acquisition and distribution.

The language of some of the charters granting lands to the queen indicates that the king was aware that the requirements of providing a dower and increasing the extent of crown estates were complementary in the long term. James granted Garioch to Mary on 26 August 1452 in recognition of the 'sincerrima et cordialissima affectione' he felt for her, a distinctive phrase used only on three other occasions in the surviving charter evidence. It appears in a charter issued in December 1451, in another dated 13 May 1453, and in a slightly altered form – 'sincerima affectione' – in a charter issued in April 1452.[36] These charters consti-tute the surviving evidence of the king's three grants of forfeited and annexed lands. They record the award of Garioch and lands held by the Livingstons and Lauder to the queen between 1451 and 1452, and the grant of lands in Edinburgh – perhaps in partial compensation for Wigtown – in May 1453. The only other grants made to the queen before 1459, according to the sources, were her dower allocations in January 1450 and July 1451, and the grant of Wigtown, for which the charter does not survive. The queen's awards thus fall into two groups: those which were ratified by parliament as dower and those which she received personally from the king in recognition of his 'affectione' for her. This affection was at its peak in 1452 when the queen was awarded Garioch following the birth of the young James III. The fact that most of the grants in this latter group are of forfeited or annexed lands and are expressed in personal terms may be indicative of an attempt by the king to divert attention from his policy of land acquisition. The king could claim that lands were needed in order to fulfil the crown's dower obligations and to acknowledge the birth of an heir. The lands thus acquired could be protected by regranting them to the queen in the knowledge that they would revert to the crown upon her death.

Most of the major grants of land were made to Mary before 1453, partly because the grants made by that time fulfilled the requirements of her dower and partly because of the need to provide for three more sons born between 1453 and 1458. The queen received no further

36 *RMS*, ii, no. 592; Edinburgh NLS, MS. Adv. 20.3.4, ff.203–4 (another copy of this charter can be found in Edinburgh NAS, RH6/330); *RMS*, ii, nos. 508, 544.

large grants after 1455, but this does not mean that her importance
to the king's policy regarding crown lands declined. The queen took a
close interest in her estates and objected to the king's promise to return
Wigtown to the earl of Douglas. The existence of these objections may
be inferred from the 'Appoyntement' between James II and Douglas of
August 1452.[37] The earl promised not to 'follow nor persew, directly
nor indirectly, be law, or any other maner of way, any entrie in the lands
of the earldome of Wigtone' without the 'speciall favour and leicence'
of the queen. In addition, he promised that 'if any thing be tane of
the good of Gallaway' he would submit to 'the Queen's will'. Douglas
further swore that he would not attempt to re-enter Stewarton without
the king's licence, underlining the separation of the powers of the king
and queen with regard to their lands. The king's powers eventually
overruled the queen's and James II promised to restore the earldom
to Douglas in January 1453. The grant of land in Edinburgh and of
income from the city's customs to Mary before June 1453 indicates that
the king was attempting to appease the queen for the loss of Wigtown.
The grants of Abercorn and Blackness to the queen before September
1456 may have been similarly made to compensate for her loss of the
earldom of Atholl, granted as dower in 1449 but later awarded to the
king's half-brother, John Stewart.[38] Blackness had been acquired from
George Crichton in 1454 as a strategic site to balance Douglas control
in Abercorn and Inveravon. The presence of the queen at the 1454
siege of the castle, the grants to her of Blackness and Abercorn, and her
role in granting lands to Crichton's heir as compensation are indicative of her involvement in, and importance to, royal policy regarding
crown land and crown-magnate relations. Her importance was clearly
visible to the Douglases who burned her dower lands of Kinclaven and
Bonnytoun before June 1455 as part of their feud with the king.[39]

The probability that the king and queen at least discussed, even if
they did not agree on, land policy is suggested in the language of three
of the king's charters which state that the king granted lands with her
consent and of lands she had 'personally resigned'.[40] An example of what
such a resignation meant in practice is provided by the king's confirmation in 1454 of his grant of the lands of Ragortoun in free barony

37 Tytler, *History of Scotland*, i, 386–7.
38 *ER*, vi, 233, 242; *Rot. Scot.*, ii, 383.
39 'Auch. Chron.', 167; McGladdery, *James II*, 84–6; *ER*, v, 674; *RMS*, ii, no.462; *APS*,
    ii, 66–7, 76.
40 *RMS*, ii, nos. 566, 702, 747

to James Crichton.[41] The transfer of lands was arranged as part of the settlement which secured Blackness, part of Crichton's inheritance, for the crown. The confirmation of Ragortoun states that the queen was currently in possession of the lands and that Crichton appealed to her to resign the lands to the king in order to secure their transfer. The queen personally resigned the lands and added her confirmation of Crichton's grant to that of the king, before both king and queen issued the act confirming the transactions. At least one of the queen's resignations was arranged to further her interests rather than those of the king. In March 1460 Mary resigned lands subsequently granted by the king to Walter and Janet Ramsay in exchange for lands they held in Dysart.[42] The lands in Dysart were then granted to the queen for one of her major building projects, Ravenscraig castle.

The public partnership of the king and queen co-existed with the separation of their income and households. The Scottish queen consort's household in the fifteenth century maintained separate chambers, wardrobes, kitchens and stables from those of the king and probably kept separate accounts. The size of the households maintained by Joan Beaufort and Mary of Guelders cannot be determined, but both would have been considerably smaller than that of Mary of Guise, which consisted of an estimated 140 people in 1542.[43] They would also have been smaller than the households of contemporary English and French queens. Joan of Navarre, for example, had 'at least nineteen grooms and seven pages to wait on her', even when she was in captivity following accusations of witchcraft.[44] The 1453–4 accounts of Margaret of Anjou's list 130 servants, more than the requested maximum of 120, while the French queen Marie of Anjou employed at least 80 people, including seventeen religious, twenty ladies, and eight masters of the hotel, over the same period. She also ran her own treasury.[45] The increasing size of the queen's household in England and France provided the consort with new opportunities to exercise influence through patronage, but also reflected the growth of

---

41 *HMC*, vii, 707, no.40.
42 *RMS*, ii, nos. 746–7.
43 Dunbar, J.G., *Scottish Royal Palaces: The architecture of the royal residences during the later medieval and early renaissance periods* (East Linton, 1999), 107, 170, 175–6, 183.
44 Myers, A.R., 'Captivity of a Royal Witch' in Myers, A.R., *Crown, Household and Parliament in Fifteenth-Century England*, ed. C.H. Clough (London, 1985), 93–133.
45 Laynesmith, *Last Medieval Queens*, 225; Myers, A.R., 'The Household of Queen Margaret of Anjou, 1452-3' in Myers, *Crown, Household and Parliament*, 146; Mooney, 'Queenship in Fifteenth-Century France', 262, 332.

the court and greater competition for access to authority. The smaller scale of the Scottish court facilitated greater daily interaction between king and queen. Lacking the mediating presence of nineteen grooms or twenty ladies to wait on her, the Scottish queen consort was more clearly involved in the life of the court, and her wishes and plans were more visible to its members.

The household accounts of Joan Beaufort and Mary of Guelders are lost – almost one third of the original exchequer rolls for the period 1425 and 1472 have not survived – but their existence is noted in the remaining records.[46] An entry in the exchequer accounts for the year beginning in July 1437 records the purchase of paper for the keeping of Joan Beaufort's accounts, but this may refer to the separation of the queen's accounts from those of her son after the murder of James I rather than to a pre-existing practice. The inclusion in the general accounts from James I's reign of purchases of luxury goods for the queen such as her ship, windows for her chamber, furs, cloth, jewels and ornaments indicates that they were treated as an element of general household expenditure rather than purchases for which she alone was responsible.[47] The luxury element of expenditure made on Joan's behalf may indicate that more mundane expenses were recorded in separate accounts, but as there is no evidence that she received an individual income until grants of land and income were made to her in 1433–5, she may have been largely dependent on the king's income before that time.

Mary of Guelders, on the other hand, was assigned a considerable income early in her reign and her books of expenses are referred to in the royal accounts for the financial year beginning in July 1454. Mary's accounts recorded both basic and luxury items of expenditure. Cloth purchases for the king and the royal children are recorded in the general accounts, for example, while those for the queen are not. Like Joan Beaufort, Mary owned a ship, but there is no record of the vessel in the exchequer accounts, an indication that at least some part of her luxury expenditure was recorded separately from that of the king.[48] Mary's expenditure and household were not, however, completely separate from those of the king. Their expenses when travelling to Wigtown in 1455–6 and 1458–9 were treated as one and the same, as were the

46 Dunbar, *Scottish Royal Palaces*, 212; *ER*, vi, 415.
47 *ER*, iv, 450, 512, 533, 626, 678–81; v, 15.
48 *ER*, vi, 5, 116, 299, 498, 583; *Calendar of the Patent Rolls*, Henry VI, 1446–1452 (London, 1909), 532.

expenses for their horses at Falkland in 1453–4. Some purchases, such as that of cloth for the windows of the queen's chamber, were recorded in the general accounts. The various payments made by Mary's mandate recorded in the general accounts and the payments to some of Mary's servants made by the king's mandate further illustrate the blurred division between the expenses and incomes of king and queen. This blurring is shown most clearly in the Edinburgh accounts for 1449–50, the period of Mary's marriage and coronation and the establishment of her household. These expenses were unique and would have been met in the first place by the king; they are not representative of long-term expenditure patterns.[49]

The partnership of king and queen is also represented, and was assisted, by their occasional sharing of royal servants. These servants were men and women associated with the royal family and household rather than those holding official posts in government, although some men were rewarded with such posts for their loyal service. David Menzies, the queen's bailie in the Appin of Dull, was in the service of both James I and Joan Beaufort. Alexander Nairn received annuities on behalf of Joan Beaufort from Haddington and Edinburgh and was paid for his services by her mandate in 1434–5 before becoming comptroller in 1436. Robert Norry, servant of the king's chamber, received payments on behalf of both king and queen in 1433–4 as well as cloth of wool and linen and other items in 1434–5. Norry also seems to have worked with the queen's servants, including Lewis, keeper of the queen's wardrobe, and Margery Nortoun, 'special servant' of the queen, on behalf of whom he received an annuity between 1429 and 1431. The annuity, from the customs of Edinburgh, was paid to Nortoun by order of the king, and Lewis was paid by James for the doubling of tapestries in Linlithgow between 1429 and 1431, further illustrating the interaction between the servants of the king and queen. George Crichton, who became sheriff of Linlithgow between 1436 and 1438 and was later the admiral and an ambassador during the reign of James II, was paid by the queen's mandate to make an offering on her behalf in England in 1427–8. The royal couple also favoured John Palmer and his wife, often stabling their horses at the Palmer house between 1427 and 1429 and appointing Palmer bailie of Linlithgow in 1435. John Turyne and his wife were also recipients of royal favour. Turyne, a custumar of Edinburgh who made various domestic and international transactions on behalf of the king, felt sufficiently confident of royal favour

49 *ER*, v, 380–8, 685–7; vi, 206, 415, 573.

to request some compensation for his losses arising from one of his journeys to Flanders. Turyne's wife assisted him in business and made purchases on behalf of Joan Beaufort including ostrich feathers, furs and velvet. She also sent Rhine wine to Perth, armour to Edinburgh castle, and spices to the comptroller, David Broun, for royal use. David Dun sent two silver seals for the king and queen from Flanders around the same time.[50]

Although a queen was expected to oversee her children's upbringing, the servants responsible for their care seem to have been in the king's employ. The future James II had his own nurse, Janet Liddale, his own household headed by his steward, John Spens, who had also held the posts of custumar of Perth and comptroller, and his own chamber and kitchen. The prince's sisters seem to have been entrusted to royal servants on a more irregular basis. Simon Logan, who escorted Margaret and Isabella from Edinburgh to Perth in 1428–9, had received payments from James I previously but does not seem to have been a regular servant of the king. According to the Edinburgh accounts for the year May 1425 to April 1426, he received two payments from the king in 1425–6, one for twelve boards, possibly for building work, and the other for an unspecified service. Similarly, Michael Ramsay was reimbursed in 1428–9 for the expenses he had incurred on behalf of the 'household of the king's sisters' and received almonds for the young prince James between 1429 and 1431. These duties were undertaken when Ramsay held the office of custumar of goods sold between Scotland and England. John Wells, 'servant of the king' and later recorded as burgess of Perth, seems to have been a more regular companion to the princesses than Logan and Ramsay, and was reimbursed for expenses incurred on their behalf in 1427–8 and for their expenses in Edinburgh and Dunfermline in 1429. He also received two other payments from the king which were unrelated to the princesses. The sources record the services of only one nurse in connection with the Stewart princesses – Annabella Leith – and she is described as the nurse of only one of James II's sisters, presumably the youngest, Annabella. Her efforts were recognised by James II with the award of an annuity from the customs of Inverkeithing at some point between 1436 and 1443, and a further payment from the same customs by the mandate of Mary of Guelders before July 1450. Such long-term interest in a royal nurse was not unusual – the accounts also reveal that James I sent beer to

50 *ER*, iv, 412, 437–8, 449–50, 472, 485, 529, 541, 575, 602, 608, 622–4, 627, 630, 679–681, 684–5.

his nurse at Dunfermline in 1434–5 – and illustrates the way in which some servants were held in long-term favour by more than one royal generation.[51]

Even those servants specifically assigned to Joan Beaufort were connected in some way with the king. Perhaps the most important of these servants to the queen were her lady companions, of whom Joan Beaufort had at least two, Margaret Manyn and Margery Nortoun. Manyn is described in the accounts as 'the queen's lady' and received an annuity from the customs of Edinburgh by order of James I in 1436. Nortoun is variously described in the accounts as 'maidservant of the queen', 'lady', and 'special servant of the queen'. She received a pension from the Edinburgh customs by order of the king between 1429 and 1431, which she was still receiving in 1447, as well as a payment by the queen's mandate in 1427–8. She seems to have been a particular favourite. The expenses of her illness were paid by the king's mandate in 1425–6 and she received salmon from Scotland in London in 1433 at the same time as the king and queen sent a gift of salmon to the duchess of Clarence, Joan Beaufort's mother. The queen maintained contact with Thomas Muktoun, servant of the Londoner Thomas Bernwell who arranged the transport of the salmon. Muktoun delivered gold rings to the queen in 1436, suggesting that he was either in her service or trying to secure her favour. Muktoun maintained his royal connection and is recorded, this time as a merchant, supplying goods for the king's household in 1447–8. Nortoun's presence in London suggests that she was English and had come to Scotland with Joan Beaufort in 1424. It may also be significant that Nortoun's journey was undertaken at a time when Scotland and England were again discussing the possibility of a royal marriage, and it is not impossible that this travel by a trusted royal servant allowed some informal communication on the matter. The esteem in which Nortoun, as trusted servant of the queen, was held is also indicated by the safe-conduct issued on 1 December 1433 for twenty Scotsmen to accompany her on her return to Scotland.[52] Robert Lyntoun was described as 'servant of the queen' in a charter confirming the grant to him of the hospital of St Mary Magdalen near Linlithgow in 1426. While the queen seems to have made this grant herself, the king confirmed the 'letters of his consort,

51 *ER*, iv, 411–3, 437–8, 472–3, 508, 516, 527, 529, 575, 603, 622, 627; v, 133, 183, 375.
52 *ER*, iv, 411, 450, 541, 567, 569, 573, 620, 678; v, 30, 221, 273, 307; *CDS*, iv, nos.1064, 1069.

Joan, Queen of Scotland' in 1430. The king's involvement can also be seen in relation to two of the queen's officers: Lewis, her wardrober, who was charged with purchasing 'diverse cloth of wool and linen, and other necessities for use in the wardrobe' and William Dicsoun, master of her stables. Dicsoun was paid on one occasion by the queen's mandate and on another by order of the king. In the accounts for 1436-7 he was described as 'servant of the king' and 'servant of the queen' when engaged in collecting and breaking horses and driving them to Dundee. Dicsoun remained in Joan's service after James I's death and in the service of her family after her own death. He received a safe-conduct for a year to travel through England with her second husband, Sir James Stewart, and their son John in November 1445. The queen also employed her own physician, Master William Forest.[53]

Some of these servants served more than one generation, as illustrated by the continuing royal favour of the Menzies and Crichton families under James II. Robert Norry, servant of the king's chamber under James I, organised payment of the king's debts after James' death, even travelling to Flanders to do so. Norry and his assistant in this task, William Bully, were reimbursed by Joan Beaufort's mandate upon their return. Norry's continued service to the dead king's family is also illustrated by his payment of the expenses of the knight of St John who brought James' heart to Perth. He held the office of comptroller in 1440, maintained his duties in the king's chamber, and was still in royal service following the arrival in Scotland of the new queen, Mary of Guelders. He received payments on Mary's behalf, as he had done for her predecessor, and was the servant who travelled from St Andrews to Edinburgh in 1452 to inform the king of the birth of the future James III. For this latter service he was rewarded by the king 'with the consent and assent of his consort, Mary, queen of Scotland' with lands in Menteith, part of the queen's dower lands. The grant is indicative of the importance of his service to both king and queen. Norry received other grants in recognition of his services, including a payment from the customs of Ayr in 1444-5 and the grant of the fermes of Torry in 1451.[54] Like Norry, William Bully also remained in favour, combining his duties as custumar of Edinburgh with royal service. He seems to have gained Mary's favour following his services at the king's marriage and the queen's coronation and became her factor. In this capacity he

53 *RMS*, ii, no.154; *ER*, iv, 508, 601, 622; v, 34, 59; *CDS*, iv, nos.1044, 1181.
54 *ER*, v, 22, 26, 32–4, 52, 84–8, 117–18, 156, 178, 386, 397, 427, 434, 438, 443, 479, 595, 627, 662, 676; *RMS*, ii, no.566.

Seal matrix of Joan Beaufort, found at Kinross, Perthshire. © The Trustees of the National Museums of Scotland (H. NM 163)

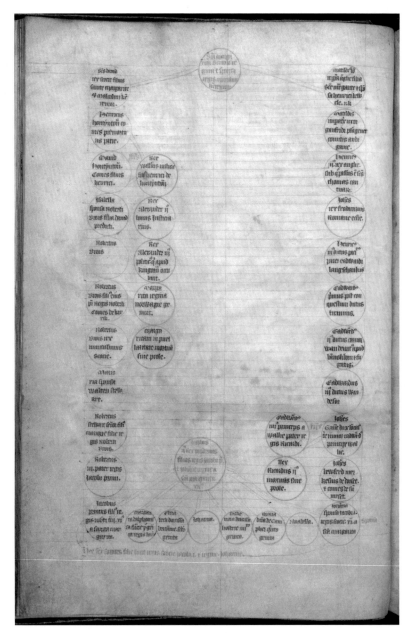

Genealogy of James II, demonstrating his descent from Saint Margaret through both paternal and maternal lines. From a fifteenth-century manuscript of Bower's Scotichronicon. Copyright © The British Library (Royal MS 13.E.x, f.26v)

Linlithgow Palace from the south east. © Crown Copyright reproduced courtesy of Historic Scotland (HS A 3209-6)

Ravenscraig Castle from the north east. © Crown Copyright reproduced courtesy of Historic Scotland (HS A 3136-11)

A Perspective View of the Trinity College Church

P. Sandby Delin.   P. Fourdrinier sculp.

Trinity College Church, 1753. Reproduced courtesy of the Royal Commission on the Ancient and Historical Monuments of Scotland (C 62936)

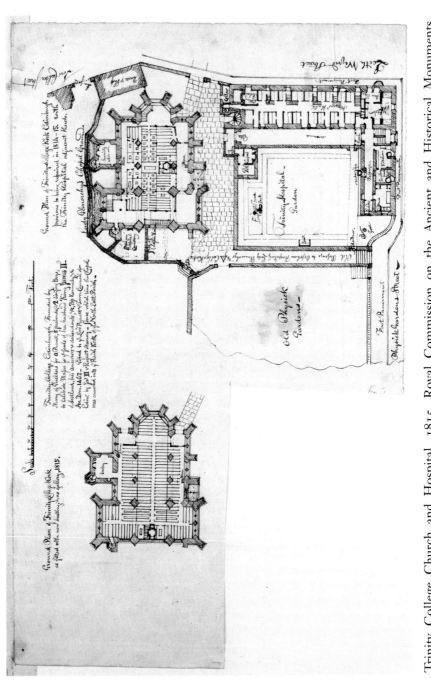

Trinity College Church and Hospital, 1815. Royal Commission on the Ancient and Historical Monuments of Scotland (C 62926)

Margaret of Denmark, from the Trinity Altarpiece by Hugo van der Goes.
The Royal Collection © 2006 Her Majesty Queen Elizabeth II

Saint Catherine presents Isabella Stewart, duchess of Brittany, to the
Virgin and child. From a book of hours owned by Isabella. Reproduction
by permission of the Syndics of the Fitzwilliam Museum, Cambridge
(MS 62, f.20r)

made payments for her confessor, provided beer, received a pension in 1451–2, and provided accommodation for her teacher, Henry van Velde, and his two sons between 1449 and 1452. Other men in long-term royal service to the king and queen included Alexander Nairn and Alexander Napier, both of whom held the office of comptroller under James II. Nairn continued to receive payments for Joan Beaufort during the minority, while Napier seems to have entered the queen's service only after the death of James I. He was rewarded by James II with lands in Filde for his services to the queen during her imprisonment and was involved in the organisation for the arrival of Mary of Guelders in 1449.[55] Neither Nairn nor Napier seem to have had any link with Mary other than those arising through their office.

In addition to those servants already in royal favour, such as Norry and Bully, James II and Mary of Guelders relied on several others. One of the most striking of these was George Schoriswood, appointed bishop of Brechin in March 1454 and chancellor by December 1456. Schoriswood's seal incorporated his personal arms plus those of Scotland and Guelders, possibly indicating that the queen, granted the lordship of Brechin in July 1451, was influential in his appointment to the see.[56] Master James Lindsay was keeper of the Privy Seal and acted as the queen's factor and chamberlain, receiving a pension from Mary in 1452–3. William Crag, 'servant of the king', delivered St Margaret's shirt to the queen for her labour in 1451 and transported three horses to her in the same year. Andrew Young, the king's steward, paid the expenses incurred by the queen during her residence at St Andrews from May to August 1452 and was reimbursed by the king's mandate. Adam Cosour, custumar of Stirling, made payments for goods delivered to the king in 1445–6 and 1447–8, and received a payment of custom on wool for the queen by the king's mandate in 1453–4. Andrew Balfour and Robert Liddale, the king's tailors, together with Robert Norry, received goods for the king and queen in 1449–50. John Dalrympil junior, burgess of Edinburgh, also paid for goods delivered to the king and for wine from Beaune and bows delivered to the queen. James Patonsoun seems to have performed a variety of duties at Falkland in his capacity of receiver of the dues of the earldom of Fife, receiving materials for building work, goods for the king and oatmeal for the horses of the king and queen. Three other men who performed services for Mary of Guelders and were paid by

55 *ER*, v, 24, 30, 133, 347–8, 493, 500, 503, 614, 616; *RMS*, ii, no.324.
56 *RMS*, ii, no.604; Dowden, J., *The Bishops of Scotland* (Glasgow, 1912), 185–6.

James II appear in the accounts. John Park was reimbursed for paying the expenses of the queen's horses at the siege of Blackness, his only mention in the records. James and John Liddale paid the expenses of the queen's horses on St Mary's Isle and provided oats for them in 1457–8. Both received various payments from the king during their careers and were the sons of Robert Liddale.[57]

In addition to these royal servants, there were also the people entrusted to care for the royal children. Agnes Colvile served prince James and the princess Mary at Edinburgh castle and was paid for her services by the mandate of both king and queen in 1452–3. James, Mary and Alexander each had their own nurse as well as other servants, but the only ones specified in the accounts are James' stewards, a courier and John Balfour, keeper of Falkland castle and 'servant of the prince', who received cloth and furs for James, Mary and David in 1455–6.[58]

Like Joan Beaufort, Mary of Guelders also had her own servants. Several of them arrived in Scotland with Mary or followed her later. They included the queen's cook, John, who was awarded the fermes of the mill of Strathmiglo by James II, and Herman, who is described as master of the queen's stable and as 'servant of the queen', made purchases on her behalf and was paid by her order. Henry Junem temporarily held the post of keeper of the queen's wardrobe and made purchases for the king and queen. Henry van Veld, 'the queen's tutor', also followed Mary to Scotland and stayed in Edinburgh from October 1449 until August 1452. He was joined by his two sons, Inglebrech and John, for shorter periods during this time. While these men seem to have been in Scotland purely to visit the queen, the king paid the expenses they incurred during their residence in the house of William Bully.[59] On her journey to Scotland in 1449, Mary was accompanied by Isabella de Lalain, member of the duchess of Burgundy's household and sister of the two Lalain brothers who had jousted with the Douglases in February of that year. Isabella remained in Scotland for a year and returned to the continent in the summer of 1450 with 22 attendants. It would seem likely that Elizabeth of Guelders also had some connection with the queen but is first referred to in the Linlithgow accounts for 1454–6 with other 'servants of the king's household'. Elizabeth is listed in the accounts after the nurse of prince James and before those

57 *RMS*, ii, nos.594–5, 597–8; *ER*, v, 227, 231–2, 274, 300, 317, 338, 386, 435, 447, 464, 466, 493, 512, 524–6, 554, 556, 603, 616, 621, 674, 679, 685; vi, 459.
58 *ER*, v, 493, 551, 590, 619, 648; vi, 116, 230, 234, 286, 291, 322–3, 331, 420, 422, 533, 629.
59 *ER*, v, 386–7, 500, 535, 688.

of Mary and Alexander, although her precise role within the household is never stated.[60]

Elizabeth of Guelders may have been one of Mary's ladies, none of whom are explicitly described as such in the accounts. It seems likely that Elizabeth Lyle, who remained in Kirkcudbright through illness when the queen continued to Edinburgh sometime in 1457–8, was either in the service of the queen or of the king's sisters, Joanna and Annabella, who made the same journey. The queen's other servants included William Clerk, who arranged the provision of feed for the queen's horses; John Rede, keeper of her horses in Cabrach; and her confessor Gerard Boot, a Carthusian monk. Boot accompanied Isabella de Lalain on her return journey from Scotland to Flanders in July 1450. Even in the case of these men the distinction between the queen's servants and 'royal' servants was blurred. Both Boot and Clerk received payments by mandate of the king or his steward, Robert Nairn. The unspecified services of two other men, Goykyn and David Ruthven, both listed in the accounts as servants of the queen, were recognised by payments from the customs of Edinburgh by the mandate of the king or the comptroller, Richard Forbes.[61] Like Joan Beaufort's servants, those of Mary of Guelders were by no means exclusively in her service or employ.

The extent of the connections between the queen and the king's servants and between the king and her servants is indicative of the status of queen consort as inferior partner to her husband rather than as a separate and autonomous political and economic actor. It is likely that many of the king's servants who performed duties for the queen were delegated to do so by the king. Many of the payments received on the queen's behalf, for example, were received by the king's mandate and many of the servants were paid by his order. The fact that the king also ordered payments to be made to several of the queen's servants further underlines her dependence upon him. On the other hand, the very acts of delegation and payment reveal the extent of discussion and co-operation between king and queen. This co-operation is most clearly indicated by the specific association of Mary of Guelders with the king in the payment of Agnes Colvile, servant of the royal children. While such association is unusual, it emphasises the fact that the queen could

---

60 D'Escouchy, *Chronique*, i, 179, 182; *CDS*, iv, nos.1225–6; *ER*, vi, 234, 322, 440, 562.

61 *ER*, v, 384, 386, 465, 500–2, 517, 597, 613–14, 616; vi, 235, 456; *PPC*, vi, 100; *CDS*, iv, nos.1225–6; v, no.1072.

order payments. Between them, Joan Beaufort and Mary of Guelders ordered payments or pensions to be made to, or on behalf of, William Bully, George Crichton, William Dicsoun, Herman, William Kemp, Annabella Leith, James Lindsay, Robert Lyntoun, and Alexander Nairn. Both queens also employed the services of, and ordered payments to be made to, four other men who are not described as royal servants or officers in the accounts. Three of these four are only recorded in the accounts with reference to the queen. Sir Alexander Berclay received Joan Beaufort's pension from the customs of Aberdeen in 1433–4, and the queen ordered that Patrick Johnson of Linlithgow receive a payment from the town's customs in 1427–8. William Nutt was paid by the mandate of Mary of Guelders in 1449–50 for his purchase of various goods on her behalf, and someone known only as Cultis was paid by her mandate for an unknown reason in 1451–2.[62]

The value of the queen's favour was evident to, and actively sought by, her servants and members of the wider community. The queen's distribution of influence is best illustrated by her use of gifts and patronage, but even in this area, much of her largesse was associated with that of the king. James I and Joan Beaufort gave money to Andrew Taillefer, a chancery clerk, to redeem his house from Robert Borthwick sometime between 1429 and 1431, possibly in recognition of his efforts in repairing the king's crossbows during his journey to the Isles in 1428–9. The king and queen made their Palm Sunday offerings together in 1427–8 and made separate offerings in church at Linlithgow in 1428–9. It is also possible that the king's foundation of a Carthusian monastery at Perth in 1426 was influenced by Joan Beaufort. The Beauforts had endowed and favoured Carthusian houses in England. Sheen, established by Henry V, was within the diocese of Cardinal Beaufort, bishop of Winchester, and he was involved in its construction. Mountgrace in Yorkshire, which oversaw the establishment of the Perth house, was founded in 1398 by Thomas Holland, duke of Surrey, and was later favoured by Thomas, duke of Exeter, maternal and paternal uncles of Joan Beaufort.[63] At the same time, the fact that Richard II and Henry V favoured the houses at Mountgrace and Sheen respectively may suggest that James I was emulating his English counterparts rather than his wife's family by endowing a Carthusian house in Scotland. Of the three gifts made solely by Joan

62 *ER*, iv, 567–8; v, 385, 449, 524–5.
63 *ER*, iv, 450, 485, 511, 529; Thompson, E.M., *The Carthusian Order in England* (London, 1930), 229–32, 238–9, 246–8.

Beaufort, two arose from spiritual and charitable rather than temporal concerns. These were the offerings made on her behalf in England by George Crichton in 1427–8 and the payment by her mandate to a woman caring for a poor child in 1434–5. The third gift – of money for drinks for the masons working at Linlithgow in 1427–8 – was a worldly one and may illustrate her interest in the building work.[64]

Like Joan Beaufort, Mary of Guelders also performed some charitable work although, in both cases, the beneficiaries were servants of the king and it is possible that the payments were made in recognition of some service they had performed. While William Kemp is always referred to in the sources as the king's cook and the queen had her own, it was she who paid the expenses arising from his illness and death in 1454. The queen also ordered the payment in 1453–4 of the expenses incurred during the illness of John de Campo, including the costs of his nurses, when he was resident in the home of John Darrach – bailie of Stirling and the king's butcher, and later his steward. Mary also used gifts to maintain her Burgundian connections and paid the transport costs of sending some horses to the duke in 1457–8.[65] Other gifts given by Mary of Guelders were probably recorded in her own accounts. Her major project as queen consort was the building of a hospital with church and other buildings at Fale in the diocese of Glasgow. Mary and James sent a petition to the pope protesting at the behaviour of the monks of the Trinitarian house originally at Fale, and the pope ordered that the house be dissolved and appropriated to the queen's foundation in November 1459.[66] While James II was a co-petitioner, the hospital would seem to be the work of the queen as the papal order suggests. Fale provides an early example of the queen's interest in charitable foundations, which was to find its best expression in the establishment of Trinity College and Hospital in Edinburgh shortly before the death of James II. The king was involved in its initial endowment, but the bulk of the work was undertaken after his death, and seems primarily to have been at Mary's direction.

Mary's interest in Fale illustrates that while the queen consort may appear from record sources to be largely a beneficiary of, or acquiescent to, the king's policy rather than a policy-maker herself, she was capable of pursuing her own strategies. The design of the Scottish queen consort's seal in the fifteenth century provides perhaps the clearest

64 *ER*, iv, 450, 627.
65 *ER*, v, 398, 457, 602, 622, 688; vi, 387.
66 *CPR. Papal Letters*, xi, 403.

indication of Joan's and Mary's awareness of their role and influence. It has been argued that the design of a seal was not only a representation of the user's identity, but that the pattern of its use acts as an 'index of the expression and extent of women's secular power'.[67] French and English queens do not seem to have acquired seals until the twelfth century, and then used them for their own rather than royal business. This distinction emphasised the separation of the queen's power from that of the king and government.[68] Little evidence of the seals of Scottish medieval queens remains. There are no surviving examples between the earliest fragment belonging to Ermengarde, queen of William the Lion, and those of Margaret Drummond and Euphemia Ross in the fourteenth century, and only four from the fifteenth century.[69] A seal and signet ring used by Joan Beaufort survive, as do two seals used by Mary of Guelders. This does not mean that other queens did not have a seal – Annabella's letter to Richard II of 1394, for example, states that it was 'given under our seal' – but rather that the seals themselves do not survive.[70]

The differentiation between the power of the queen and that of the royal government was emphasised in earlier centuries by the design of the seal itself. French and English seals represented the queen as a standing female figure, wearing a crown and occasionally holding a sceptre. Kings were depicted enthroned. By the mid-fourteenth century, the design of seals used by English queens had changed. The seals of Philippa of Hainault and Anne of Bohemia, queens of Edward III and Richard II, depicted shields incorporating the arms of the queen and her husband, a design also employed by Elizabeth Woodville, queen of Edward IV in 1467.[71] The change in designs of English seals is echoed

67 Bedos-Rezak, B., 'Women, Seals, and Power in Medieval France, 1150–1350' in Erler and Kowaleski, *Women and Power*, 61.

68 Bedos-Rezak, 'Women, Seals, and Power', 63–4; Bedos-Rezak, B., 'Medieval Women in French Sigillographic Sources' in J.T. Rosenthal (ed.), *Medieval Women and the Sources of Medieval History* (Athens, Georgia, 1990), 4; Danbury, E., 'Images of English Queens in the Later Middle Ages', *The Historian*, 46 (Summer 1995), 4.

69 Laing, H. (ed.), *Descriptive Catalogue of Impressions From Ancient Scottish Seals, Royal, Baronial, Ecclesiastical, and Municipal (1094–1707)* (Edinburgh, 1850–66), i, 9, 11–12, 219; ii, 3-4; Stevenson, J.H. and Wood, M. (eds), *Scottish Heraldic Seals. Royal, Official, Ecclesiastical, Collegiate, Burghal, Personal* (Glasgow, 1940), i, 37–9.

70 *Nat. MSS. Scot.*, ii, 42.

71 Bedos-Rezak, 'Women, Seals, and Power', 75; Bedos-Rezak, 'French Sigillographic Sources', 8–9; Danbury, 'Images of English Queens', 4; W.de G. Birch, *Catalogue of Seals in the Department of Manuscripts in the British Museum* (London, 1887), i, 101–2, nos. 801, 804, 807.

in fourteenth- and fifteenth-century Scottish seals. The image depicted on Margaret Drummond's seal was of a queen standing beneath the Scottish arms with the Stewart arms to her right and the Drummond arms to her left. Similarly, the seal of Euphemia Ross featured a full-length female figure wearing a crown and holding a sceptre, with the Scottish arms to her right and the Ross arms to her left.[72] The seals of their husbands, David II and Robert II, portrayed the king in armour on one side and enthroned on the other. Their successors Robert III, James I and James II employed the same images on their seals.[73] The style of armour worn by the king varies on each of the seals and, from Robert II onwards, the soldier-king was seated on a galloping horse, but otherwise the design of the king's seal remained consistent through the five reigns.

While the seals of fifteenth-century Scottish kings continued to depict them enthroned in majesty, those of Joan Beaufort and Mary of Guelders deviate from the fourteenth-century design of queens' seals by moving away from the use of a female figure. Joan Beaufort's seal was lozenge-shaped, like those of many of her English counterparts, and represented a unicorn as a bearer of a coat of arms. The seal and her signet displayed the arms of Scotland and Beaufort instead of featuring a female figure.[74] Similarly, Mary of Guelders' seal, a 'rich and beautiful design, executed in the highest style of art', depicts the arms of Scotland and Guelders on a shield beneath an open crown and supported by an angel. Her privy seal retained the shield and crown but omitted the angel.[75] While the seals of the queens consort differ from those of their predecessors, they display some similarities to those of their husbands. Joan's seal, which depicts a shield supported by a unicorn, is broadly similar in design to the privy seal of James I, which consists of the Scottish arms supported by two lions rampant.[76] Similarly, Mary's seal – a shield bearing the arms of Scotland and Guelders beneath an open crown – resembles the privy seal of James II, which represents a shield of the Scottish arms supported by two lions rampant beneath a crown.[77] The broad resemblance between the

72 Laing, *Ancient Scottish Seals*, i, 9 no.36; ii, 3 no.8.
73 Laing, *Ancient Scottish Seals*, i, 7–14, nos.27–9, 33–5, 37–43, 45–7.
74 Laing, *Ancient Scottish Seals*, i, 11 no.44; ii, 4 no.11; Danbury, 'Images of English Queens', 4.
75 Laing, *Ancient Scottish Seals*, i, 12 nos.48–9. See also the damaged example attached to Edinburgh NLS, MS. Adv. Ch. B 73 dated 10 May 1462.
76 Laing, *Ancient Scottish Seals*, i, 11 no.43.
77 Laing, *Ancient Scottish Seals*, i, 12 no.47.

king's privy seals and the seals of the queen consort is indicative of the queen's increasing status in the first half of the fifteenth century. The establishment of a coronation ceremony for Scottish queens in the fourteenth century, the developing cults of monarchy and dynasty and the resulting growing symbolic importance of the queen in late medieval Europe all contributed to this change in status. The Scottish queen consort could not exercise authority, but her power as represented by her seal was visibly related to that of her husband.

The seals of Joan Beaufort and Mary of Guelders, like those of their European counterparts, emphasised their family connections and omitted traditional imagery borrowed from Marian iconography. Such iconography, it has been argued, represented women by their gender rather than by their places in the social order and in so doing 'radically differentiated [them] from males and conceptually dissociated [them] from property, rules of succession, and other discriminations linked to paternity.'[78] The development of new seal designs representing family connections and social status embodied the queens' – and perhaps their husbands' – understanding of their practical and earthly situation. This new emphasis on status suggests that queens consort wished and expected to be actively involved in public life. Their wishes and expectations contributed to the strong working partnership of the Scottish king and his consort in the fifteenth century.

---

78 Bedos-Rezak, 'French Sigillographic Sources', 2, 11.

SEVEN

Royal birth, motherhood and regency

'. . . children are the greatest haven, security and ornament
that she can have'

The roles of royal wife and mother were inseparable. European
ceremonies of coronation and intercession not only emphasised the
subordinate status of the queen as wife, they also relied heavily on
maternal imagery. Prayers for the birth of heirs were said at the coronation of English queens. Chroniclers invented pregnancies for added
drama and symbolism in their descriptions of acts of intercession
performed by queens. Royal births were regarded as ideal opportunities for petitioners to approach the queen with requests for her assistance.[1] The iconography and symbolism drawing these roles of queen,
intercessor and mother together were explicitly Marian. Mary's power
was explicitly acquired through motherhood, and Marian imagery was
a potent reminder that it was the queen's role as mother that provided
her with her greatest opportunities to intervene in public life.

Both Joan Beaufort and Mary of Guelders were able to take advantage of these opportunities. By James I, Joan had six daughters and
twin sons, one of whom died in infancy: a total of seven pregnancies
in a maximum of thirteen years. By James Stewart of Lorne, whom
she married in 1439, she had three more sons. Mary of Guelders had
five sons and three daughters, including a son and daughter who died
in infancy: a total of eight pregnancies in a maximum of eleven years.
Their childbearing efforts went, for the most part, unrecorded. Only
a few of the births are explicitly noted and the existence of most of the
children is only known from their adult lives. Of Joan Beaufort's eight
children by James I, Bower recorded the births of only three, noting
that Margaret was born in 1424 and that James and Alexander were
born on 16 October 1430 at Holyrood.[2] The Auchinleck chronicler

1 Parsons, 'The Pregnant Queen', 40–2, 45; Parsons, 'Ritual and Symbol', 67;
McCracken, *Romance of Adultery*, 6–7.
2 *Scotichronicon*, viii, 247, 263.

did not provide dates of birth for Joan's children but recorded that she had twin sons called James and Alexander and six daughters, of whom he named two, Margaret and Eleanor. He did, however, confuse Eleanor with Isabella, describing her as the second-born daughter who married the duke of Brittany. The chronicler also provided a date for the premature birth of Mary of Guelders' first child, which lived only for a few hours after its birth at Stirling on 19 May 1450.[3] The precision of this date is unique for the births of Mary's children. The queen bore a child in the months before July 1451 and another before June 1452 but none of the other births was recorded. The first of these children was probably the princess Mary, who travelled from Stirling to join her mother in St Andrews in May 1452. In the following month, James II granted lands in Menteith to Robert Norry who had brought him news of the birth of Prince James.[4] The pattern of recorded births is the same for both generations: the much-anticipated first birth, proof of the queen's fertility, was noted and celebrated, but interest in subsequent arrivals dissipated following the birth of a son and heir.

The birth of a daughter, while less significant than that of a son, was not without political import. Bower noted that in 1424 'the king's eldest child Margaret was born, who later became dauphiness of France'.[5] This information was intended to preface the subsequent account of the French mission to Scotland to arrange her marriage rather than to signify a general delight in the arrival of the king's first-born. While the birth of a son secured the succession, the description of Margaret in terms of her subsequent marriage emphasises the political advantages a daughter possessed. The importance of a daughter's marriage is underlined in the genealogy of James II included in a manuscript of the *Scotichronicon* currently held in the British Library.[6] All of James' six sisters are included in the diagram, but the two unmarried princesses – Joanna and Annabella – are described by their names only. The other four – Margaret, Isabella, Eleanor and Mary – are listed by their names, the titles they acquired through marriage and the order of their birth: first, second, fourth and fifth respectively. The two unmarried princesses literally did not count. The Auchinleck chronicler recorded

3 'Auch. Chron.', 162, 172.
4 *ER*, v, 447, 512, 537, 685; *RMS*, no. 566; Angus, W. and Dunlop, A.I., 'The Date of the Birth of James III', *SHR*, xxx, 199–204; Riis, T., *Should Auld Acquaintance Be Forgot…Scottish-Danish Relations c.1450-1707* (Odense, 1988), i, 245–6; McGladdery, *James II*, 76; Macdougall, *James III*, 7.
5 *Scotichronicon*, viii, 247.
6 London BL, MS. Royal 13.E.x, f.26b.

that James I had six daughters but listed only two by name, one of them incorrectly, while the *Liber Pluscardensis* listed all six daughters and their marriages without error.[7] It is possible that the increased importance of Scottish royal daughters as European brides in the first half of the fifteenth century contributed to a heightened recognition of their status. Daughters of Scottish kings were generally referred to as 'domina', but Mary, elder daughter of Mary of Guelders and James II, was described as 'dominam Mariam principissam' in the Stirling exchequer accounts of 1460–2.[8]

The descriptions of the birth of James II reflect the greater political significance of the birth of a son. In the 'Auchinleck Chronicle', James' birth is described before those of his sisters are mentioned. Bower noted the specific date and place of birth, the death in infancy of James' twin, Alexander, and that both boys were knighted on the occasion of their baptism. Even more than the sheer amount of information Bower includes, it is this last piece of information and the inclusion of a listing of the other boys knighted at the same ceremony that clearly illustrates the importance of the birth of a son and heir. Earlier in his work, Bower wrote that the king created twenty-seven knights on the day of his coronation, including the duke of Albany's youngest son and the earls of Douglas, Angus, and March. It is unlikely that Bower's account is reliable – many of the men listed may already have been knighted by 1424 – but it is noticeable that many of the boys listed by Bower as being knighted at James' baptism in 1430 were the sons and heirs of the men knighted at his father's coronation in 1424. It would seem that Bower was drawing parallels between the two kings, emphasising the continuity of line between them and between the kings and their closest advisors. James II, a minor when Bower was writing, was implicitly as much a king at his baptism as was his father at coronation, and the nobility were to treat him as such, just as the loyal boys knighted with him were still his 'commilitones'.[9] Bower's descriptions of the births of James and Margaret are used in part to illustrate the king's relationship with the nobility and his foreign policy respectively. The queen is not mentioned. The 'Auchinleck Chronicle', for all its brevity, treats the births of James I's children in much the same fashion. The chronicler's statement that James I married Joan Beaufort and 'gat

7 'Auch. Chron.', 162; *Liber Pluscardensis*, i, 377.
8 *ER*, vii, 38.
9 *Scotichronicon*, viii, 243, 263; Brown, *James I*, 117, 132–3. See also the *Liber Pluscardensis*, i, 376.

on hir' two sons and 'gat with hir vi dochteris' indicates that the queen was of only secondary importance.[10]

There was no contemporary expectation that a queen should withdraw from court life until she chose to do so at the end of her pregnancy. In most cases it was the queen herself who decided how active she would be before that time. Eleanor of Castile, queen of Edward I, bore at least fifteen children, and 'despite almost constant child-bearing...went everywhere with the king', including accompanying him on crusade in 1270–2. Marie of Anjou, who bore fourteen children by Charles VII, 'played no evident political role' but this seems to have been by choice rather than through physical incapacity. Anne of Cyprus, duchess of Savoy, bore eighteen children between 1435 and 1454 and was politically active throughout her married life. Her successor as duchess, Yolande of France, bore ten children between 1453 and 1470 and was named regent in 1469 in response to her husband's failing health.[11] Even if they did not travel everywhere with the king during pregnancy, it is unlikely that Joan Beaufort and Mary of Guelders resigned their interest in the political life of the kingdom at that time. If they had done so, given the amount of time both women spent pregnant, they would rarely have participated in political life at all.

Pregnancy and birth placed the queen at the centre of attention. The interest in royal births, although it may have decreased after the birth of an heir, ensured that the occasion of every birth was surrounded by ceremonies and symbolism intended to glorify the king and honour the queen. The content of Scottish ceremonies for royal births and can be inferred from the highly ritualised celebrations in the courts of England, France and Burgundy. These celebrations shared the same basic elements of the queen's withdrawal from court, the birth and baptism of the royal infant, and the queen's purification and return to court. In England the queen withdrew from court – 'when it plessithe the Queen to take to hir chambre' – about four to six weeks before the expected birth. The queen, accompanied by two earls or dukes, joined a procession to attend mass before returning to her great chamber to take spices and wine with the lords and ladies of court. She then withdrew to a private suite of chambers with her ladies and female servants; men were not permitted in this suite and could proceed no further than the outer chamber. It was in this latter chamber that Elizabeth of York

10 'Auch. Chron.', 162.
11 Crawford, *Letters of the Queens of England*, 68; Vale, M.G.A., *Charles VII* (London, 1974), 91; Jori, *Genealogia Sabauda*, 58–9, 63–4.

received a French embassy while awaiting the birth of Margaret Tudor in 1489.[12]

The queen's chambers reflected the wealth and prestige of the court and royal family: the walls were hung with expensive tapestries, the floors covered in rugs and the beds covered in the finest brightly-coloured fabrics and furs. A dresser in the central or state room displayed the 'vaisselles de cristalle garnies d'or' and gold cups and dishes.[13] The queen's chambers in Scottish royal palaces were similarly but less lavishly decorated and equipped. The queen's chamber at Perth had glazed windows, while the windows of the queen's chamber at Stirling were covered in cloth. Furs, tapestries and rugs were purchased for the royal chambers. A guest at James IV's wedding to Margaret Tudor in 1503 reported seeing dressers of a distinctively Scottish design in the chambers of both king and queen.[14] It was not only the objects displayed on the dresser which illustrated the status and honour of the royal family but the dresser itself, as the degree of honour was represented by the number of display shelves it contained. Burgundian sources suggest that the duke was entitled to six shelves, the queen of France to five, the duchess of Burgundy to four and so on.[15]

The most important part of the queen's great chamber was the bed. The bed acted as a visual reminder to visitors of the sources of the queen's power: she was the wife of a king and the mother of kings. The bed was, in effect, the queen's 'real throne'. In England, the procession to church for a mass marking the queen's purification and her return to court began from her bed of state, further emphasising the way in which the queen's roles as wife and mother were the basis of her privileged status in the court.[16] The bed did not simply illustrate the source of the queen's power but demonstrated her social status. Beds of state were

12 Staniland, K., 'Royal Entry into the World' in D. Williams (ed.), *England in the Fifteenth Century: Proceedings of the 1986 Harlaxton Symposium* (Woodbridge, 1987), 301, 303.

13 De Poitiers, A., 'Les Honneurs de la Cour' in M. de la Curne de Saint-Palaye (ed.), *Mémoires sur l'ancienne chevalerie; Considerée comme un éstablissement politique et militaire* (Paris, 1759), ii, 217–22; Eames, P., 'Furniture in England, France and the Netherlands from the twelfth to the fifteenth century', *Furniture History*, xiii (1977), 256–72; Staniland, 'Royal Entry into the World', 309.

14 Dunbar, *Scottish Royal Palaces*, 132–3, 172–4; *ER*, iv, 533; vi, 415.

15 Eames, 'Furniture in England, France and the Netherlands', 56–7, 239–40, 253, 259, 272; Dunbar, *Scottish Royal Palaces*, 173–4.

16 Duby, G., *The Knight, the Lady and the Priest. The Making of Modern Marriage in Medieval France* (London, 1984), 234; Parsons, 'Ritual and Symbol', 67–8; Staniland, 'Royal Entry into the World', 308.

objects of display rather than furniture in which to sleep; in addition to the bed of state in the central chamber, there were other beds for sleeping in the personal chamber of the queen or duchess. The total number of beds varied between courts, with the French queen having five beds and the duchess of Burgundy and English queen having three in their chambers.[17] The position of the beds, the size of the canopy and the kind of coverings denoted further subtleties of rank. James I's purchase of bed-linen from Flanders in 1436 included a sperver, a conical canopy for the bed 'particularly favoured in great households in the fifteenth century' and hence an important sign of status. More than £386 was spent on hangings of gold cloth and other trimmings for Margaret Tudor's bed of state in 1503.[18]

Royal births were celebrated with mass and announced throughout the kingdom by the ringing of church bells and the lighting of bonfires and torches. James II's birth at Holyrood was a great state occasion, with the news of his birth celebrated with bonfires, music and free wine and food.[19] Royal baptisms were more formal. In England and Burgundy, the church was specially decorated with rich tapestries and rugs, and a duchess or princess, accompanied by other important members of the nobility, carried the baby to the church and to the font. The queen, who was isolated from court and prevented from attending church until her purification, remained in her private suite with the king.[20] Other features of baptismal celebrations could include processions or, in the case of the birth of James II, the investiture of knights. The king derived direct political benefit from these ceremonies. The involvement of the upper nobility in the ceremonies provided the king with the opportunity to express his favour by selecting particular noblemen to lead the processions, carry the infant or act as godparent. The king could also show his pleasure in a more concrete fashion. James II awarded Robert Norry, who had brought the news of the birth of the future James III to the king at Edinburgh, lands in Menteith in June 1452. A fortnight later he issued Bishop Kennedy with a charter confirming land grants

---

17 Eames, 'Furniture in England, France and the Netherlands', 77, 85–7, 240–1, 272; Willard, 'A Fifteenth Century View', 108; de Poitiers, 'Les Honneurs de la Cour', 217, 224; Staniland, 'Royal Entry into the World', 312; Dunbar, *Scottish Royal Palaces*, 134–5.
18 *ER*, iv, 682; Eames, 'Furniture in England, France and the Netherlands', 83; Dunbar, *Scottish Royal Palaces*, 133, 172.
19 *Liber Pluscardensis*, i, 376.
20 Staniland, 'Royal Entry into the World', 303–5; de Poitiers, 'Les Honneurs de la Cour', 227–31.

and privileges in recognition of the bishop's services in providing his castle at St Andrews for the queen's safety and the delivery of the heir to the throne.[21] This kind of display of wealth and power reflected well upon a king, and reminded participants and onlookers of his exalted status in the kingdom.

The importance of birth and baptismal ceremonies to the maintenance of a sense of hierarchy is revealed by Christine de Pizan's horror at the grandeur of the lying-in of a merchant's wife. She wrote that

> It would be better for them [the merchants] if the king imposed some aide, impost or tax on them to prevent their wives from going about comparing themselves with the queen of France who scarcely looks any grander. Now, such a circumstance is not in the right order of things and comes from presumption and not from good sense ... It is very great folly ... to take up the grander style that belongs to another and not to oneself.[22]

This criticism also reveals the way in which a wife's behaviour reflected on her husband and, by implication, how the queen's status and the ceremonies celebrating that status augmented the king's own. The queen's maternity was clearly important but the ceremonies surrounding it, like those for coronation and intercession, often emphasised the glory and power of the king rather than the queen. This emphasis reflects in part the Aristotelian bias of medieval medicine which stressed the role of the father as the giver of life and the mother as passive bearer of life. The Auchinleck chronicler, for example, wrote that James I 'gat on hir [Joan] James that was king and ane nother son callit alexander and scho baire baith thir sonis on a nycht. Item he gat with hir vi dochteris ... '[23]

Contemporary chroniclers' treatment of royal maternity and the rituals celebrating royal birth performed similar functions to their representations of the ceremonies of marriage, coronation and intercession. They emphasised the complementary relationship of king and queen in which the king was an active and the queen a passive political figure.

The relative absence of the mother in these accounts and the king's use of birth celebrations for political ends cannot disguise the fact that the queen was the focus of those celebrations rather than a bit player

21 *RMS*, ii, nos. 566, 1444.
22 *Treasure*, 155.
23 'Auch. Chron.', 162.

as she was in the other rituals. Like other mothers, the queen occupied centre stage during her churching or purification ritual. Following the birth of her child, the queen remained in her private rooms for around forty days. Her return to the life of the court was marked by lavish celebrations. In England, the queen lay in her bed of state while courtiers assembled in the outer chamber. Two duchesses drew back the curtains and covers of the bed and two dukes raised the queen from the bed and escorted her to church. The procession for Queen Elizabeth Woodville's churching in 1465 included priests carrying relics, scholars singing and bearing candles, and sixty female attendants of the queen. After a special mass, the procession returned to the queen's great chamber for a celebratory feast over which she presided. Sometimes jousts and masques were also staged to mark the occasion. Fifteenth-century churching rituals were for, and starred, the new mother and her female attendants; as such, they empowered and acknowledged female corporate identity.[24] This acknowledgement would not have been lost on a queen. Even more than the other royal birth ceremonies – withdrawal from court, birth, and baptism – churching celebrated the queen's power rather than its subordination to the king's authority. It was this power of the queen as mother that provided her with great opportunities to exercise her influence on political life, particularly during a minority.

The potential power of the queen as mother was regarded in a different light from her power as wife. While a wife represented Eve the temptress, a mother was portrayed as another Mary, a woman of pure intentions and selfless devotion to her children. The acceptability of the queen's involvement in political matters relating to her children is illustrated by James I's responses to the French ambassadors in February 1435 and September 1435. He wanted 'to speak to the queen' about Margaret's marriage and he wished to show a letter from the French king 'to the queen and his council'.[25] Joan Beaufort had already been officially included in the negotiations as early as July 1428 when she was named after the king and before key members of the nobility in the letter in which the Scots agreed to observe the Franco–Scottish alliance. Similarly, the French queen, Marie of Anjou, was named in

24 Staniland, 'Royal Entry into the World', 308; Gibson, G.M., 'Blessing from Sun and Moon: Churching as Women's Theater' in B.A. Hanawalt and D. Wallace (eds), *Bodies and Disciplines: Intersections of Literature and History in Fifteenth-Century England* (Minneapolis, 1996), 147–51.
25 Paris BN, MS. Fr. 17330, ff.129r., 140v

Charles VII's ratification of the marriage treaty in October 1428. Both the Scottish and French political communities accepted and expected the queens' involvement in the marriage negotiations for their children. Marie of Anjou, not known for her involvement in political matters, was also present at the proxy marriage of Eleanor Stewart to Sigismund of Austria in 1448.[26]

While the queen as mother could expect to be included in the discussions leading to her children's marriages, not all cases of maternal political involvement were regarded as acceptable. The coronation of Euphemia Ross may have been delayed until the potential succession problem was debated and her sons' claims to the throne explicitly recognised as inferior to those of their step-brothers. The problems generated by Robert II's second marriage were not unique; many second wives across medieval Europe fought for the rights of their children and sought the exclusion from succession and favour of the children of a first marriage.[27] This behaviour does not represent the desire of a queen to achieve power for herself so much as a desire to secure her future through that of her children. Christine de Pizan wrote that

> children are the greatest haven, security and ornament that she [the princess] can have. It often happens that someone would greatly like to harm the mother but would not dare to do it out of fear of the children; she ought to hold them very dear.[28]

As a royal bride, the queen was in many ways an outsider to her birth family as well as to her husband's family. As a royal mother, the queen was not an outsider. Her children were bound to her and, unlike her father or husband, could not dispose of her by marriage or divorce. In the event of her husband's death, the queen's acceptability to, and role in, her adopted kingdom was dependent upon the survival of her children, especially of her eldest son, the new king. When Isabel of Portugal, duchess of Burgundy, allied with her son in his dispute with her husband in 1457 she is reported to have explained that she feared the duke would attack their son. She asked for his forgiveness 'for she was a stranger in these parts and had no one to support her save

26 Paris AN, J678/24, 26; Vienna HHSA, Fam. Urk. 608.
27 Stafford, P., 'Sons and Mothers: Family Politics in the Early Middle Ages' in D. Baker (ed.), *Medieval Women: Essays Presented to Rosalind M.T. Hill on the Occasion of her Seventieth Birthday* (Oxford, 1978), 81–2; Stafford, *Queens, Concubines and Dowagers*, 151–2; Stafford, P., 'The Portrayal of Royal Women in England, Mid-Tenth to Mid-Twelfth Centuries' in Parsons, *Medieval Queenship*, 144–6.
28 *Treasure*, 67.

her son.'[29] She had then been resident in Burgundy for twenty-seven years and had exercised extensive powers as her husband's deputy. The socio-political practice of dynastic marriage reinforced the ideological alliance of mother and children, which in turn justified the queen's intervention on her children's behalf.

In medieval France the queen's interest in promoting her children and political circumstance united to create a strong tradition of female regency. Medieval Scotland did not develop such a tradition. There were only three minorities before the fifteenth century, those of Malcolm IV, Alexander III and David II, and only one in which the queen consort outlived her husband. Alexander II died in July 1249 and was succeeded by Alexander III, then aged seven. The queen mother, Marie de Coucy, does not appear to have sought, or to have been awarded, regency powers and returned to France after her son's tenth birthday in September 1250. She subsequently married the son of the king of Jerusalem in 1257, but retained some influence over Alexander, spending Christmas with him at York in 1251 and returning to Scotland with her husband in 1257 to be included in the minority government of 1258. The fact that Alexander was seventeen years old when the plans for this government were formulated suggests that the powers of the regency council were largely theoretical and that 'for most practical purposes the minority of Alexander III ended in 1258.'[30] Whatever powers Marie may have been granted during the minority, it seems clear that the Scottish political community did not regard her, or indeed any one person, as a possible regent. In this respect, the community may have been guided by the English arrangements for the minority of Henry III in 1216, in which government was in the hands of a council that did not include the queen, rather than by contemporary French practice in which Blanche of Castile was regent for her son.

The Scottish preference for nominating a council rather than an individual to govern the kingdom in the event of a minority or an inter-regnum continued throughout the thirteenth century. When Margaret Plantagenet, queen of Alexander III, returned to England for the birth of her first child in 1260–1, her father, Henry III, agreed to return Margaret and her child to Scotland forty days after the birth. At the same time, Alexander III arranged that should he die before the birth

29 Stafford, *Queens, Concubines and Dowagers*, 155; Vaughan, *Philip the Good*, 339.
30 Watt, D.E.R., 'The Minority of Alexander III of Scotland', *TRHS*, xxi (1971), 6, 18–20; Duncan, *The Making of the Kingdom*, 558–60, 570, 573.

of his heir, a council composed of men selected from a specified group of four bishops, five earls and four barons would receive the child in his stead.[31] The selection in 1286 of two bishops, two earls and two barons to act as guardians during the minority of Margaret, Maid of Norway, echoes the arrangements made by Alexander III in 1260 and further suggests that the earlier plan implicitly encompassed arrangements for a minority government. The four surviving guardians of the six appointed in 1286 continued to govern Scotland in the 1290–2 interregnum, and guardians were again chosen by the Scots to govern during the 1296–1306 interregnum.

This second interregnum did, however, display a relatively new form of regency government in Scottish terms: individuals could claim to be sole guardian of the kingdom. It was this form of regency that was adopted during the frequent periods of the king's absence or incapacity in the following century. The person charged with government during these periods could be chosen by the reigning monarch or, in the event of his death, by prominent members of the political community. Thomas Randolph, earl of Moray, was chosen by Robert I to act as 'custos' or guardian for the young David II during the minority. There was no nominated regent following Randolph's death in July 1332, and it fell to the political community to choose a regent.[32] As a result of deaths and captures on the battlefield, the office was held by five men in six years: Donald, earl of Mar, Andrew Moray, Archibald Douglas, John Randolph, earl of Moray and Robert Stewart. These men were either related to Robert I – Mar was a nephew, Moray a brother-in-law, Robert Stewart a grandson – or to the men Robert had relied upon to rule after his death. Douglas was the younger brother of 'Good Sir James' and Randolph the younger son of Thomas, the first appointed guardian. Robert Stewart, heir-apparent to David II, was the longest-serving of these guardians, holding the position not only during the minority but also during the king's captivity in England between 1346 and 1357. This practice of appointing the next adult male in the succession to rule in the king's minority or captivity was used again during James I's captivity in England between 1406 and 1424 but, on this occasion, the post was described as 'gubernator' or governor rather than guardian. Robert, duke of Albany, younger brother of Robert III

31 *CDS*, i, no.2229.
32 Webster, B., 'Scotland Without a King, 1329-41' in A. Grant and K.J. Stringer (eds), *Medieval Scotland: Crown, Lordship and Community* (Edinburgh, 1993), 223–38; McNeill, P.G.B., 'The Scottish Regency', *Juridical Review*, 12 (1967), 127–48.

and uncle to James I, became governor in 1406 and was succeeded in 1420 by his son, Murdac.

The choice of regent before 1437, whether by king or government, therefore favoured male relatives of the king or, in their absence, prominent members of the political community. The only feature of the regency that remained constant regardless of the circumstances or the available choices was the official separation of powers between the regent, who ran the government, and the person entrusted with custody of the child-king.[33] The queen mother, according to contemporary views of maternal behaviour, was seen primarily as the natural custodian of her son rather than as a potential governor of the kingdom. Although she was not necessarily regarded as the leader of a regency government, the queen mother, as custodian of the young king, was still a member of that government. This was the case, at least initially, during the minorities of both James II and James III. As queen mother, neither Joan Beaufort nor Mary of Guelders could succeed to the throne. As women of foreign birth whose only natural allies in Scotland were their children, their interest in acting as guardians for their sons arose from self-protection rather than self-promotion. It was this very interest and the perceived strength of the maternal bond that made them ideal custodians of their sons. Male relatives were entrusted with powers to govern the kingdom, but their place in the succession made those who sought to secure the role of guardian also potential competitors for the throne itself. It was not until 1513, when James IV nominated his queen, Margaret Tudor, to become regent in the event of his death, that the two powers of government and custody were legally united in one person. The queen was explicitly bound to include her council in any decision but the importance of her appointment should not be underestimated. Not only was Margaret the first female regent, she was the first person to be called regent rather than guardian or governor.[34]

Margaret Tudor's appointment as regent in 1513 formally acknowledged the expansion of the queen mother's role and power during the fifteenth-century minorities. This expansion in turn reflected the tendency of potential male regents to make themselves unacceptable to the political community. The probable involvement of Robert Stewart, duke of Albany in the death of the heir-apparent, the duke of Rothesay, in 1402, the lack of effort on the part of the Albany Stewarts to secure

33 McNeill, 'The Scottish Regency', 134.
34 McNeill, 'The Scottish Regency', 128, 134, 145.

the release of James I from English captivity and Atholl's complicity in the plot to murder his nephew – James I – contributed to a lack of confidence in the practice of assigning regency to the next adult male in the line of succession. The Livingston custody of James II and his sisters in the 1440s was also regarded in subsequent years as unacceptable. James III reported that during his father's reign, any such custody that had not been approved by parliament was to be regarded as treason.[35] This decision is indicative of the way in which the rules and practice of regency evolved in response to particular circumstances, and illustrates how the rights and powers of the queen mother could be increased in response to the behaviour of male guardians. Even as those powers increased, however, they were still limited by the requirement that the queen mother work in association with a council formed of prominent men in government. Neither Joan Beaufort nor Mary of Guelders exercised power or authority in her own right during a minority.

35 Armstrong, C.A.J., 'A Letter of James III to the Duke of Burgundy' in Armstrong, *England, France and Burgundy*, 399.

EIGHT

Joan Beaufort, 1437–45

'Alsua the said princess sal haue access to visit our said
soueryn lord hir son'

The murder of James I at Blackfriars in Perth on 21 February 1437
represented an attempt to win control of the kingdom. Its success
depended upon acquiring custody of the heir to the throne as soon after
the murder as possible, ensuring that the immediate battle for political
control was fought between two factions centred on the two possible
guardians of the young James II. These were the earl of Atholl, next male
in line to the throne, and the queen, who possessed a 'natural' right to
custody as the king's mother and to whom the political community had
sworn oaths of loyalty in 1428 and 1435. The faction supporting the
queen quickly gained the upper hand. The queen herself was specifically noted in contemporary accounts for her 'diligence in pursuing
the saide traytours'.[1] John Shirley continued, writing that 'The queene
[did] herselfe grett worschipp for hir trewe aquitayle in this mater. But
hathe not ofte be seene to-foore this tyme so sodaine vengeaunce taken
uppon soo hoorrible and cruelle a deede.' Justice and the re-establish-
ment of government could not, however, be achieved solely through
the anger of the queen but required the involvement of at least some
members of the nobility and the authority of parliament. The queen
attempted to influence the nobility and parliament in their actions, but
she lacked the authority to order or undertake these actions herself.
It is therefore important to distinguish between the queen's personal
desire for vengeance and her wider political power and role in the
aftermath of James I's assassination.

Contemporary accounts of the events at Blackfriars indicate that the
initial response to the murder was spontaneous; it was only at a meeting
after the king's burial that formal decisions were made. Shirley records
that the court and townspeople were drawn to the scene when 'noys
aros and sprange owte, bethe into the courte and into the towne, of this

---

1 Connolly, 'Dethe of the Kynge of Scotis', 63.

orrible fette'. Waurin and Monstrelet also wrote that the queen's cries and those of her attendants drew the crowds to the king's chamber.[2] According to the *Liber Pluscardensis*, the bishop of Urbino, to whom the king had confessed eight days previously, publicly declared the king to be a martyr. This declaration was critical to the chronicler's representation of James I as an 'agnus innocens ad victimam ductus', a wise and good king who died without sin with his hands raised towards heaven, giving thanks to and begging for mercy from God. There is no evidence that Joan Beaufort ordered or forced the bishop to declare that her husband had died a martyr. Even if James I had previously imprisoned the bishop, as the papal tax collector in England alleged, there is no reason to assume that the queen similarly exercised power over him following the king's death. On the contrary, the legate worked with the queen and the earl of Angus to punish the criminals and re-establish government. He was in Edinburgh with the queen within a week of the murder, he wrote to the bishop of St Andrews advocating peace, and he heard the confessions of the condemned conspirators.[3]

Like the bishop's declaration of the king's martyrdom, Joan Beaufort's letter informing the English government of the events in Perth secured moral support for her future actions.[4] The queen's actions immediately after the king's burial were undertaken following consultation, and in association, with those members of council present at Blackfriars. Both Waurin and Monstrelet recorded that the lords present at Blackfriars met with the queen after James' burial and agreed that his murderers should be immediately found and punished.[5] Many of those present at the General Council held in Perth a few weeks earlier had already left the town before the murder, but some royal allies such as the earl of Orkney met with the queen and members of the royal council and household to debate future actions. The chamberlain, keeper of the

2 Connolly, '*Dethe of the Kynge of Scotis*', 62; de Waurin, J., *Recueil des Croniques et Anchiennes Istories de la Grant Bretaigne* (1431–1447), eds W. Hardy and E.L.C.P. Hardy (London, 1884), 210–11; *The Chronicles of Enguerrand de Monstrelet*, ed. and trans. Johnes, T. (London, 1849), ii, 47. See also Chartier, J., *Chronique de Charles VII*, ed. V. de Viriville (Paris 1858), i, 238–9.

3 *Liber Pluscardensis*, i, 390; Brown, M., '"That Old Serpent and Ancient of Evil Days": Walter, Earl of Atholl and the Death of James I', *SHR*, 71 (1992), 43; Weiss, R., 'The Earliest Account of the Murder of James I of Scotland', *EHR*, 52 (1937), 490 n.4; *Copiale Prioratus Sanctiandree*, ed. Baxter, J.H. (Oxford, 1930), 146–7; Connolly, '*Dethe of the Kynge of Scotis*', 65.

4 Weiss, 'The Murder of James I of Scotland', 480–1, 491.

5 Waurin, *Recueil des Croniques* (1431–47), 210–11; *Chronicles of Enguerrand de Monstrelet*, ii, 47.

privy seal, and William Crichton may have been among this latter group. The presence at Blackfriars of Crichton, keeper of Edinburgh castle, would have been particularly significant. The heir to the throne, the duke of Rothesay, was resident in the castle in the care of his steward, John Spens, who was himself in the service of Atholl.[6] In making her plans, the queen had to consider her own safety in addition to that of her son; she had been wounded in the attack at Blackfriars and may still have been at risk, particularly if she remained in the clearly unsafe environment of Perth. Safety concerns and political astuteness saw the queen remove to Edinburgh, where she could protect her son and rely on the local support of Crichton, Orkney and Angus.

The queen and council were in Edinburgh within a week of the murder. The papal legate's letter urging the 'consilium atque presidium' to seek peace was issued from the city on 27 February.[7] The bishop's reference to the 'presidium' or guardian does not indicate who held the position nor whether the guardian in this case had charge of the king or of the kingdom. Precedent suggested that under 'normal' circumstances, the queen would have been awarded custody of the king and Atholl would have been appointed governor of the kingdom. In the unusual circumstances created by James' apparent choice of Joan as regent and Atholl's involvement in the king's death, it is possible that the queen was temporarily guardian of both king and kingdom. Neither Angus nor Douglas was given any official role until after Atholl's death and the coronation of James II at the end of March. Angus was one of the few members of the nobility who had remained on good terms with James I for most of his reign and he remained a strong supporter of the queen after the king's death. He captured Atholl and returned with him to Edinburgh where parliament had been called for Atholl's trial and the coronation of James II. The new king was crowned at Holyrood on 25 March by the bishop of Dunblane, another loyal supporter of the late king. Atholl, protesting his innocence and wearing 'a corowne of iren', was executed the following day.[8] The coincidence of these two events demonstrates that the coronation and restoration of government could not take place until Atholl had been dealt with; while he remained free, only short-term arrangements for government could be made.

6 Connolly, 'Dethe of the Kynge of Scotis', 56; Edinburgh NAS, RH6/295; *ER*, iv, 603, 622; v, 31; Brown, 'Walter, Earl of Atholl', 41–2; Brown, *James I*, 195–6.
7 *Copiale*, 146–7.
8 *APS*, ii, 31; Connolly, 'Dethe of the Kynge of Scotis', 65.

The logical person to lead an interim council was Joan Beaufort, who wanted to avenge her husband as well as to protect her son and his inheritance. Unlike the king's male relatives, she could not gain personal advantage through the temporary expansion of her role and power and could be more easily forced into the background when the crisis had ended. Although James I appeared to favour the queen as potential regent in the oaths sworn to the queen in 1428 and 1435, there is no evidence that even the most loyal supporters of the royal family attempted to appoint her as regent in 1437. In view of the lack of precedent for female regency in Scotland, it is unlikely that the political community regarded Joan Beaufort as a potential regent during the minority despite these oaths. The level of dissatisfaction with the policies of James I would also suggest that the appointment of someone guaranteed to endorse and perpetuate them would be avoided at all costs. It is probable, however, that the queen mother's right to custody of the king was immediately recognised and possible that this role enabled her to play a leading role as 'presidium' in the interim council. On the other hand, this is the only reference to such a position. A letter ordering the fortification of Perth was issued in the name of James II at Edinburgh on 7 March 1437 and refers only to 'oure conseil'.[9]

If the queen did play a leading role in council in the weeks between her husband's murder and the coronation of her son, she did not do so for long. Just as prominent members of the nobility supported the queen in February and March before reverting to their more usual allegiances once the immediate emergency had passed, so the queen returned to her more accustomed role as guardian of the young king. The first two parliaments of the minority, in March and May 1437, endorsed the punishment of James I's assassins, established 'the authority of the new government' and appointed Douglas as lieutenant-general. The continuity of government between the reigns of James I and James II is illustrated by the roles of Douglas and Angus, Bishop Cameron, who retained the office of chancellor, and James Douglas of Balvenie, a supporter of James I who was created earl of Avandale in May 1437. The ongoing service of men such as John Forrester, Walter Ogilvy, William Crichton, Robert Norry and Alexander Nairn similarly represented the relatively smooth transition to minority government.[10] The

9 Marshall, D., 'Notes on the Record Room of the City of Perth', *Proceedings of the Society of Antiquaries of Scotland*, 33 (1899), 425.
10 Tanner, *Scottish Parliament*, 86; *ER*, iv, 644, 671; v, 12, 78, 84, 108; Brown, *James I*, 199.

queen, according to her 1439 'Appoyntement' with the Livingstons, was granted custody of the young king and princesses and provided with Stirling castle for their residence and 4000 marks for their care.[11] If the undated reference in the 'Auchinleck Chronicle' to the decision that 'the king suld come be him selfe and his and the Queen be hir self and hirris bot the king suld ay remane with the Queen Bot scho suld nocht Intromet with his proffettis bot allanerlie with his person' does refer to Joan Beaufort rather than to Mary of Guelders as Macdougall suggests, it is not proof that Joan had attempted to acquire an unacceptable level of power in the early years of the minority.[12] The entry specifically states that the queen could retain custody of the king but that their finances were to be administered separately, suggesting that it describes the regency arrangements of 1437 rather than the changes made to those arrangements in 1439 when Joan Beaufort was deprived of the custody of her children. The only reference to Joan Beaufort's accounts – a record of purchases of wax and paper – dates from the financial year 1437–8, indicating that the queen's finances were formally separated from her son's in line with the division of responsibilities on the regency council.[13] Similar arrangements were made to differentiate between the accounts of James III and his mother, Mary of Guelders, in 1461.

As custodian of the young king, Joan Beaufort retained a role in government in the early years of the minority, particularly during the negotiations for the nine-year Anglo–Scottish truce from May 1438. The queen wrote to her uncle, Cardinal Beaufort, before November 1437 to inform him of the imminent arrival of the Scottish embassy, and she was presumably involved in the decision to pledge some royal jewels to lord Hailes to cover the expenses of the ambassadors.[14] There is no other evidence of the queen's political involvement between late 1437 and summer 1439, but given the continuity of personnel and policies from James I's reign, it is likely that her role in government during the minority was relatively unchanged, at

11 *APS*, ii, 54–5.
12 'Auch. Chron.', 171; Macdougall, N., 'Bishop *James Kennedy* of St Andrews: a reassessment of his political career' in N. Macdougall (ed.), *Church, Politics and Society: Scotland 1408–1929* (Edinburgh, 1983), 19 n.16. Macdougall argues that this entry follows a gap in the manuscript and needs to be read in the context of the entries which follow – dated 1420, 1436, 1438 and 1440 – rather than those which precede it, dated 1461.
13 *ER*, v, 15.
14 *Foedera*, x, 679–80, 695–6; *PPC*, v, 81; *ER*, v, 93.

least in an official sense. Unofficially, however, there are indications that Joan Beaufort's role in political life was diminishing from about the summer of 1438. The queen continued to receive her annual pension of £100 from Aberdeen until her death, but payments of her pensions from Edinburgh and Haddington, worth a combined income of £220 annually, are only recorded in 1438. There is a two-year gap in the Edinburgh accounts between 1438 and 1440, but the absence of any mention to the queen's pension in the apparently complete Haddington accounts suggests that both payments stopped after July 1438. The queen was partially compensated for this loss of income with a payment of £30 from the earldom of Mar between 1436 and 1438, a payment of £27 from Inverkeithing between 1436 and 1443, and annual payments of £3 or £4 from Kinghorn between 1436 and 1445.[15] The shortfall in the queen's income may have been offset by the Linlithgow customs, worth just over £300 in 1446, which were granted to her for life by James I some time after July 1436. This grant was recorded in the Linlithgow accounts rendered by the custumars, Robert Livingston and John Waltoun, in July 1438 but there is a gap in the burgh's customs accounts until 6 July 1445, nine days before Joan's death, making it impossible to ascertain whether payments continued to be made. It has been argued that Robert Livingston took financial advantage of his post during the minority, raising doubts about the amount of revenue the queen received from Linlithgow after 1438.[16] Upon Livingston's execution in 1450, the customs were conferred on Mary of Guelders as part of her dower allocation. It is possible that other elements of the queen's income were recorded in her own accounts, separated from those of James II in 1437, but the continuing references to her income from Aberdeen and Kinghorn in the general accounts suggest that this is not the case. The impression given by the accounts is that the queen's income decreased after July 1438.

This loss of income had significant implications for the queen's political power: her ability to dispense patronage and exercise economic influence was curtailed at a time when it was most required. The depletion of the upper ranks of the nobility at the start of the minority provided several lesser individuals and families with considerable opportunities for advancement. Tensions and feuds became evident towards the end of 1438, but the death of the earl of Douglas in June 1439 marked the

15 *ER*, v, 16, 24, 30, 56, 70–1, 92, 117, 123, 133, 155, 187–8, 199.
16 *ER*, v, 20, 223; Dunlop, *James Kennedy*, 109, 330–2.

onset of intense factionalism in the Scottish court and government.[17] Douglas' death allowed individuals such as Crichton, Livingston and Avandale to seek an increase in power, but also forced them to defend the power and offices they had already acquired from their competitors. No lieutenant was appointed following Douglas' death. This was partly due to the lack of available candidates – the earl left a fifteen year-old heir and the next adult male in the succession, Malise Graham, earl of Menteith, was still a hostage in England – but also reflects the readiness of members of council to take advantage of the opportunities his death afforded. The queen was particularly vulnerable in this environment. Although she remained official custodian of the king, she was unable to exercise this role in practice in summer 1439. James II was resident in Edinburgh castle, held by Crichton, in early July, and the story of continental chroniclers that the queen had to remove James from the castle without Crichton's knowledge indicates that he held effective custody of the king.[18] The possible involvement of the Crichton and Livingston families in the erosion of Joan's income would also have been a matter for concern. The two greatest elements of that income, the pension from Edinburgh and the customs of Linlithgow, were paid by towns dominated by William Crichton and Robert Livingston respectively, and the latter in particular was able to withhold payments from town revenues to the queen.

The actions and fortunes of Joan Beaufort in summer 1439 need to be seen in this context. At some point over the summer, she married James Stewart of Lorne. The papal dispensation for the marriage was granted on 21 September but indicates that the queen and Stewart had been privately married some time before seeking the dispensation. The queen removed her son from Edinburgh to Stirling between 10 July and 13 August, probably with the assistance of Stewart and at least one of his brothers, suggesting that the queen may have remarried in early July.[19] The timing of both the marriage and the removal of the king to Stirling indicates that the queen acted quickly to defend herself and her son following Douglas' death in June. While Douglas was powerful in his own right, men such as Crichton and Livingston were more dependent on the custody of the king for the exercise of power. The queen, too, needed to maintain custody of her son to play

17 Tanner, *Scottish Parliament*, 89–91.
18 *RMS*, ii, 201–2; Waurin, *Recueil des Croniques* (1431–47), 214; Monstrelet, *Chronicles*, ii, 47–8.
19 *CPR Letters*, viii, 255–6; *RMS*, ii, nos. 202–3.

any role in the minority government. She may also have felt, given her husband's wishes and the absence of any close male relative to act as lieutenant-general, that she should assume a leadership role as she did immediately following her husband's death in 1437. It is debatable, however, whether she intended to assume leadership of the regency government by establishing her own council at Stirling.[20] Having been marginalised after the crisis had passed in 1437, the queen was aware of what she could realistically achieve, particularly as she was in a weaker position in 1439 than at the start of the minority, unable to rely on an Angus or even a Douglas. By removing James II from Crichton's custody in Edinburgh, the queen was in some ways simply restoring the status quo of 1437 when she had been awarded custody of the king and his sisters and granted Stirling for their residence. She aimed to protect her son and his inheritance by resuming custody and acquiring influence on the government her enemies were actively seeking to dominate. It would have taken far greater support than the queen could muster, and a considerably less effective opposition than she faced, to have converted custody of the king into the establishment and leadership of an alternative council in 1439. Her resumption of the king's custody was a dangerous act. It was achieved by means of the high-risk strategy of remarriage, which, in the end, was not to her political advantage. The fact that the queen chose to remarry despite the risks suggests that she was in desperate need of protection and support, not that she saw it as a means of moving from the margins to the centre of power.

For a well-dowered and independent-minded woman in the fifteenth century, a second marriage entailed the surrendering of the legal and economic independence she had acquired on the death of her husband. Not only did she enjoy the income from her dower lands, a widow acquired the legal right to control her affairs, giving her more independence than she had ever experienced before. Only half of the young noble widows in fifteenth-century England chose to remarry, and the rate of remarriage among widowed peeresses as a group declined with age.[21] Christine de Pizan, herself a widow, admitted that 'there is so much hardship in the state of widowhood' that some people thought

---

20 Brown, *Black Douglases*, 249, 257.

21 Rosenthal, J.T., 'Fifteenth-Century Widows and Widowhood: Bereavement, Reintegration and Life Choices', 33–7, and Brundage, J.A., 'Widows and Remarriage: Moral Conflicts and Their Resolution in Classical Canon Law', 25, in S.S. Walker (ed.), *Wife and Widow in Medieval England* (Ann Arbor, 1993).

that all widows should remarry. Christine responded:

> This assumption could be countered by saying that if in married
> life everything were all repose and peace, truly it would be
> sensible for a woman to enter it again, but because one sees quite
> the contrary, any woman ought to be very wary of remarriage,
> although for young women it may be a necessity or anyway very
> convenient. But for those who have already passed their youth
> and who are well enough off and are not constrained by poverty,
> it is sheer folly, although some women who wish to remarry say
> that it is no life for a woman on her own'.[22]

What Christine's view of remarriage meant in practice is illustrated by
the case of Isabella Stewart, who clearly felt that it was not an option for
her following the death of the duke of Brittany in 1450. The Bretons
began negotiations with Navarre regarding Isabella's remarriage – the
need to provide dower income for Isabella as well as for her successor
imposed a huge financial burden on the duchy – but James II objected.
He secured the support of Charles VII of France for his plans and a joint
Franco–Scottish embassy went to Brittany in March 1453 to discuss
three key issues: Isabella, whom James claimed had been deprived of
her dower following her husband's death; her daughters, whom James
claimed had been deprived of their inheritance; and James' claim to the
duchy itself. Charles VII also wrote directly to Pierre, duke of Brittany,
asking him to suspend negotiations for Isabella's marriage. Isabella
assured the embassy that she had been well treated by the duke and
had no desire to leave Brittany, effectively ruling out her remarriage to
Navarre or within Scotland. More importantly, she took advantage of
the opportunity to complain that far from being deprived of her rights
by the duke of Brittany, she had been treated poorly by her own family
as James II had never paid her dowry. She then sent a letter to Charles
VII in April 1453 in which she reiterated her claims that she had been
well-treated by Brittany and sought the assistance of the French king
in retrieving her dowry. Isabella thus resisted the efforts of the duke
of Brittany, the prince of Navarre, James II and Charles VII to control
her future and was sufficiently strong-willed, and economically independent, to make demands of them instead. She never remarried and
lived on her dower lands of Succinio until her death sometime after
1495. Isabella did not want to remarry and had the legal and economic

22 *Treasure*, 159–60.

independence, not to mention the will, to reject any marriage plans put to her.[23]

A queen, on the other hand, possessed a significant degree of economic and legal independence even as a consort. She was endowed with lands and income at her marriage in order to ensure that her household did not constitute a drain on crown resources, she used her own signet to transact business and she could appoint her own officers. The disadvantages of remarriage for a widowed queen were related more to her status within the kingdom than to her economic and legal independence. In discussing the options of a young and childless widowed princess, Christine de Pizan wrote that 'if she [re-]married by her own choice' without the consent of her family and friends, 'she would be greatly at fault'. If 'she made a bad match and no good came of it...she would lose her friends' favour'. Christine did not discuss the possibility of a queen mother's remarriage. In the event of a minority, she advised the queen mother to keep the peace between her children – potentially jealous of their sibling's elevation in status – and amongst the barons. Christine also recommended that the queen be prepared to face the threat of foreign attack.[24] The queen mother's energies were to be devoted to preserving the peace and stability of the kingdom for her son, and it was these duties that permitted her to undertake tasks not normally assigned to her, such as the preparation for war. These views reflect French perceptions of the queen mother's role, but are nevertheless striking in their silence on the question of remarriage and their assumption that the queen would not act to secure power for herself.

The secret remarriage of a young widowed princess, according to Christine, was improper and would result in the loss of favour. The drawbacks of a second marriage were even greater for a queen mother entrusted with the custody of her son during his minority as her remarriage could result in the loss of custody or influence. A statute was

---

23 Trévédy, J., 'Trois duchesses douairières de Bretagne', *Bulletin Archéologique de l'Association Bretonne*, Troisième Série, 27 (1909), 3–49; Nantes ADLA, E13/1; Paris AN, K1151/1; Dom H. Morice, *Mémoires pour servir de preuves à l'histoire Ecclesiastique et Civile de Bretagne* (reprint Paris, 1974), ii, 1629–30. Dunlop suggests that James intended to marry Isabella to Orkney to pacify him for the loss of Garioch (*James Kennedy*, 185 n.3), but Crawford argues that Orkney had no claim on the earldom and that the parallel arrangements for Isabella's return were purely coincidental (Crawford, B.E., 'The Earls of Orkney-Caithness and their relations with Norway and Scotland: 1158–1470' (unpublished PhD thesis, University of St Andrews, 1971), 297).

24 *Treasure*, 82, 85.

enacted in the English parliament of 1427–8 prohibiting the queen mother, Katherine of Valois, from remarrying without the consent of her son, then aged seven.[25] He could not give such consent until he reached his majority, by which time the queen's second husband would not be in a position to exert any undue influence over him. It was not only the possibility that a man who was not related to the king and had not been appointed by parliament would acquire power over the king that raised problems but also the unsuitability of the queen mother marrying an inferior. The social and political hierarchy had to be maintained, particularly as any attack on the queen's honour was implicitly an attack on the honour of the monarchy and her son. Similar prohibitions on the queen's remarriage were enacted in France in 1294 and 1374 and, in Scotland, Margaret Tudor was appointed regent in 1513 on the condition that she did not remarry.[26] Joan Beaufort was only the second Scottish queen mother to remarry. No law prevented her from doing so and the only other queen to remarry, Marie de Coucy, had managed to retain a role in government despite her remarriage in 1257. Joan Beaufort's remarriage, however, provided Alexander Livingston with grounds for depriving the queen of custody of her son. The fact that this act was publicly sanctioned – regardless of whether such sanction was given voluntarily or by force – indicates that the occasion of the queen's remarriage was regarded as suitable grounds for transferring custody. Joan must have been aware that her marriage to a relative unknown might meet with disapproval, particularly given the ongoing competition to dominate government, and it is unlikely that she contracted the marriage in the belief that it would secure her leadership of the minority government. The probability that the marriage was contracted two months before a papal dispensation was granted may indicate that it was kept secret. If this was the case, it indicates an awareness that the marriage could have negative consequences for the queen's power.

Remarriage was unnecessary, even unattractive, to a widow of independent means and, in the case of a queen mother, could result in the loss of custody of her son. Yet Joan Beaufort chose to remarry. Given the events at Blackfriars, her physical safety and that of her children may

25 Griffiths, R.A., 'Queen Katherine of Valois and a Missing Statute of the Realm', *Law Quarterly Review*, xciii (1977), 253, 257–8; G.O. Sayles, 'The royal marriages act, 1428', *Law Quarterly Review*, 94 (1978), 188–92.
26 Poulet, A., 'Capetian Women and the Regency: the Genesis of a Vocation' in Parsons, *Medieval Queenship*, 110, 114; McNeill, 'The Scottish Regency', 138.

still have been a primary concern in 1439, but unlike 1437, the queen now had no obvious source of protection. At the beginning of June she issued a letter from Falkland renouncing her right to the third year of revenue granted to her from the church at Haddington.[27] She claimed that she had earlier renounced the initial two years 'for gude and resonabile causis moving us' in favour of the prior of St Andrews and that this final renunciation was made 'nochtwitstandyng ony clam that schir Alexander Hume pretendis of tak tharof throw our graunt or promisse.' The letter may indicate that Hume had initially been a supporter of the queen and had fallen from favour, perhaps by seeking an alternative and stronger alliance. The queen's renunciation of some potentially helpful revenue in order to maintain the support of St Andrews was in keeping with her general search for allies which was concentrated in Perthshire, where she held lands, and the neighbouring earldoms of Strathearn and Fife. Her marriage to James Stewart of Lorne created links between the queen and landowners and officers in Perthshire. Stewart's brother, Archibald, was deputy sheriff of Perth in 1439 when he received a payment for the queen by her mandate, while the eldest brother, Robert, lord of Lorne, and Robert's brother-in-law, David Murray of Tullibardine, held lands in Perthshire.[28] Murray was also campaigning to be appointed steward of the earldom of Strathearn, vacant since the death of Atholl.

Another landholder in Perthshire was *James Kennedy*, bishop of Dunkeld, nephew of James I and cousin of the earl of Douglas, who was charged with securing the papal dispensation for the queen's marriage to James Stewart. Kennedy's uncle, Hugh (who had fought in France and was a member of the French embassy to Scotland in 1434), Robert Stewart and David Murray were members of the royal council in September 1439, presumably representing the queen's interests. The Stewart brothers and David Murray were all with Joan Beaufort at Falkland in March 1440.[29] It is likely that upon the death of the bishop of St Andrews the following month, this group lent its weight to the installation of *James Kennedy* as his replacement. Kennedy was elected by the chapter of St Andrews on 22 April and was provided to the see by Pope Eugenius IV but faced a competitor in the person of James Ogilvy, appointed by Pope Felix V. This latter appointment would have been agreeable to Avandale and the Livingstons, who supported Felix

27 *Copiale*, 171.
28 *ER*, v, 110; Brown, *Black Douglases*, 257.
29 *RMS*, ii, no. 205; Edinburgh NAS, GD 20/301.

and the council at Basel in order to secure promotions for members of their families. Kennedy was the preferred candidate for the queen and her allies. Kennedy had secured the papal dispensation for the queen's marriage and could have expected her assistance and that of her new family in achieving his installation. The queen was resident in the St Andrews diocese and had already displayed favour towards its prior by renouncing her claim to the Haddington tithes. The chapter may have sought her support for its choice of bishop. Bishop Cameron, chancellor of James I and early patron of Kennedy, returned to court at the end of April, perhaps to lend his support to Kennedy's installation.[30]

The queen was seeking allies in 1439 but this search was primarily a defensive rather than an offensive measure. Her opponents were men such as Avandale, Crichton and Livingston who collaborated in the imprisonment of the queen and her husband in August 1439 and in the murder of the young earl of Douglas and his brother at the Black Dinner in November 1440. The ambitions of these men and the Crichton-Livingston control of several key offices in government made them formidable opponents. The queen, for all her strength and support in and around Perthshire, could not overcome them. Her supporters could not dominate or form an alternative council, nor could they oust the Crichtons and Livingstons from their posts. The opportunity for Alexander Livingston to imprison the queen and her husband arose because he controlled Stirling, indicating that the queen could not, and may not even have attempted to, exclude her opponents from power. The queen's motive in remarrying and securing custody of the king was the need to remain in the political arena and protect her son. Without custody, the queen would have found it difficult, if not impossible, to retain a role in a government composed of men determined to maintain and maximise their power at their competitors' expense. The competition for dominance fought by these men could be won through gaining custody of the king, making his safety a primary concern. The presence of Stewart and his brother at Stirling during the king's residence further suggests that the queen was trying to ensure the king's safety as well as her own.

In the event the plan was unsuccessful. The queen's marriage and her probable involvement in the removal of the king from Edinburgh to Stirling prompted her opponents to take action. In Stirling castle on 3 August 1439, Alexander Livingston 'Tuke the qwene and put hir in ane chalmere and kepit hir stratlye thairin/ till scho was lowsit be the thre estatis at the counsall haldin at striuling that samyn zere the last day of august'.[31] Livingston's willingness to arrest the queen and take illegal custody of the king indicates that Joan Beaufort remarried to secure physical protection for her family and its interests, despite the possibility that her marriage might deprive her of official custody of her son. Her supporters were no match for Livingston, who 'tuke sir James Stewart the lord of lornis brother and William Stewart and put tham in pittis and bollit thaim'.[32] His actions were undertaken with the knowledge and approval of Avandale and William and George Crichton, who joined him at Stirling by by 13 August, over a fortnight before the queen's release. The General Council that released her included several of her allies – Robert Stewart, David Murray and Hugh Kennedy – but was unable to prevent the queen losing custody of her children. The queen was forced to make an 'appoyntement' with Livingston and his accomplices in which she promised not to seek revenge for their actions, surrendered custody of her children and renounced the pension granted to her for their care.[33] Livingston effectively secured a position in the minority government by depriving the queen of custody of the young king. The witnesses to this agreement included the young earl of Douglas, Crichton, his ally Gordon, and Avandale's brother-in-law, Walter Haliburton, lord of Dirlton.

Their victory over the queen was not as complete as the terms of the 'appoyntement' may suggest. In the first place, the coalition of Livingston, Avandale, Crichton and their supporters was itself unstable, breaking and reforming in different combinations during the decade after the queen's arrest. Secondly, the network of support around the queen continued to function in the months after her imprisonment and the loss of her custodial rights. The probable involvement of this network in the installation of Kennedy as bishop of St Andrews and the return to court of Cameron at the end of April 1440 are indications that the queen had not been sidelined from power by losing custody of the king. The betrothal of the princess Joanna to the earl of Angus in October 1440 was probably supported by the queen and indicates that the network continued to seek new sources of support.[34] Joanna, however, was officially in the custody of the Livingstons at the time, and the betrothal was not acceptable to the queen's opponents. Angus was

---

31 'Auch. Chron.', 160.
32 'Auch. Chron.', 160.
33 *RMS*, ii, nos. 203–5; *APS*, ii, 54–5.
34 Fraser, W., *The Douglas Book* (Edinburgh, 1885), ii, 42.

deprived of his new pensions after 1441 and the Douglas–Livingston faction sent Joanna uninvited to France with her sister Eleanor in July 1445. Kennedy's return to Scotland in spring 1441 further strengthened the network around the queen, and the charge made in March that Cameron and 'several others of the king's council' were engaged in a conspiracy against the king's life is indicative of the friction within council.[35] Douglas' efforts to increase his power and promote his family saw Crichton ally with both Kennedy and Angus in the dispute over Coldingham in 1442, and the power of this alliance was still felt at the beginning of the following year. The list of lords of council who heard a case at Stirling in January 1443 included David Murray and procurators for the queen and Angus, as well as opponents of the queen such as Robert, James and William Livingston.[36] The queen therefore retained some presence in council, however limited it may have been in practice, as late as 1443.

Angus, Kennedy, Crichton and Murray were members of the General Council which met at Stirling in February 1443, but the accession of the eighth earl of Douglas in March altered the balance of power within government. Angus disappears from the surviving government records for a time after February, while Douglas and Alexander Livingston joined forces to oppose the power of William Crichton. On 16 August 1443, Livingston swore under oath that he had not been involved in the execution of Sir Malcolm Fleming following the Black Dinner, a declaration which implicitly placed the blame on Crichton and paved the way for the Douglas-Livingston alliance in government.[37] Livingston's declaration was witnessed by Kennedy and Cameron, among others, suggesting that the subsequent attack on Crichton had relatively broad support. In August Crichton ceased to be chancellor and Douglas laid siege to George Crichton's house in Barnton 'at the command of James II'. In November a General Council 'blewe out on sir William of Crichton and sir George of Crichton'.[38] The same Council also declared Scottish obedience to Pope Eugenius IV, thus removing the major obstacle which had prevented an alliance between Kennedy and Douglas' predecessor as earl. After six years of fluctuations in the balance of power within the minority government, one faction had finally become dominant.

35 *Cal. Scot. Supp.*, iv, no.748
36 Dunlop, *James Kennedy*, 48–54; HMC, x, Appendix I, 63–4.
37 *APS*, ii, 58–9; *RMS*, ii, no.270; Brown, *Black Douglases*, 260–5.
38 'Auch. Chron.', 161; McGladdery, *James II*, 28.

The eighth earl of Douglas' success in sidelining or forging alliances with his opponents in government in 1443 overpowered the queen and her supporters. Without the assistance of men such as Kennedy, Crichton and Angus in council the queen could do little to reverse her situation. The Douglas–Livingston faction was able to exploit its custody of the king as it had done at Barnton, and proceeded to arrange the marriages of those of his sisters still in Scotland, despatching them to the continent in 1444-5. The Savoy embassy negotiating Annabella's betrothal spent time with the king at Stirling, controlled by Livingston, and met the earls of Douglas, Crawford and Orkney and the Lord of the Isles on a number of occasions between September 1444 and April 1445. A fortnight after Annabella's marriage contract was sealed, the ambassadors spent Christmas and New Year with the king and Douglas at Stirling. Kennedy and Angus each met the ambassadors only once, on 1 October and 9 February respectively, and played little role in the negotiations. The queen was not mentioned.[39] The queen had reason to act but her re-emergence into active political life in November 1444 was only made possible by the renewal of her alliance with Bishop Kennedy. Kennedy would appear to have been allied with the Douglas–Livingston faction on 1 October when he met the Savoy embassy, but by 17 November, he had joined with Joan Beaufort to write to the burgh of Aberdeen and order the town not to pay revenues to 'tha persownis that nw has the kyng in gouernance'. The queen and Kennedy were soon joined by Crichton, Angus and Adam Hepburn. Hepburn had been associated with Angus and Kennedy in the Coldingham dispute between 1442 and 1444. Like them, he had been trusted by James I, who had appointed him keeper of Dunbar castle in 1435, and had an uneasy relationship with the earls of Douglas, the previous holders of the castle.[40] This network of support for the queen enabled her to protest about the Douglas–Livingston control of her son and of government generally. But the opposition campaign was doomed to failure. On 20 November the alderman of Aberdeen declared that the letter from the queen and Kennedy should not be read or obeyed. This order was followed by a letter from James II a few days later which ordered that the revenues should be paid and collected as usual.[41] The king, or those who ruled in his name, could overrule any attempt made by the opposition to regain some influence in government.

39 Turin AS(1), Inv.16 Reg.93, ff.372v.–373v.
40 *ER*, iv, 620; Dunlop, *James Kennedy*, 75.
41 *Council Register of the Burgh of Aberdeen*, i, 399.

The Douglas–Livingston faction was able to defend itself legally, by force, and in parliament. Attacks were made in November and January on Methven castle near Perth and on Kennedy's lands in Fife. The first attack was made in the presence of the king and members of his council, while the second was headed by 'The erll of Crawford, [and] James of Livingston, that tyme kepar to the king and captain of Stirling'.[42] Crichton was besieged in Edinburgh castle 'on the kingis behalf' in June 1445 while the queen took refuge in the castle of Dunbar, held by Hepburn.[43] The Douglas-dominated parliament held in June threatened Angus with forfeiture and may have considered punishing Kennedy for his activities but settled for denying him any office in government.[44] The queen's husband, James Stewart, was also threatened with forfeiture and Crichton lost the captaincy of Edinburgh castle.[45] The opposition was formally over when, on 15 July 1445, 'the qwene his moder deit in Dunbar and was erdit in the charterhous of Perth and incontinent the lord Hailes gaf our the castell of Dunbar throu trety'.[46] It is likely that the Douglas–Livingston faction would have claimed victory during the summer regardless of the queen's fate, having effectively isolated the king and secured their control over him with the departure of his remaining unmarried sisters to the continent and the arrests of Angus and James Stewart.

James I publicly displayed his trust in the queen with the oaths of loyalty sworn to her in 1428 and 1435. The oaths did not specifically mention Joan's rights during a minority, but they demonstrated the king's belief that she would carry out his wishes and ensure the safe transmission of the crown to James II. While the queen may have felt entitled to an official role in the minority government as a result of her husband's trust and actions, she settled for pursuing a long-term strategy to maintain a role on council. Joan aimed to use her position as mother and custodian of the king to represent the plans of her murdered husband and the interests of her son, a strategy which was in keeping with the behaviour and values expected of royal women in the fifteenth century. But converting her 'natural' rights as the king's mother into a

---

42 'Auch. Chron.', 162; *ER*, v, 186–7, 230; *RMS*, ii, no.283.
43 'Auch. Chron.', 162.
44 Edinburgh NAS, GD 52/1042; *APS*, ii, 59–60; Macdougall, 'Bishop James Kennedy of St Andrews', 11.
45 Pinkerton, J., *The History of Scotland from the Accession of the House of Stuart to that of Mary, with Appendices of Original Papers* (London, 1797), i, 477, Appendix xiv; *ER*, v, 259, 305.
46 'Auch. Chron.', 162; *ER*, v, 184.

position on the minority council was far from easy. The Appoyntement of 1439 demonstrated the challenges faced by the queen and the limits of her strategy. While formally depriving Joan Beaufort of her position as the king's custodian, Livingston agreed that she would continue to 'haue access to visit our said soueryn lord hir son'. Her biological and emotional rights as the king's mother were explicitly recognised at the same time as her legitimate right to custody of the king, and hence a role in the minority government, was denied. The possibility that her maternal status could again be allied with custodial rights ensured that the queen was a focus for forces of differentiation and opposition for the remainder of the minority. Those who opposed the dominant faction in government gravitated to the queen, the possessor of a clearly legitimate right to custody and a leading role in government. The Douglas–Livingston faction would have emerged triumphant in the summer of 1445 even without the queen's death, but the focus of opposition to their dominance died with her.

The queen's political role during the minority was greatest when she worked in coalition with Angus and Douglas immediately following her husband's murder. She was represented on council as late as January 1443 and managed to retain some influence through the membership on council of her allies in subsequent months. But in the final two years of her life, the queen lost most of her remaining influence as her supporters were finally overpowered by the Douglas faction. The success of the queen's strategy to maintain a role in the minority government was dependent upon the recognition, assistance and political fortunes of leading members of the political community. The widespread recognition of Joan Beaufort's rights as the king's mother and the reference to her 'men and retenewe' in the Appoyntement of 1439 demonstrate that her power was associated with that of other men right from the start of the minority. Her decision to remarry and her alliances throughout the minority with men who were personally opposed to the Douglas–Livingston faction reveal her awareness that she could not retain influence over the king on her own. Her very dependence on men who might, and sometimes did, change their allegiance indicates that Joan Beaufort never regarded herself, and nor was she regarded by others, as a separate and autonomous political figure.

NINE

Mary of Guelders, 1460–3

'Thai left the King in keping with his modere the queen and governing of all the kinrik'

The experiences of Mary of Guelders during the minority of James III were fundamentally different from those of Joan Beaufort. James II was killed by an exploding cannon at the siege of Roxburgh on 3 August 1460, but the 'lordis' leading the army continued and won the siege five days later. The transition to minority government was similarly successful, and the 'Prince with his modere the quene and bischopis and uther nobillis' arrived in Kelso for the coronation ceremony two days after the victory.[1] The success of the campaign bore little resemblance to the divided and abandoned effort mounted at Roxburgh by James I in 1436. The division betwÞen king and nobility made public on the battlefield culminated in the murder of James I six months later, and continued into his son's minority. The different circumstances and legacies of each king's death created different problems and opportunities for their widows. Unlike Joan Beaufort, Mary of Guelders was able to retain her access to her son, the young James III, and to claim and maintain a leading role in a stable minority government.

Mary of Guelders' considerable political ability during the minority has traditionally been overlooked in favour of tales of her emotional instability and personal rivalry with Bishop Kennedy. In the nineteenth century, the queen's intelligence and character were the subjects of detailed debate in the pages of the *Proceedings of the Society of Antiquaries of Scotland*. The debate was ignited by the discovery in 1848 of two female skeletons during the demolition of Trinity College church in Edinburgh, burial place of Mary of Guelders. Daniel Wilson noted that one of the skulls indicated 'acute cerebral disease' but argued, on the basis of its location within the church, that it was not that of the queen.[2]

---

1 'Auch. Chron.', 169.
2 Wilson, D., 'Notes on the Search for the Tomb of the Royal Foundress of the College Church of the Holy Trinity at Edinburgh', *PSAS*, iv (1860–2), 559–62.

David Laing argued that the diseased skull was that of the queen and that she had 'inherited the dispositions and weakness, in other words the insanity, of her nearest relatives'. He did, however, stop short of a 'supposition of absolute imbecility'. Laing's diagnosis is closely related to his belief that Mary's name was 'not so much as once mentioned in connexion with any public event' between 1449 and 1460. He acknowledged that Mary of Guelders played a greater role in public life after 1460 but claimed that this role was confined to educating the royal children, causing dissent and conducting love affairs. Bishop Kennedy was entrusted with political matters.[3]

The belief that Kennedy managed political life during the minority, already centuries old in 1860, continued to be the dominant view for another 120 years. In 1939, Macrae argued that the 'mere fact that her political opponent, Bishop Kennedy, supported Henry VI would of itself prompt the queen to champion a policy of friendship with Edward IV.'[4] Macrae represented Scottish policy during the early minority as subject to personal rivalries and portrayed Kennedy's actions as the outcome of a careful consideration of political circumstances. He argued that the queen's actions were the result of her emotional and implicitly unstable response to the bishop's rational policy. Annie Dunlop took a similar view in her eulogy of Kennedy, published in 1950. While she noted that it was difficult to know 'how far her passions influenced politics during the years of her marriage', Dunlop argued that the queen's actions as a widow 'reveal her as ambitious and susceptible, headstrong and unstable.'[5] Ranald Nicholson's history of late medieval Scotland, published in 1974, described the queen's foreign policy as 'wayward' and 'perhaps not uninfluenced by personal factors', namely her rumoured affairs with Somerset and Hailes. He further accused the queen of acting 'independently' and concluded that she was 'doubtless the source of the "evil and peril" and "great division" of which Bishop Kennedy complained'.[6] A major reassessment of the queen's mental

---

For a more recent analysis of the probable location of the queen's tomb, see Tolley, T., 'Hugo van der Goes's Altarpiece for Trinity College Church in Edinburgh and Mary of Guelders, Queen of Scotland' in J. Higgitt (ed.), *Medieval Art and Architecture in the Diocese of St Andrews* (Leeds, 1994), 219–21.

3 Laing, D., 'Remarks on the Character of Mary of Gueldres, Consort of King James the Second of Scotland; in connexion with an attempt to determine the Place of her Interment in Trinity College Church, Edinburgh', *PSAS*, iv (1860–2), 574–7.

4 Macrae, C., 'Scotland and the Wars of the Roses' (unpublished DPhil thesis, Oxford University, 1939), 313.

5 Dunlop, *James Kennedy*, 240.

6 Nicholson, *Scotland*, 399, 403–4.

health and contribution to the minority government was published in 1982. In his study of James III, Norman Macdougall associated the queen mother with 'pragmatism' and Kennedy with 'tradition'. In addition, he suggested that Kennedy's opposition to Mary following his return to Scotland in 1461 arose because he was jealous at his exclusion from the minority government. This government, according to Macdougall, displayed 'remarkable stability and continuity of service in the higher echelons' and Kennedy played little official role in it until the latter half of 1463.[7] This interpretation of Kennedy's public role in the early years of the minority has been modified by Roland Tanner in his recent book on the medieval Scottish parliament. Tanner argues that Kennedy exercised considerable influence on government policy as leader of a parliamentary faction opposing the queen and dates his success in undermining her policies from late 1462.[8]

Bishop Kennedy is himself largely responsible for the emphasis on personal rivalry in Scottish political affairs in the early years of the minority. The most detailed contemporary account of Scottish foreign policy and its domestic effects 1461–4 is contained in Kennedy's instructions to Monypenny regarding the Scottish embassy to Louis XI in 1464.[9] Kennedy was a long-standing supporter of the Lancastrians but, following the exclusion of Scotland from the truce concluded between Louis, nominally pro-Lancastrian, and Yorkist England in October 1463, he was forced to support the negotiations for a separate Scottish–Yorkist truce. Discussions began in the winter of 1463–4 and were postponed until March – the month in which Kennedy sent Monypenny to France to justify the bishop's apparent change of heart to the French king. The instructions thus emphasise the 'grant discencion entre ladite royne et moy' from the time of the bishop's return to Scotland in summer 1461 and the efforts he had made since then to promote the Lancastrian cause and the traditional French alliance, despite the opposition of many of the 'grans seigeurs du royaulme'. His acknowledgement of the role of 'grans seigeurs' and those advisers of the queen who were 'contraires au dit roy Henry' exposes the internal contradictions of the letter: the queen was at once the chief architect of dispute and a cipher dominated by her counsellors.[10] Kennedy also

7 Macdougall, *James III*, 51; Macdougall, 'Bishop James Kennedy of St Andrews', 15–16.
8 Tanner, *Scottish Parliament*, 169–80.
9 De Waurin, J., *Anchiennes Cronicques d'Engleterre*, ed. E. Dupont (Paris, 1858–63), iii, 164–75.
10 Waurin, *Anchiennes Cronicques*, iii, 166–7.

claimed that the queen and council intended to support the Lancastrians in 1462, but reconsidered when they believed the French king had withdrawn his support for Henry VI.[11] The bishop's version of events represented him as a tireless Franco–Lancastrian campaigner who had failed in his quest through fault of circumstance and Louis' ambivalence. The queen, as his main opponent, was implicitly in error as a pro-Yorkist and explicitly at fault as the cause of 'grant division' in the kingdom. This negative characterisation favoured Kennedy, particularly as his account exaggerated his own role in government between 1461 and 1463, and downplayed the strength of pro-Yorkist support within Scotland.

James II's policy during the Yorkist–Lancastrian conflict was to lend his support to whichever side offered him the greater opportunity to recover Berwick and Roxburgh, and to advance Scottish interests generally. He initially supported the Lancastrian cause, communicating with his imprisoned uncle, the duke of Somerset, in 1454 and using Somerset's death and the imprisonment of his cousin, Henry VI, as excuses to besiege Berwick in June 1455. James' awareness of the potential of the English conflict was revealed in a letter he sent to Charles VII asking him to join the war against England on behalf of their shared kinsman, Henry VI. The letter emphasised that the division within England provided the kings of Scotland and France with the ideal opportunity to attack the kingdom, and stated specifically that a combined effort could reclaim Berwick for the Scots and Calais for the French.[12] James' apparent change of allegiance from Lancaster to York in 1459–60 seems to have been the result of the better terms offered by the duke of York. Following the rout of the Yorkists at Lumford Bridge in October 1459, York fled to Ireland where he attempted to win foreign support for his cause. Given the perception of Scotland as England's natural enemy and James II's marital relationship with Burgundy – York's ally – it seems likely that York also approached the Scottish king for his support. The king sent Archibald Whitelaw to Ireland in 1460 to negotiate a secret treaty promising Scottish support for York's claim, and was rumoured to be planning a marriage between one of his daughters and York's son.[13] James attacked England as York's ally, and wrote to Charles

11 Waurin, *Anchiennes Cronicques*, iii, 168–9.
12 Macrae, 'Scotland and the Wars of the Roses', 192, 198–9; Stevenson, *Letters and Papers*, i, 319–22.
13 Macrae, 'Scotland and the Wars of the Roses', 268–9; *Cal. State Papers (Milan)*, i, 27.

VII and the duke of Milan encouraging them to do likewise, again reminding the French king of the advantages of a divided England.[14] As in 1455, it seems clear that James II was seeking an opportunity to reclaim Berwick and Roxburgh rather than to assist either Lancaster or York to claim victory. Similarly, York was interested in the English throne rather than in offering concessions to the Scots. Following the Yorkist victory at Northampton in July 1460, York left Ireland to press his claim and in November was proclaimed heir-apparent to Henry VI and protector of England. The Yorkist successes and James' death at Roxburgh removed the need to make concessions to the Scots, which in turn created the opportunity for the Lancastrians to promise similar concessions in order to regain Scottish support. The attraction of the Lancastrian cause and the likelihood that its leaders would be able to fulfil their promises increased with the death of the duke of York at the battle of Wakefield in December 1460. The meeting between Mary of Guelders and Margaret of Anjou at Lincluden in the following month was intended to renew the Scottish-Lancastrian alliance to Scottish advantage and, as such, did not signify the Scottish queen's inconstancy but the perpetuation of James II's policy.

The queens of Scotland and England met for 'x or xii days and thai said that thai war accordit on baith the sydis'.[15] The queens are reported to have discussed a marriage alliance between Mary, sister of James III, and the prince of Wales at the meeting, and it is possible that Margaret offered to restore Berwick to the Scots in exchange for their support.[16] It is unclear whether the restoration to the Scots of Berwick in April 1461 was the result of promises made three months earlier or whether the Lancastrians were forced to make this concession following their defeat at Towton and flight to Scotland in March. York's son had been installed as Edward IV at the beginning of March, but the Lancastrian promises and the possibility that Yorkist fortunes might again fail persuaded the Scots to continue providing a refuge for the family and supporters of Henry VI without becoming involved in a full-scale war.[17] This policy was sound. A papal legate, reporting in June 1461, stated that neither the Yorkists nor the Lancastrians were

14 Stevenson, *Letters and Papers*, i, 323–6; *Cal. State Papers (Milan)*, i, 23; Macrae, 'Scotland and the Wars of the Roses', 258–72; Appendix A, no.3, pp.461–70.
15 'Auch. Chron.', 170.
16 Waurin, *Anchiennes Croniques*, ii, 301–2; iii, 166; *Cal. State Papers (Milan)*, i, 90, 93, 98.
17 *The Paston Letters AD 1422–1509*, ed. Gairdner, J. (London, 1904), iii, 267, 307; *ER*, vii, 49, 60, 62, 84–5, 139, 145, 211.

strong, and that 'if they begin again, it is considered most likely that no young man or certainly very few will see the end'. He also noted that the balance of power between the competing royal claims was matched by an international balance between Scottish and French support for Henry VI, and the support of the duke of Burgundy and the dauphin for the Yorkists.[18] The Yorkists attempted to open negotiations with the Scots as early as April 1461. Although these attempts were unsuccessful, the Milanese ambassador to France reported on 18 June 1461 that the court felt that 'the Queen of Scotland will give up the idea' of attacking England.[19] This assumption was erroneous given the Scottish support for an attack on Carlisle in June, but it reflects the reluctance of the queen and regency council to commit Scotland fully to the provision of military assistance for a long-running and potentially doomed cause.

This reluctance gradually became a move towards the Yorkists following the failure of the Scottish–Lancastrian campaigns on Carlisle (which may have been promised to the Scots) and on Durham in June 1461. The coronation of Edward IV at the end of June, and the Yorkist attempts to create division within Scotland by supporting the earls of Ross and Douglas further strengthened the Yorkist position. The Yorkists, however, also continued to offer opportunities for negotiation and, in August and November 1461, Edward IV appointed the earl of Warwick and Robert Ogle to discuss the possibility of an Anglo–Scottish truce.[20] Two Scottish embassies were appointed in September and November 1461. The ambassadors included men associated with the queen and regency council: Lindsay, appointed keeper of the privy seal by the queen; Orkney, guardian of James III in June 1461; Lord Livingston, chamberlain; and George Liddale, secretary to James III. The Scottish treasurer, David Guthrie, was also in England sometime before July 1462.[21] An Anglo–Scottish truce for a year was concluded in November, but negotiations and threats continued. The English government continued its negotiations with Douglas and Ross during the winter of 1461–2. In March 1462 an envoy of Edward IV reported that the king had gone north 'to have peace or war with the Scots'. He recorded that some people felt 'that the Scots want to come and

18 *Cal. State Papers (Milan)*, i, 90–1.
19 *ER*, vii, 63, 145, 147, 189; *Rot. Scot.*, ii, 402; *Cal. State Papers (Milan)*, i, 98–9.
20 Macrae, 'Scotland and the Wars of the Roses', 292, 296–7, 303–8; *Rot. Scot.*, ii, 402, 404.
21 *Foedera*, xi, 476; *Rot. Scot.*, ii, 390, 403; *CDS*, iv, no.1326; *ER*, vii, 127.

make war, but I can hardly credit this because the Scottish ambassadors left here with a different conclusion'.[22] In April, Margaret of Anjou left Scotland for France with the intention of winning the support of foreign princes and raising funds to enable her to continue pressing the Lancastrian claim. Her departure recognised that Scottish support for her cause was limited and, even at its strongest, would not be sufficient to defeat the Yorkists. More importantly, it removed a major obstacle to the success of the Scottish negotiations with Edward IV. Edward's interest in evicting the Lancastrians from their Scottish refuge had earlier been indicated in a letter sent to James III in the winter of 1461–2, asking him to return the royal family and its supporters if they had not become subjects of the Scottish king. The departure of Margaret of Anjou for France in April represented a significant victory for Edward in his relations with Scotland, and was followed by the meeting at the end of that month between Warwick, Mary of Guelders and James III at Dumfries.[23]

Kennedy reported that the object of the talks held in Dumfries was to secure 'longues treves et de faire doubles aliances et amitiez'.[24] It was also rumoured that marital alliances between Scotland and the Yorkists were suggested. The meeting was unsuccessful, but plans for further talks were soon underway. Several English knights were sent to Scotland, Warwick received a safe-conduct to visit Scotland in June, and Mary of Guelders travelled to Coldingham in the following month. Warwick became impatient with the lack of progress and opted for a more direct approach to the negotiations. Before 3 July, he entered Scotland and took 'a castell of the Skoots; and upon thys ther came the Quene of Skoots with other Lords of her contre … in basetry to my seyd Lord of Werwek, and a trews is take betwyx this and Seynt Bertylmew Day in August'.[25] Warwick and Mary of Guelders continued their discussions at Carlisle in July. According to a letter written to John Paston, the English promised to cease giving support to the earl of Douglas, and the Scots promised that 'Kyng Harry and his Aderents in Scotland schall be delyvered'.[26] The letter also suggested

22 *Foedera*, xi, 477; Macrae, 'Scotland and the Wars of the Roses', 303–8; *Cal. State Papers (Milan)*, i, 106.
23 Macrae, 'Scotland and the Wars of the Roses', 301, 312–13; Waurin, *Anchiennes Cronicques*, iii, 167.
24 Waurin, *Anchiennes Cronicques*, iii, 167.
25 *ER*, vii, 152; *Paston Letters*, iv, 44; Macrae, 'Scotland and the Wars of the Roses', 315, 317.
26 *Paston Letters*, iv, 50–1.

that these decisions were taken by the pro-Yorkist regency council rather than the pro-Lancastrian parliamentary faction in Scotland led by Bishop Kennedy. The council sent an embassy to London at the beginning of October but the return of Margaret of Anjou to Scotland and the letters of Louis XI encouraging James III and Kennedy to support Henry VI strengthened Kennedy's faction and ensured that the negotiations with the Yorkists were not immediately successful.[27] Margaret of Anjou's mission to secure French support for the Lancastrian cause had been a minor success, and she had returned to Scotland with ships and men under the command of Pierre de Brezé, seneschal of Normandy. They sailed for England with Henry VI to seize the castles of Alnwick, Dunstanburgh and Bamburgh but were sent back to Scotland by mid-November following a Yorkist counter-attack. The Scots were reported to be planning to 'rescue these iij. castellys' from Yorkist sieges in December, and Angus and de Brezé attacked Alnwick to rescue its Lancastrian garrison in January 1463.[28] Scottish support for the Lancastrian campaign in late 1462 was muted, with Margaret of Anjou relying primarily on French assistance and staunch Scottish supporters such as the earl of Angus. Official policy remained relatively unchanged, despite Kennedy's best efforts.

Conflict between the Yorkists and Lancastrians within England and factionalism between their supporters in Scotland continued throughout the winter of 1462–3, but a Scottish embassy was in London by March. This was soon followed by the issue of English safe-conducts to various members of the Scottish government and royal family, including the earl of Atholl and Sir James Stewart, uncles of James III, and Duncan Dundas, a participant in earlier missions to England.[29] Not all of these visits were necessarily concerned with discussions of a truce, but are indications that Anglo–Scottish relations during the summer of 1463 were not entirely hostile, despite the growing threat of full-scale war. The growing hostility and the Scottish involvement in the Lancastrian siege of Norham reflected the growing influence in government of the pro-Lancastrian Bishop Kennedy and declining involvement of Mary of Guelders.[30] Kennedy later claimed that the Scots took action in the summer of 1463 because Edward IV was attempting to take advantage

27 *CDS*, iv, nos.1332–3; *Rot. Scot.*, ii, 404; Waurin, *Anchiennes Cronicques*, iii, 167–8; Macrae, 'Scotland and the Wars of the Roses', 321–2.

28 *The Paston Letters*, iv, 59; Nicholson, *Scotland*, 404–5.

29 *CDS*, iv, nos. 1328, 1338; *Rot. Scot.*, ii, 408.

30 Macdougall, 'Bishop James Kennedy of St Andrews', 16; Macrae, 'Scotland and the Wars of the Roses', 336–41; Dunlop, *James Kennedy*, 236–8.

of the division within Scotland created by the rivalry between himself and the queen, and by Edward's support of the earl of Douglas. The bishop also declared he was himself ready to take the field at Norham, although 'ne accoustumé d'aler en guerre', with his sovereign lord. Mary of Guelders accompanied her son to Norham, but it is unlikely that she actively supported the campaign. Kennedy, on the other hand, was believed by Edward IV to have authorised it. More significantly, the English king believed that Kennedy had met with James III and Margaret of Anjou before the siege, indicating that the Scottish queen was no longer a force in government.[31]

The Norham campaign was an embarrassing failure, with Margaret of Anjou and the prince of Wales departing for Burgundy before its disastrous conclusion. Scotland was then excluded from the Anglo–French truce of October 1463, a move which caused considerable disquiet and forced the Scots back into negotiations with Yorkist England.[32] The truce was not only threatening to Scotland's external security, but also affected the balance of power within the kingdom, as it represented the cessation of French support for the Lancastrian cause supported by Kennedy. On 5 December 1463, four days after the death of Mary of Guelders, a Scottish embassy was issued with an English safe-conduct. A truce lasting until the end of October 1464 was concluded at York four days later on 9 December.[33] Negotiations were to continue the following March and postponed to April before a fifteen-year truce was finally concluded at York in June 1464.[34] The involvement in the negotiations of 1463–4 of Lindsay, keeper of the privy seal since 1461, Colin Campbell, earl of Argyll and a prominent figure in government since the late 1450s, and Whitelaw, royal secretary since 1462, reveals that the regency council had maintained its pro-Yorkist policies despite the growing and opposing influence of Kennedy. This continuity of policy is also indicated by the appointments of the chancellor, Lindsay, Argyll, the bishops of Glasgow and Aberdeen, Lord Livingston and others, to travel to England for further negotiations in March 1465. Despite his best efforts, Kennedy's increased role in government between 1463 and 1465 made little long-term impact on policy. The negotiations, including the discussion of a possible English marriage

31 Waurin, *Anchiennes Cronicques*, iii, 172; *ER*, vii, 289; Macrae, 'Scotland and the Wars of the Roses', 338; Tanner, *Scottish Parliament*, 177.
32 Waurin, *Anchiennes Cronicques*, iii, 173.
33 *Rot. Scot.*, ii, 409; *Foedera*, xi, 509–11.
34 Waurin, *Anchiennes Cronicques*, iii, 174; *Rot. Scot.*, ii, 412; *Foedera*, xi, 525; *CDS*, iv, no.1337 (misdated to 1463).

alliance for James III, continued with more success after the bishop's death in June.[35]

Official policy regarding the English conflict between 1455 and 1465 consisted of not committing Scotland to either the Lancastrian or Yorkist cause, but playing the two against each other to Scottish advantage. Kennedy's 'stubborn adherence to the unpopular Franco–Lancastrian axis' was not in keeping with official policy.[36] The queen's flexible approach represented the perpetuation of her late husband's policy as well as that of the regency council. Kennedy was not alone in his pro-Lancastrian sympathies – the alliance of the earl of Angus with Margaret of Anjou in 1462–3 provides the most notable example of the division of Scottish support – and was able to rely on his family and supporters in parliament to ensure that his views were heard. He was unable to translate his views into policy until 1463 because he held no office in government, but was eventually rewarded with leadership of the kingdom after Mary of Guelders' death. The personnel of the regency government 1460–3, like its policy, remained consistent. Several of its key figures, such as the chancellor and the earl of Argyll, were appointed by or had served James II, and several of them continued royal service under James III. The appointments of Scottish embassies to England also reflected this continuity of policy and personnel. James Lindsay, keeper of the privy seal in 1453 and from 1461, was nominated as ambassador in August 1460, September and November 1461, and in 1462. The chancellor was a member of the August 1460 embassy, the Scottish treasurer, David Guthrie, visited England before July 1462, and the earl of Orkney, appointed guardian of James III in summer 1461 and James II's ambassador to England in 1459, was an ambassador in September and November 1461. Archibald Whitelaw, secretary of James III from 1462 and James II's agent for negotiating a secret pact with the duke of York in 1460, was a member of the Scottish embassy to England in August 1460 and spent the winter of 1463–4 in England negotiating a truce.[37]

Several other men were regular ambassadors: Thomas Spens, bishop of Aberdeen in September and November 1461, and June 1463; the bishop of Glasgow in 1459 and November 1461; Lord Livingston in August 1460 and September and November 1461; Lord Hamilton in August 1460, and April, September and November 1461; Lord Borth-

35 *Foedera*, xi, 541; *Rot. Scot.*, ii, 416; Dunlop, *James Kennedy*, 248.
36 Macdougall, 'Bishop James Kennedy of St Andrews', 16.
37 *CDS*, iv, no.1310; *Rot. Scot.*, ii, 390, 403; *Foedera*, xi, 476; *ER*, vii, 127, 152, 284.

wick in 1458 and September 1461; and Duncan Dundas in August 1460, April, September and November 1461 and June 1463.[38] The bishop of Aberdeen in particular had a long history of ambassadorial service. He was involved in the negotiations for the marriages of James II and Eleanor and discussions of the marital prospects of Isabella and Annabella in 1453 and 1455. He arranged the return journeys to Scotland of Joanna and Annabella from France in 1457 and of the duke of Albany, brother of James III, from Guelders in 1464. He had negotiated with Charles VII and Louis XI on other matters in 1448–9 and 1462, and with Edward IV in 1461 and 1464, receiving a pension from him in the same year. His associates on the two embassies of 1461 included lords Livingston and Hamilton and James Lindsay, participants of other missions to England. Most of these ambassadors had served James II and all of them – with the exception of Dundas – continued their involvement in discussions with the Yorkists following the death of Mary of Guelders on 1 December 1463. On 5 December, Kennedy, Lindsay, the earl of Argyll, the bishop of Glasgow, the abbot of Holyrood, Lords Livingston, Hamilton, Borthwick, Boyd, and Alexander Boyd of Drumcoll were issued with a safe-conduct to travel to England. Kennedy did not go to the talks, and does not seem to have been directly involved in the subsequent Anglo–Scottish talks from April 1464, at which the Scottish representatives were Lindsay, Argyll, the bishop of Glasgow, the abbot of Holyrood and Alexander Boyd. Lords Borthwick and Boyd were also nominated as commissioners in April, but do not appear to have been involved in the actual negotiations. The efforts of the Scottish government to secure a truce with the Yorkists – with the approval but not the direct participation of Kennedy – is indicated by the ongoing service of its ambassadors. The chancellor, Lindsay, Argyll, Lord Livingston, Alexander Boyd, the bishops of Glasgow and Aberdeen and the abbot of Holyrood were chosen to participate in further negotiations with the Yorkists in March 1465.[39] Kennedy's role in government had increased in 1463 and he had been appointed to a leading role following the queen's death, but his ability to change foreign policy was limited by the continued service of men such as Chancellor Avandale, Lindsay, Guthrie and Whitelaw. He could stall, but not prevent, negotiations with Yorkist England.

This continuity of service is further underlined in the charter evidence.

38 *Rot. Scot.*, ii, 390, 402–3, 408–9; *CDS*, iv, nos.1301, 1310, 1338; Dunlop, *James Kennedy*, 203 n.3.
39 *Rot. Scot.*, ii, 409, 416; *Foedera*, xi, 509–10, 517–18, 541; *CDS*, iv, no. 1341.

Of those men participating in Anglo–Scottish negotiations 1460–3, Lords Livingston, Hamilton, Borthwick and Boyd, Avandale, the abbot of Holyrood and the bishop of Aberdeen all witnessed charters in the last two years of James II's reign.[40] The queen's foundation charter for Holy Trinity church and hospital of March 1462 was witnessed by the bishop of Glasgow and Avandale, while another charter issued by the queen in May 1462 was witnessed by Avandale, Lindsay, Guthrie and Lord Livingston.[41] In the months following August 1463, Avandale, Lindsay, Whitelaw, and the bishop of Glasgow – all of whom were involved in negotiations – were regular witnesses to charters. Two further participants in the Anglo–Scottish talks, Lord Boyd and the abbot of Holyrood, each witnessed two charters between August and December 1463. Colin Campbell, earl of Argyll, does not seem to have participated in Anglo-Scottish negotiations until December 1463 but was prominent throughout the minority, witnessing the foundation charter of Holy Trinity and acting as a regular charter witness from August 1463 onwards. It is only after January 1464 that substantial changes in witness lists occur with the inclusion of Bishop Kennedy, the earl of Crawford, Gilbert Kennedy, and Lords Gray and Darnley, but the constant presence of Avandale, Whitelaw, Argyll, Guthrie and, to a lesser degree, Lindsay, indicates a distinct degree of continuity from 1460–3.[42] Similarly, the auditors of the exchequer in the last two years of James II's reign included Thomas Spens, later bishop of Aberdeen, Ninian Spot, later bishop of Galloway, Lord Livingston and Avandale, while the bishops of Glasgow and Galloway, Avandale, Argyll, Lindsay, Guthrie and Whitelaw were nominated as auditors in 1462. In 1464, the auditors included Kennedy, serving for the first time since 1456, Avandale, the abbot of Holyrood and Guthrie, and the same men, with the exception of Kennedy and addition of the bishop of Galloway, also served in 1465.[43] The bishops of Aberdeen, Glasgow and Galloway, the abbot of Holyrood, Argyll, Lindsay, Lords Avandale, Livingston and Borthwick, among others, attended at least one of the parliaments held in October 1459, March 1461, October 1463 and January 1464.[44]

---

40 *RMS*, ii, nos. 607–11, 614–20, 625–6, 628–36, 638–40, 645–6, 649, 656–67, 669–70, 672, 674–6, 683–7, 693–4, 699–704, 706, 731, 734–7, 739–54.
41 *Charters and Documents relating to the Collegiate Church and Hospital of the Holy Trinity, and the Trinity Hospital, Edinburgh, AD. 1460–1661* (Scottish Burgh Records Society, 1871), 27; Edinburgh NLS, MS. Adv. Ch.B 73.
42 *RMS*, ii, nos. 756–843.
43 *ER*, vi, 113, 382, 488; vii, 107, 229, 308.
44 *APS*, xii, 25–30.

This continuity of personnel places Mary of Guelders' political role during the minority in perspective. She was granted a leading role in 1461 as a member of a regency government that did not significantly deviate from the policies or personnel of the government of James II. She did not rule the kingdom or determine policy alone, and her policy of negotiating with both Yorkists and Lancastrians to Scottish advantage was in keeping with that of the regency council, unlike Kennedy's rigidly pro-Lancastrian stance. In opposing the regency government he represented other Scottish supporters of the Lancastrian cause as well as those 'lordis' mentioned by the Auchinleck chronicler who 'said that thai war littill gud worth bath spirituale and temporall That gaf the keping of the kinrik till a woman'.[45] The queen's decisions, on the other hand, were supported by those of the regency council, as Thomas Playter recognised in his description of the meeting between Mary of Guelders and Warwick at Carlisle in July 1462. Playter reported the promises rumoured to have been made at the meeting and stated that he had heard that 'these appoyntements were take by the yong Lords of Scotland, but not by the old'.[46] This report indicates that two factions existed, but recognised that the queen was associated with the 'yong Lords', and it was this party that was responsible for negotiations, directed policy and controlled government. The association of the queen with the regency government was underlined when the chancellor, Lord Avandale, acted as the queen's justiciary sometime between July 1460 and December 1463.[47] Kennedy himself recognised that the queen did not act alone but was advised 'par aucuns qui estoient contraires au dit roy Henry' to take James III to the border for talks with the Yorkists in 1462.[48]

The statements of Playter and Kennedy and the evidence for much of the talks also emphasise that, in the absence of an adult king, Mary of Guelders was the representative of the minority government. Margaret of Anjou and the earl of Warwick negotiated directly with the Scottish queen in their attempts to secure her support for the Lancastrian and Yorkist causes. Their continental allies also wrote to Mary soliciting her assistance. The duke of Burgundy sent Louis de Bruges, Sieur de la Gruthuyse, to Scotland on 11 December 1460 in support of the Yorkists, but the ambassador's arrival in Scotland must have been coincident with, or soon after, that of Margaret of Anjou,

45 'Auch. Chron.', 170.
46 *Paston Letters*, iv, 51.
47 *ER*, vii, 281.
48 Waurin, *Anchiennes Cronicques*, iii, 167.

and his mission was unsuccessful.[49] Charles VII sent an embassy to Scotland in support of Margaret around the same time. According to Kennedy, the French king also sent an envoy to the bishop, then at Bruges, encouraging him to return to Scotland 'pour tenir la main et aider au roy Henry'.[50] Burgundy sent another embassy to Scotland in May, perhaps to advise against the proposed marriage between the prince of Wales and the sister of James III and the Scottish–Franco–Lancastrian alliance it represented. The marriage did not proceed, but as 'tous les grans seigneurs du royaulme' of Scotland opposed the match and accused Kennedy of placing the kingdom 'en perdicion' to please the French king, it is likely that the Burgundian advice was superfluous.[51] The Milanese ambassador to France reported in June 1461 that the dauphin and the duke of Brittany had also sent embassies 'to the Queen of Scotland to dissuade her' from attacking England on behalf of the Lancastrians.[52] The Veere accounts record that the duke of Guelders also sent an embassy to Scotland in the middle of 1461 but its purpose was not stated.[53] The deaths of Charles VII and the duke of Burgundy in 1461 and the more ambivalent attitudes of their successors towards the English conflict contributed to a declining interest in soliciting Scottish support in subsequent years. There is little evidence of embassies from the continent seeking Scottish support for either Lancastrians or Yorkists between 1461 and 1465. Louis XI wrote to Kennedy and the young James III in the summer of 1462 encouraging them to support the Lancastrians, but the French king's own lack of effort on their behalf suggests that these letters did not represent a serious attempt to influence Scottish policy.[54] The loss of interest in soliciting Scottish support may also indicate that the government was seen as generally pro-Yorkist after 1461.

Mary was widely regarded as the leader of the government in the early years of the minority and, despite the factionalism, government remained relatively stable. The first parliament of the reign began at Edinburgh on 22 February 1461 and formalised the arrangements for government during the minority, leaving 'the King in keping with his

---

49 Waurin, *Anchiennes Cronicques*, ii, 302–4; Macrae, 'Scotland and the Wars of the Roses', 283, Appendix B no.18.
50 Waurin, *Anchiennes Cronicques*, iii, 165–6; Macrae, 'Scotland and the Wars of the Roses', 285.
51 *Cal. State Papers (Milan)*, i, 90; Waurin, *Anchiennes Cronicques*, iii, 166.
52 *Cal. State Papers (Milan)*, i, 94.
53 Macrae, 'Scotland and the Wars of the Roses', Appendix C no.8.
54 Waurin, *Anchiennes Cronicques*, iii, 167–8.

modere the queen and governing of all the kinrik.'[55] If the 'Auchinleck Chronicle' is correct, the traditional separation of responsibilities
between the guardian of the young king and governor of the realm was
overturned in 1460–1. Ten years later, James III stated that the Estates
had awarded custody of his person to Mary of Guelders and the lords
of her council and, following the queen's death, to Bishop Kennedy
and the royal council.[56] This suggests that the king's guardian and the
royal council were together responsible for the government of the
kingdom and that their duties were not separated. Without extensive
parliamentary records for the minority it is difficult to ascertain the
queen's official role and title in 1461 with any precision, but she was
clearly accorded a greater role in the regency government than was her
predecessor. In the absence of a senior male relative of the king who
could act as lieutenant, Mary of Guelders was in a position to claim a
leading role in the minority government. This does not mean, however,
that she was granted regency powers. The fact that she continued to be
described as 'domine regine' during the minority renders the task of
determining the nature and extent of her powers even more difficult.[57]
The earl of Douglas, for example, was referred to as 'locumtenente' or
lieutenant-general in the accounts of 1437–8, his changed title a clear
indicator of the kind of powers he had been granted.

The ambiguous and debated nature of Mary's role is underlined by
the fact that her title did not change to reflect her expanded powers
and by the opposition her 'appointment' generated. The Auchinleck
chronicler, who recorded the decisions of the first parliament of the
minority to place the king and kingdom under the care of the queen
mother, also stated that 'thairfor the lordis said that thai war littill gud
worth bath spirituale and temporall That gaf the keping of the kinrik till
a woman'.[58] The queen clearly did not have universal approval for her
role in the minority government, but commanded sufficient support to
continue in her new role. Before June 1461, William Sinclair, earl of
Orkney, was

> personally residing with the most serene prince, James, illustrious
> King of the Scots, for the purpose of keeping his royal person
> during his tender age by the desire and anxious care of the three
> estates of the realm of Scotland … [59]

55 'Auch. Chron.', 170.
56 Armstrong, 'A Letter of James III', 399.
57 For example, *ER*, vii, 8, 47.
58 'Auch. Chron.', 170.
59 *Records of the Earldom of Orkney 1299–1614* (Scottish History Society, 1914), 54.

This change in custody arrangements was in keeping with Scottish precedents for the separation of guardianship and regency: the queen was free to play a more prominent role in the regency government, with Orkney acting as guardian for the king. This separation of responsibilities and the overall duty of care accorded to the Estates may also explain the reference to the king being in the possession of Kennedy and the Estates in summer 1463.[60] If the queen had initially been entrusted with both roles in February 1461 and custody of the king had been granted to Orkney by June, it would seem that the queen did command significant support for her role in government and that the opposition described by the Auchinleck chronicler was limited. If the opposition to the queen's political presence had been greater, it is more likely that she would have been required to surrender 'the keping of the kinrik' rather than the role of the king's guardian, a role regarded as naturally appropriate for a mother.

While resistance to the scope of Mary of Guelders' powers during the minority could not prevent her from utilising those powers, the Auchinleck chronicler suggests that it did provoke her to 'put in new keparis in the castellis of Edinburgh, Stirling and Dunbar viz. in Edinburgh Androw keyre In Dunbar lord Hailes In Blackness and Stirling Robert Liddale'.[61] The queen may well have been 'Incontinent' at the reaction of some to her role in government and, as these appointments were attributed to her and made 'eftir this parliament', it would seem that she was at least partly responsible for them. They should not, however, be seen as rash or as proof of her inability to govern. The men appointed keepers of Edinburgh, Stirling and Dunbar castles had all served James II at some point during his reign. Andrew Kerr, custodian of Edinburgh castle from 1461 to 1463, had been one of the commissioners appointed to secure the Anglo–Scottish truce sealed at Reddenburn in September 1458. In this capacity he was associated with Lord Hailes, who had sworn to be a conservator of the 1451 Anglo–Scottish truce, was created a lord of parliament by James II in 1452, was a charter witness in 1458 and was appointed keeper of Blackness in 1461.[62] Hailes' links with the royal family were long-standing – his father had been keeper of Dunbar castle during the minority of James II and had been a supporter of Joan Beaufort during the civil

---

60 Waurin, *Anchiennes Cronicques*, iii, 162–4.
61 'Auch. Chron.', 170.
62 *ER*, vii, 136, 148, 211; *RMS*, ii, nos. 619–20, 625–6, 630–3; Dunlop, *James Kennedy*, 129 n.4, 137, 203 n.3.

war – and he also seems to have had links with Bishop Kennedy.[63] Robert Liddale held Tantallon castle in 1438, and was a household servant of James II in 1450 before becoming keeper of Dunbar castle between July 1451 and December 1452 and 1455–60, and from 1458 was one of the bailies of the earldom of March, conferred on the king's second son, Alexander, in 1455. His appointment to Stirling castle in 1461 could hardly have been regarded as an attempt by the queen to display her will contrary to the wishes of the political community. All three of these men had served James II in some capacity and were not – with the possible exception of Kerr – newcomers to royal office. More significantly, all three men had been involved in Anglo–Scottish peace negotiations: Kerr in 1458, Hailes in 1451 and 1458 and Liddale in 1453–4, when he spent some time in England negotiating for peace.[64] They were men likely to support the moves of both Mary of Guelders and the regency council, and in this respect their appointments would seem to be acceptable to that council. In short, there is little reason to suppose that any of the three appointments were as disruptive or as unpopular as the Auchinleck chronicler suggests.

The chronicler's treatment of these appointments may shed some light on his statement that

> the said Queen efter the deid of king James the secund tuke master James Lindesay for principal counsellor and gart him kepe the preve sele notwithstanding that the said master James was excludit fra the counsall of the forsaid king and fra the court and for his werray helynes and had been slane for his demeritis had nocht bene he was redemit with gold.[65]

Lindsay had previously been keeper of the privy seal under James II in 1453, but his associations with the Douglases may have cost him the post in the lead-up to the forfeiture of the family in 1455. His return to favour following Mary's appointment as guardian was perhaps to be expected, as he had acted as the queen's factor and chamberlain between 1451 and 1453. He received a pension from her in 1452–3 and, in his capacity as provost of Lincluden, had hosted her talks with Margaret of Anjou at the church in January 1461.[66] The queen's

63 Dunlop, *James Kennedy*, 117 n.2, 403.
64 *ER*, v, 53, 386, 429, 506, 536, 580, 622, 644; vi, 60, 227, 258, 539–40, 625; *Foedera*, xi, 335–6; *Rot. Scot.*, ii, 367–8.
65 'Auch. Chron.', 170.
66 *RMS*, ii, nos. 594–5, 597–8; *ER*, v, 524–5, 554, 556; 'Auch. Chron.', 169–70; McGladdery, *James II*, 107–8; *ER*, vii, 234, 287.

gratitude for Lindsay's services is represented by payments made to him by her order from lands in Kincleven and the Linlithgow customs in autumn 1463. Lindsay's appointment as keeper of the privy seal in 1461 was not, however, the first sign of his rehabilitation into political life. On 26 August 1460 he was nominated with the chancellor and Archibald Whitelaw, both of whom had served James II, as member of an embassy to England. Lindsay's appointment to the 1460 embassy associated him with political figures who had served James II, as well as with a pro-English party that remained in power throughout the minority, despite the opposition of Bishop Kennedy. Lindsay continued as a regular member of embassies to England and as keeper of the privy seal following the death of Mary of Guelders, and was appointed treasurer in 1468. Any anger aroused by his reinstatement to political office was limited, short-lived and, most likely, exaggerated by the Auchinleck chronicler.[67] His re-emerging career was evident within weeks of James' death, and was assisted by Mary of Guelders, to whom he was a loyal servant, but cannot be solely attributed to her.

Mary of Guelders' appointment to a leading role in government and her tenure of this role until the last months of her life indicate that she commanded considerable support from her colleagues in government. Any opposition to her power and actions was limited to a vocal parliamentary faction and, if Kennedy's leadership of the opposition is representative, was not generated from within the regency council. Kennedy was limited to undermining the queen from outside the council, particularly by mustering his friends and family in parliament.[68] The queen was not, however, invulnerable to attack. Kennedy's statement that he found 'grant division ou dit pays mise par la royne' upon his return to Scotland in 1461 reflects contemporary concerns that women were disruptive influences in government and temperamentally ill-suited to rule.[69] The presence of James III at Dumfries for the queen's talks with the Yorkists in April 1462 and at the siege of Norham in summer 1463 allayed some of the threat represented by female power. Mary and James III were also together at Haddington before Mary travelled to Coldingham for talks in 1462, and it is likely that the king accompanied her on her journey. Margaret of Anjou similarly travelled with

67 *CDS*, iv, no.1310; *RMS*, ii, nos.756–72, 775–84, 786, 788, 796, 811, 813–9, 821–2, 826–7, 834–5, 862–5, 868, 879, 881–4, 893, 895–901, 903–16, 920–6, 928, 932–5, 937–8, 942, 944–9, 951–64; *ER*, vii, 593; Macdougall, *James III*, 52.
68 Tanner, *Scottish Parliament*, 172, 177–8, 190.
69 Waurin, *Anchiennes Cronicques*, iii, 166.

her son to negotiations and battles. The combined presence of queen mother and king indicated to domestic and foreign audiences alike that the queen's ability to negotiate terms or to accompany an army was based upon her role as mother and did not signify an attempt to claim power in her own right.[70] The linking of the queen's power to that of her son also allowed her to move beyond the limits imposed by her gender. The queen's involvement in military matters had already been indicated during the reign of James II by her presence at the siege of Blackness in 1454. During the minority it continued with her purchase of bombards and employment of gunners, the building of her defensive castle, Ravenscraig, and her presence at the siege of Norham in summer 1463.[71] The association of the queen's power with that of the king is also indicated by the language of the accounts which not only refer to 'regis et regine' on several occasions, but also designate them 'dominorum regis et regine'.[72] This nomenclature is shorthand rather than an explicit description of their associated power, but the implicit effect of such shorthand was to elevate the queen's status and power to that of a male monarch by linking her title to that of her son.

The public linking of the queen's power to her son's authority could not prevent rumours about Mary of Guelders' personal immorality circulating from 1463. The development of these early rumours by sixteenth-century writers and their retelling in more recent times clearly illustrates the intention and success of the original story-tellers: the queen's political and historical reputations have only recently shaken off the suggestion that her 'passions' ruled her politics.[73] The earliest story about Mary's immorality linked the queen and Patrick Hepburn, lord Hailes. A Frenchman, Phillipe de Cran, reported in July 1463 that there was 'grande discension' in Scotland following the queen's marriage to 'le seigneur de Heyller' and his attack on Kennedy and the Estates, who held possession of the king.[74] The letter was issued from Boulogne, indicating that the rumours were widely circulated. Sixteenth-century versions of the rumour claimed that the object of the queen's affection was Hailes' son, Adam Hepburn, and it is these later stories that have occupied historians for centuries. While the truth

---

70 Waurin, *Anchiennes Cronicques*, iii, 167; *ER*, vii, 152, 289; 'Auch. Chron.', 169–70; *Cal. State Papers (Milan)*, i, 90; *Paston Letters*, iii, 267, 307, iv, 51; Macrae, 'Scotland and the Wars of the Roses', 331–8.

71 *ER*, v, 674; vii, 32, 99, 289.

72 See for example *ER*, vii, 68, 82, 84.

73 Macdougall, *James III*, 54–7.

74 Waurin, *Anchiennes Cronicques*, iii, 162–4.

of the rumours is debatable, it is clear that both father and son were close supporters of the queen. Lord Hailes had attended parliament and witnessed charters during the minority but disappears from the parliamentary records with the queen's death. His son was the keeper of Dunbar, residence of the queen and James III on their way to or from the battles with the Yorkists in Northumbria in summer 1463. Unfortunately for the queen's later reputation, Hepburn was seeking a divorce in 1463 but apparently allowed the suit to lapse following the queen's death. Like his father, he too fell from favour.[75]

The linking of the queen's remarriage with an attempt to gain custody of the king from Kennedy and the Estates may be an elaboration on the changing balance of power between the bishop and the queen at the time, represented most clearly by the abortive campaigns against the Yorkists which Kennedy supported. At the same time, the suggestion that the king was in the possession of Kennedy and the Estates echoes the arrangements made for the minority in 1461, when Orkney was appointed guardian of James III 'by the desire and anxious care of the three estates'. Furthermore, the queen made at least part of the journey to Norham with her son in summer 1463, and it is hard to give credence to the claim that Hailes used his rumoured relationship with the queen to wrest custody of the king from Kennedy and the Estates at that time. The queen's public role certainly diminished in 1463 but it is highly unlikely that she found herself in what would have been a civil war for custody of her son. Whatever the basis of the rumours, their content effectively represented her claim to custody and a role in the minority government as invalid. As Joan Beaufort had discovered, a queen's remarriage constituted grounds for loss of custody and its attendant power.

It is difficult to ascertain how widespread and damaging these rumours were during the queen's lifetime. They clearly existed in Boulogne, but the two most detailed Scottish sources for the period do not record any rumours about the queen's morality or battles for the custody of the king. The 'Auchinleck Chronicle', as Macdougall points out, is not sympathetic to Mary of Guelders but does not mention a relationship between the queen and Hailes, although this omission may be explained by the fact that the surviving manuscript is incomplete.[76] Kennedy's account of his rivalry with the queen is similarly silent on

75 Tanner, *Scottish Parliament*, 176–7; *ER*, vii, 178, 214; *CPR. Papal Letters*, xi, 484–5, 459–60; Dunlop, *James Kennedy*, 77 n.4.
76 Macdougall, *James III*, 56; McGladdery, *James II*, 117.

the queen's morality and, given the potential advantage to be gained from condemning her in his capacity as bishop, this silence is notable. His omission of any suggestion that the king's custody was contested is similarly significant. The only other evidence of such rumours from the fifteenth century is found in the annals attributed to Worcester. The annals record that lord Hailes was recruited to kill the duke of Somerset because he had informed Louis XI of his own affair with the queen.[77] The addition of yet another lover for the queen in this story illustrates that its primary intent was to blacken her name and undermine her power. The story is apparently of French origin and spread to England, a chain of rumour which raises the possibility – given that the earliest evidence was recorded in Boulogne – that the stories originally circulated outside Scotland and were spread by European princes, most likely the Lancastrians and their supporters, to discredit the queen and so advance their cause. Kennedy's silence on the subject would suggest that the rumours were intended for, and appealed to, an international audience with limited knowledge of Scottish domestic politics.

While the queen's public role and influence diminished from the end of 1462, her considerable personal income and power as a major landowner was maintained throughout the minority. Unlike her books of expenses as consort, some of Mary's accounts for the period 1461–63 survive. Their existence provides a more detailed picture of her finances as queen mother than as consort, and in so doing exaggerate the apparent change in the extent of Mary's power during the minority.[78] Her household was separated from that of James III between March 1461 and July 1462, and it is possible that the Auchinleck chronicler's remark that 'the king suld come be him selfe and and his and the Queen be hir self and hirris bot the king suld ay remane with the Queen Bot scho suld nocht Intromet with his proffettis bot allanerlie with his person' refers to this separation.[79] While it is difficult to reconcile Orkney's appointment as guardian in summer 1461 with the statement that 'the king suld ay remane with the Queen', it is indicative of a general concern to avoid placing executive power over the crown and personal control of the king in the hands of one individual.

The queen's accounts 1461–63 suggest that she may have received the £5000 annual income – almost £4000 from land and the remainder

77 Stevenson, *Letters and Papers*, ii, Part II, 779.
78 *ER*, vi, 5.
79 'Auch. Chron.', 171; *ER*, vii, p.xlvii; Macdougall, *James III*, 54; Macdougall, 'Bishop James Kennedy of St Andrews', 18–19 n.16.

from goods in kind – promised her as dower in 1449. The queen's coinage and her grants of £10 in 1461 and 1462 to William Goldsmith, also employed by James II, imply that she was keen to utilise her wealth and indicates that she exercised considerable political and economic power.[80] The basic elements of her expenditure, although recorded in more detail in 1461–3 than between 1449 and 1460, remained relatively constant. In terms of servants, for example, the patterns of long-term service to the royal family and the interaction between servants of king and queen continued during the minority. These trends are, of course, more pronounced before the separation of Mary of Guelders' household from that of James III sometime in 1461–2. Before the households were separated, stewards, bakers and brewers were described as servants of 'dominorum regis et regine'.[81] The long-term careers in royal service of James Lindsay, keeper of the privy seal, and Alexander Napier, comptroller, have been mentioned elsewhere, and are by no means unique. John Carlile, for example, was master of the queen's stable in 1460–61, keeper of Lochmaben castle from 1460–65, and performed various services for James II and the duke of Albany. James II's doctor, Serapion, remained in royal service after the king's death and provided the queen with medicine sometime between 1460 and 1462. Andrew Lesouris, the king's carpenter, completed building works on the queen's new chamber at Falkland in 1461–2 and worked at Ravenscraig, Stirling and Linlithgow in the following decade. The queen's baker, Patrick Purdy, remained in royal service after her death, becoming the king's baker in 1464–5 and remaining in that post until 1467–8. Robert Mure, the queen's chamberlain in Stirlingshire, Menteith, Methven and Strathearn also collected fermes for James II and was chamberlain in Strathearn under James III.[82] Some of these long-term servants are also notable because other members of their families were in royal service. John Darrach was James II's butcher and steward before becoming steward to Mary of Guelders in 1461, while Mariot Darrach was nurse to the princess Margaret.[83] John Balfour was servant to the young James II in 1438, keeper of Falkland from 1453 and servant to the young James III in 1456. His son, Michael, was

80 *ER*, vii, p.xlvi, 47–106, 161–200, 227–8, 292; Macdougall, *James III*, 67 n.15;. Stahl, A.M., 'Coinage in the Name of Medieval Women' in Rosenthal, *Medieval Women and the Sources of Medieval History*, 321, 323; *ER*, vii, 292.
81 *ER*, vii, 61, 68, 82, 106.
82 *ER*, vi, 3, 12, 293, 572–3, 580, 617; vii, 8, 25, 34, 49, 75, 77, 138, 144, 150, 181–2, 200, 247, 280, 309, 335, 384, 442, 449, 457, 544, 549, 571, 613, 657.
83 *ER*, v, 457, 464, 485, 602, 619, 622–4, 638; vi, 38, 132; vii, 61, 138, 146.

receiver of the fermes of Fife for Mary of Guelders and then James III, and Michael's wife, Margaret, received payments for the queen and one occasion attested her mandate.[84]

Mary of Guelders also continued to employ some European servants during the minority. Elizabeth of Guelders received her fee by mandate of the queen in 1461–2 and a doctor from Guelders was reimbursed for his expenses by order of the queen in the same year. Another servant, Hakkinet, is described in the accounts as 'Teutonico' and seems to have been involved in trade. Another 'Teutonico', Dederic Grutare, initially employed by James II, occasionally paid by Mary of Guelders and retained by James III, was a gunner.[85] The queen's accounts 1461–3 indicate a continuity in employment patterns, but also provide additional information about several servants in the queen's household and about those responsible for the administration of her lands. The queen employed a secretary, John Laing, and two legal experts – Gilbert Hering, an advocate, and Thomas Laing, a pleader – presumably to oversee her transactions, as well as administrators for each of her major land-holdings.[86] In the February 1462 audit of her accounts, she employed seven chamberlains and receivers of fermes: Robert Mure, Michael Balfour, Thomas Carmichael, Henry Kinghorn, Thomas Wardropare, Oswald Weire and Simon Salmon. In August 1463 six men – Mure, Balfour, Salmon, Andrew Lyell, William Rynde and John Moray – submitted accounts. Of these ten men, Mure, Balfour, Carmichael and Wardropare administered the king's lands at the same time as the queen's, while all of these men, with the exception of Carmichael and addition of Rynde and Moray, administered the king's lands after the queen's death. Carmichael, Wardropare and Salmon had also administered lands for James II. The most important of these men was Henry Kinghorn, chamberlain in Garioch and Brechin and the queen's steward, who made various payments and commercial transactions on her behalf, acted as her ambassador to Veere in 1461, and incurred some expenses for her funeral.[87] The queen's other important servants were

84 John: *ER*, v, 35, 535, 689; vi, 79, 116, 252, 369, 417, 565, 613; vii, 75, 196, 242, 268, 383, 455, 569, 654. Michael: *ibid.*, vii, 70, 101, 191, 241. Margaret: *ibid.*, vii, 59, 66, 81, 86–7, 172, 174–5, 189, 191, 197–8, 342.

85 *ER*, vi, 385, 496, 498–9, 581; vii, 32, 34, 48–9, 66, 84, 91, 144, 211, 218–19, 287, 289, 362, 422, 501, 589–90, 663.

86 *RMS*, ii, no.766; *ER*, vii, 59, 81, 94.

87 *ER*, vii, 47–106, 128, 137, 139, 153–4, 161–200, 217–20, 224, 227–8, 241, 243–4, 254, 259, 276, 286, 303; *CPR. Papal Letters*, xi, 211–12; Macrae, 'Scotland and the Wars of the Roses', Appendix C no.8.

David Boys and John Halkerstoun, employed to oversee her various building projects at Ravenscraig and Trinity Hospital respectively.[88]

The queen's interest in building, demonstrated in her husband's reign, flourished during the minority of her son and underlined her status as an economic and cultural leader in the kingdom. In March 1460 Mary of Guelders resigned some of her lands in exchange for lands in Dysart, the site for the castle of Ravenscraig, one of her major projects. The queen was the driving force behind its construction: building began after the king's death and the castle was unfinished when work ceased soon after the death of the queen. The payments for work on the castle were recorded in the queen's accounts, were made by the queen's mandate, and came from her own funds.[89] Minor repairs at Stirling were also carried out at the queen's expense. The work undertaken at Falkland in 1461–2 seems to have been at the queen's direction, and consisted primarily of building and furnishing a new chamber with glass windows for the queen. In the course of 80 days' work, a new lawn was created outside the queen's chamber, repairs were made to the hall and great chamber, and a gallery was installed. This is the first record of such a structure in Scotland, and it has been suggested that it was 'an innovation commissioned by the queen-mother', who grew up in Burgundy, where galleries were 'not uncommon'.[90]

The queen's greatest project was the building of Holy Trinity collegiate church which, like Ravenscraig, was planned before the death of James II. The queen had a particular interest in hospitals – an interest she shared with her kinswoman the duchess of Burgundy – and supported institutions in Stirling and at Fale.[91] The king and queen had co-petitioned the pope in 1459 for the dissolution and annexation of the Trinitarian house at Fale to the queen's new foundation, and it is likely that the annexation of Soutra (which was under James' patronage) to Holy Trinity in 1460 was arranged in the same manner. The first reference to the church occurs in a papal bull dated 23 October 1460, authorising the annexation of the 'hospitalis pauperum de Soltre' to Holy Trinity, indicating that the church was planned or established before the king's death at the beginning of August. This does not mean, however, that its foundation was originally planned

88 *ER*, vii, 59, 77, 84, 91, 138, 153, 164, 167, 171–5, 197, 216–7, 243.
89 *RMS*, ii, no.746; *ER*, vii, 59, 243; Dunbar, *Scottish Royal Palaces*, 103.
90 *ER*, vii, 75, 78–9, 106; Dunbar, *Scottish Royal Palaces*, 23.
91 *ER*, vii, 60, 85; *CPR. Papal Letters*, xi, 403; Willard, 'Patronage of Isabel of Portugal', 314.

by James II. Bishop Kennedy stated in 1462 that the queen wished
to found a collegiate church and made no reference to the late king's
involvement, while the queen's foundation charter reveals her personal
interest in the church and its organisation.[92] She specified how the
church and hospital were to be founded, the number of prebendaries
and their duties, how vacancies were to be filled, and the number of
services to be said. The queen paid particular attention to the ability and
character of the prebendaries, forbidding them from keeping concubines or housekeepers and ruling that they must be capable of reading
and singing. She instructed that after mass, the prebendaries were to
approach the tomb of the foundress for further prayers to encourage
the congregation's devotion. The charter concluded with the stipula-
tion that the queen reserved the right to make changes and additions
to its provisions, emphasising the queen's interest in and control of her
new foundation. There is no reference to the queen continuing the
work of her late husband. This omission is made more noticeable by
her dedication of the church to the Trinity, the saints and the kings and
queens of Scotland, specifically mentioning the soul of James II, and by
her order that the prebendaries observe his anniversary.

While the foundation was the work of the queen, it is noticeable that
James III's consent to her plans for the dissolution and annexation of
Soutra is emphasised in the papal bulls approving the foundation. His
consent, like that of Bishop Kennedy, was necessary because Soutra
was under the king's patronage and was held by the cathedral of St
Andrews, but it also suggests that even in undertaking charitable work
at her own expense the queen did not possess complete freedom of
action. The foundation charter issued under the queen's seal reserved
the right to change its provisions but stated that such changes would be
in accordance with the counsel of 'iurisperitorum et virorum pruden-
cium'. The very process of petitioning the pope and establishing the
church and hospital forced her to rely upon Kennedy and the bishop
of Glasgow to promote her plans. The inability of the queen to be
universally recognised as sole foundress of the church and hospital is
most clearly shown in the papal bull issued by Pius II in August 1463,
which declared that Mary of Guelders had founded Holy Trinity and
that her son, James III, intended to complete the work.[93]

92 *Charters and Documents relating to the Collegiate Church and Hospital of the Holy Trinity*, 3–4, 15–29; Macdougall, *James III*, 62.
93 *Charters and Documents relating to the Collegiate Church and Hospital of the Holy Trinity*, 6, 8, 12, 31, 37, 40.

The only acts of piety and charity that were recognised as the queen's alone were of a relatively minor and standard nature. She undertook a pilgrimage to the shrine of St Ninian at Whithorn before March 1461, made several offerings to religious orders and gave alms to the poor in the same year, and supported six paupers at Stirling throughout the minority. It has also been suggested that Mary was connected with the establishment of Observant Franciscanism in Scotland.[94] The survival of Mary's accounts for the minority exaggerates the extent of her patronage and charity as widow compared to the work she undertook as consort. Recent studies have, however, noted the correlation between the legal and financial independence of widowhood and the levels of patronage of medieval women.[95] The extent of Mary's patronage can also be seen as an indication of her perception of her own role and importance. In undertaking major building projects the queen was able to promote values and cultural standards of importance to her, display them to others and leave them to influence future generations. Mary's specific requirement that prayers be said over her tomb to encourage devotion indicates a strong self-awareness of her status and her responsibility to ensure the spiritual wellbeing of her subjects. If the high altar of Trinity College church was positioned directly in front of her tomb under an image of the coronation of the Virgin, as suggested by Thomas Tolley, the congregation would have been continually exhorted to regard the foundress as a queen of the highest virtue and power.[96] As a noted patron, Mary publicly demonstrated her status as queen and engaged in an enterprise typical of medieval princes and wealthy nobles. The queen's building works and charitable foundations prominently displayed her wealth and status and underlined her Christian virtue. Denied the authority of her male contemporaries, Mary's patronage constituted one means by which she could join their ranks.

Mary of Guelders died on 1 December 1463 at the age of thirty.[97] Her premature death may have been the result of a long illness, a possibility which would partly explain her diminishing public role in 1463. She

94 *ER*, vii, 66, 69, 78–80, 188; Durkan, J., 'The Observant Franciscan Province in Scotland', *The Innes Review*, xxxv (1984), 55.

95 McCash, J.H., 'The Cultural Patronage of Medieval Women: An Overview' (8–10) and Jambeck, K.K., 'Patterns of Women's Literary Patronage: England, 1200–ca.1475' in McCash, *Cultural Patronage of Medieval Women* (244–5).

96 Tolley, 'Hugo van der Goes's Altarpiece', 221–3.

97 *ER*, vii, pp.liv–lv, 389. See Nijsten, *In the Shadow of Burgundy* (372–4) for details of the funeral service held in Arnhem on 13 March 1464, attended by Mary's father and her son, Alexander, duke of Albany.

died only weeks after Scotland's exclusion from the Anglo–French truce vindicated the wisdom of her policy regarding the Yorkist-Lancastrian conflict, and days before the leading opponent of that policy, Bishop Kennedy, was forced to open negotiations with Yorkist England. The success of her policy and the ability with which Mary negotiated with English and continental leaders during the minority distinguish her as an extremely capable politician and diplomat. At the same time, the official policy regarding England with which Mary is associated was modelled on that of her late husband, was followed through by the regency council of which she was an important member, and was finally achieved after her death. The mark of Mary's political aptitude is therefore not only the development and pursuit of policy but also her ability to work with, and represent, the minority government. At the beginning of the minority Mary acquired greater powers than any of her predecessors as queen mother, and she retained these powers despite the opposition of a section of the Scottish political community and the circulation of rumours about her morality. Her partners in government accepted her unusually extensive powers and resisted the pro-Lancastrian faction led by Kennedy and its attacks on the suitability of a woman as a leader. Mary's predecessors as queen mother numbered only two and the results of comparisons can only be tenuous at best, particularly given the different circumstances in which each queen was widowed. But the extent of Mary's power and its acceptability to the minority government were distinctive in Scottish terms, and contributed to the further expansion of the queen mother's role in the sixteenth century.

TEN

Connections, consciousness and conclusions

'Ce qu'elle vit et ouyt dire à sa dicte mere durant le temps
qu'elles résidérent en laditte Cour'

A queen's power was derived from that of her husband or son and
was dependent upon the support and recognition of powerful men.
But queens were also part of a female world and dependent upon the
advice, support and network of female relatives and of powerful women
in other courts and within their own. The existence and workings of
this female world are virtually invisible in the surviving evidence. Even
Christine de Pizan's *The Treasure of the City of Ladies* recognised the
existence of a 'whole world of women', but aimed to educate women
about how to live successfully in a male-dominated world rather
than to record the workings of their own.[1] One contemporary work
describing the activities of the 'world of women' in fifteenth-century
courts is Aliénor de Poitier's account of Burgundian rituals celebrating
the female-dominated events of childbirth and baptism. This work is
notable for the relative absence of men from the text, yet their influence is still present in the form of a female hierarchy, based upon the
status and titles of their husbands. The importance of male hierarchy
to the relationships of their wives is emphasised by de Poitiers' inclusion of information about these men in order to explain the rigid rules
governing precedence, greeting and etiquette.

The apparent lack of male interest in, or knowledge of, the female
world described by de Poitiers explains why it has not been described
in the surviving sources, written almost entirely by men. These men
described the aims and achievements of a male world in which women
only rarely made an impact. De Poitiers reversed this focus in her work
and provides unique evidence about a world dominated by women, yet
its very uniqueness means that it is difficult to place that world in its
proper perspective and to ascertain its importance in women's lives.
The other notable feature of de Poitiers' work is that it recorded her

1 *Treasure*, 180.

experiences and those of her 'mere durant le temps qu'elles résidérent en laditte Cour de Bourgongne'.[2] Her mother, Isabelle de Souze, came to Burgundy with her daughter, then aged seven, as one of the ladies attending Isabel of Portugal at the time of her marriage to the duke of Burgundy in 1430. The work thus records the transmission of experiences from woman to woman and mother to daughter, and illustrates one of the ways in which women were trained in matters relating to court life. It also reveals the importance of verbal rather than written communication in recording the experiences of women, a factor which further obscures the existence and workings of their world. At the same time, it suggests that women felt that their experiences were worth communicating, at least to other women which, in turn, reveals an awareness of their roles in society. De Poitiers' work raises several issues regarding women in the courts of the fifteenth century: the ways in which they were prepared for their future roles in society, the creation of networks of support between women and courts, and their awareness of their status, roles and power.

Children were born into a predominantly female environment and while boys left that environment at the age of about seven, girls did not. De Pizan advised that the princess should supervise the 'appearance, actions and speech' of her children herself, and observe and investigate the conduct and reputation of the ladies appointed to govern her daughters to ensure that they knew 'how to demonstrate the good manners and deportment fitting for the daughter of a prince.' Christine included further advice regarding the instruction of daughters in recognition of the princess' responsibility for their upbringing, stating that when 'the girl is old enough, the princess will wish her to learn to read.' She advised that girls be taught to read religious, devotional and moral works and stated that the

> princess will not tolerate books containing any vain things, follies or dissipation to be brought before her daughter, for the doctrine and teaching that the girl absorbs in her early childhood she usually remembers all her life.[3]

Christine thus emphasised two kinds of education: a formal education which included training in literacy, and a form of apprenticeship, in which girls learned about court life and acceptable behaviour by example and experience. Both forms of education relied heavily on the

2 De Poitiers, 'Les Honneurs de la Cour', 184–215, 227–33.
3 *Treasure*, 67–8.

teaching of girls by older women.

Christine's education was unusual by the standards of her contemporaries – few girls were taught Latin and science as she had been by her father – but her emphasis on reading as an important aspect of a girl's upbringing is supported by other evidence. The late medieval popularity of the image of St Anne teaching the Virgin in which one or both figures hold a book is representative of a growing practice of mothers teaching daughters to read. The connection between popular practice and the image is indicated by the absence of a scriptural or textual basis for the image, suggesting its secular origins, and by the fact that the book is open rather than closed, indicating that it was an active rather than passive image.[4] The specific link between the teaching of daughters and the image is suggested by the choice of saint – both Anne and Mary were important symbols of family and motherhood – and by the growth of female literacy and patronage from the fourteenth century.[5] Much of this patronage was directed towards the production of books of hours which, in addition to their religious content, could contain advice about the conduct and speech expected of women. One of Isabella Stewart's books of hours outlines some recommended teaching for young girls, while another contains verses promoting the duty of a princess to contract a foreign marriage and the honour she acquired in doing so.[6] Most of the surviving evidence regarding books owned by women reveals the importance of religious and devotional works, but some women also owned copies of histories, secular verse, romances and didactic treatises.[7]

While no evidence of books associated with Joan Beaufort survives,

4 Bell, S.G., 'Medieval Women Book Owners: Arbiters of Lay Piety and Ambassadors of Culture' in Erler and Kowalseki, *Women and Power*, 162–4, 168, 173; Sheingorn, P., '"The Wise Mother": The Image of St. Anne Teaching the Virgin Mary', *Gesta*, 32 (1993), 69–80.

5 Sheingorn, '"The Wise Mother"', 72–5; Bell, 'Medieval Women Book Owners', 149–87; Meale, C.M., '" … alle the bokes that I haue of latyn, englisch, and frensch": laywomen and their books in late medieval England' and Boffey, J.,'Women authors and women's literacy in fourteenth- and fifteenth-century England' in C. Meale (ed.), *Women and Literature in Britain, 1150-1500* (Cambridge, 1993), 128–58, 159–182; Jambeck, 'Patterns of Women's Literary Patronage', 228–65; Rosenthal, J., 'Aristocratic Cultural Patronage and Book Bequests, 1350–1500', *Bulletin of the John Rylands University Library of Manchester*, 64 (1982), 522–48.

6 Bell, 'Medieval Women Book Owners', 160–2; Paris BN, MS. n.a. Latin 588, ff.206r.–213r.; MS. Latin 1369, ff.447–8.

7 Jambeck, 'Patterns of Women's Literary Patronage', 246–8; Bell, 'Medieval Women Book Owners', 157–8; Meale, '" … alle the bokes that I haue"', 134–44; Mombello, 'Christine de Pizan and the House of Savoy', 191–2.

there is substantial evidence for the literacy of several of her daughters. Margaret Stewart wrote a great deal of poetry, and the inquiry held to investigate her premature death heard that her intense writing activity had contributed to her frailty. None of her work survives, and it is alleged that the dauphin ordered the destruction of his wife's papers.[8] Isabella owned at least four books of hours and a copy of a work entitled *Le Livre des Vices et Vertus*. The portraits of Isabella and members of her family, combined with the incorporation of the arms of Scotland and Brittany in her books of hours, suggests that she requested their production or adaptation. Isabella could also sign her name. Her signature survives on several pages of one of her books of hours, a letter to her sister Eleanor and some official documents including her husband's will, of which she was an executor, and the letter giving her consent to her daughter's marriage.[9] Eleanor acquired several books, including a psalter incorporating the arms of Scotland and Austria, a Lancelot romance and an edition of Jerome's *Epistolae*. In addition, a translation of Boccaccio's *De Claris Mulieribus* was dedicated to her. A manuscript of Virgil, now held in Edinburgh, may also have belonged to Eleanor. Her letters and literary work indicate that she knew several languages, adding German to her Scots, French and Latin after marrying the archduke of Austria-Tyrol in 1448. The late fifteenth-century translation from French to German of the romance *Pontus und Sidonia* was made either by her or at her direction and, in either case, is indicative of her literary and linguistic interests and abilities.[10] Nothing is known about the literary interests of Mary, Joanna and Annabella, but those of their sisters suggest that they were at least able to read. If Annabella could not read when she left Scotland at a young age it seems likely that she acquired that skill in Savoy. The court had an extensive library

---

8 Paris BN, MS. Dupuy 762, f.46r.; Beaucourt, *Charles VII*, iv, 189.

9 Paris BN, MS. Latin 1369, ff. 38, 55, 299, 301, 303, 305, 307, 312, 316, 318, 320, 339, 346, 348, 379, 382; MS. n.a. Lat. 588, f.33v.; MS. Fr. 958 (*Le Livere des Vices et Vertus*), f.1; Cambridge Fitzwilliam, MS. 62, ff.20r., 24r.; Innsbruck TLA, Sigm. IVa 181/11; Nantes ADLA, E25/1, E12/15; Bawcutt, P. and Henisch, B., 'Scots Abroad in the Fifteenth Century: The Princesses Margaret, Isabella and Eleanor', in Ewan, E. and Meikle, M.M. (eds), *Women in Scotland 1100–1750* (East Linton, 1999), 48–9.

10 Köfler, 'Eleonore von Schottland', 90–1, 94–5, 98; Cherry, A., *Princes, Poets and Patrons: the Stuarts and Scotland* (Edinburgh, 1987), 18; Innsbruck TLA, Sigm.IVa 8/1–9, 31/1478, 181/1–19; Stewart, A.M., 'The Austrian Connection c.1450–1483: Eleonora and the Intertextuality of *Pontus und Sidonia*' in J.D. McClure and M.R.G. Spiller (eds), *Bryght Lanternis. Essays on the Language and Literature of Medieval and Renaissance Scotland* (Aberdeen, 1989), 138–9.

which was supplemented by the three boxes of books brought by Yolande of France when she came to the court for her marriage to Amadeus IX in 1452. As queen of France, Charlotte of Savoy continued her family's literary interests by acquiring 115 books, including Christine de Pizan's *The Book of the City of Ladies* and *The Treasure of the City of Ladies*, and histories by Chastellain and Froissart.[11]

Margaret's literary ability and love of poetry have been attributed to those of her father, the reputed author of *The Kingis Quair*, but Joan Beaufort's influence on her daughters' literary interests should not be overlooked. The practice of mothers and older women supervising and training daughters resulted in the transmission of cultural values and interests between generations of women. Joan's aunt, Joan Beaufort, countess of Westmorland, was a noted patron of literature and owner of works of devotional literature and history, two of which she lent to Henry VI. Two of her daughters and a granddaughter were also patrons and owners of books. The evidence for the countess of Westmorland's literary interests dates from 1425, a year after her niece's departure for Scotland. But there is no reason to assume that her interests did not predate this time, particularly as the evidence itself exists because the countess was then a widow with more direct control over her affairs.[12] The literary interests of the Beauforts, James I and the Stewart princesses, combined with the important role played by mothers to their daughters' education, indicate that the queen shared some of those interests.

Mary of Guelders could sign her name – her signature appears on a letter of 1450 to Charles VII – and her literary interests can be inferred from her childhood. Mary's family accumulated an extensive library for its time, and her mother, Catherine of Cleves, is thought to have possessed at least five books. The contents of one of her books of hours, made in the decade after her marriage, emphasised the duties and behavior expected of a wife and mother, including her responsibility for the education of her children. It seems likely that Catherine taught her daughters to read, and there is a reference in the Guelders accounts for 1441 to a psalter belonging to 'my young lady', assumed

11 Mombello, 'Christine de Pizan and the House of Savoy', 191–2; Bell, 'Medieval Women Book Owners', 176; Mooney, 'Queenship in Fifteenth-Century France', 124.
12 Barbé, *Margaret of Scotland*, 117; Bawcutt and Henisch, 'Scots Abroad in the Fifteenth Century', 46; Jambeck, 'Patterns of Literary Patronage', 239–42, 244–6; Meale, '" … alle the bokes that I haue', 144–5; McCash, 'The Cultural Patronage of Medieval Women', 8–10, 14.

to be Mary, the eldest.[13] Mary's early literacy exposure and training would have been reinforced during her long residency in the Burgundian court. The Burgundian interest in literary patronage is shown most clearly by the dissemination of Christine de Pizan's *Treasure of the City of Ladies* throughout the continent, effected partly by Burgundian marriage alliances and by the efforts of Isabel of Portugal, duchess of Burgundy, who may have sent copies to her nieces in Portugal and the imperial court. Christine herself desired, and contributed to, the dissemination of her work. She concludes that she would 'distribute many copies of this work throughout the world whatever the cost, and it would be presented in various places to queens, princesses and great ladies … and it might be spread among other women'.[14] The Stewart, Beaufort and Burgundian literary networks were not unique, and current research is revealing more such networks, all of which are linked by women and reflect the effects of the practice of mothers teaching daughters to read.

The interest in reading, the choice of reading material, the relationships forged in the process of learning and the gifts of books of hours as wedding gifts to daughters were all factors in the development of female networks.[15] The role of the mother in the commissioning and giving of books of hours as wedding gifts was of enormous importance to establishing and maintaining international family networks. Given the importance of books of hours in the literacy training of young girls and their familiarity with their contents, the production and gift of a similar book in another language aided in the acquisition of that language. In addition, the incorporation of illustrations and calendars emphasising local saints familiarised a young bride with the customs of her new home. The books of hours of Isabella Stewart, for example, lay particular emphasis on St Francis of Assisi, her husband's patron saint. Isabella developed her own literary networks in turn, and gave two of her books of hours to her daughters, Marguerite and Marie.[16]

13 Paris BN, MS. Latin 10187, f.15, printed in Stevenson, *Letters and Papers*, i, 303–4; Nijsten, *The Shadow of Burgundy*, 240, 424–6; Bell, 'Medieval Women Book Owners', 161.

14 *Treasure*, 180.

15 Bell, 'Medieval Women Book Owners', 163–5, 176, 179; McCash, 'The Cultural Patronage of Medieval Women', 14–16; Parsons, 'Of Queens, Courts, and Books', 175–201; Jambeck, 'Patterns of Women's Literary Patronage', 228–65; Meale, '" … alle the bokes that I haue"', 137–8, 143–5.

16 Bell, 'Medieval Women Book Owners', 173; Paris BN, MS. Lat. 1369, ff.38, 55, 320; Bawcutt and Henisch, 'Scots Abroad in the Fifteenth Century', 49.

Through books and literacy training, a mother could educate her daughter directly in her own court and prepare her for future her role as a foreign bride.

Daughters were also prepared for marriage with a form of apprenticeship. Christine de Pizan noted that a princess should be more careful in her supervision of her daughters as they grew older and that she should 'have them around her most of the time and keep them respectful.'[17] Because many royal and noble daughters were married or sent to other courts at a relatively young age, they grew up as the surrogate daughters of women other than their mothers. Following their betrothals, Margaret and Annabella Stewart were sent to the courts of France and Savoy respectively in order to learn the habits and customs of their future homes and families. James I attempted to safeguard Margaret's welfare in the course of negotiations in 1434–5, requesting that upon her arrival in France, she be accommodated in her own household with her own people, but conceded that she might stay with the French king and queen when they desired it. While he wanted her to have her own people about her, he recognised that the king and queen would select for his daughter French gentlemen and ladies so that she would learn the customs and habits of her new home. Charles refused these requests, saying that before her marriage Margaret should live with the French queen 'comme sa fille' in order to learn 'les estaz et manieres de france'. He argued that it was not possible or acceptable for her to live elsewhere. Charles later specified that while Margaret could travel with as many Scots as James wished, only one or two women and the same number of men could remain with her in France, because if she were surrounded by people of her own nation she would not willingly or easily learn 'francoys ne lestat de ce Royaulme'.[18] Both men thus tried to accommodate the needs of an eleven-year-old girl far from home, while at the same time recognising the necessity of adapting to her new environment as quickly as possible. The key feature of the negotiations was, however, the understanding that Margaret would reside in the queen's household before her marriage. When she arrived at the French court, then at Tours, Margaret was received by its leading ladies – she was introduced to the French queen, Marie of Anjou, by Marie's mother, Yolande of Aragon, Queen of Sicily – before meeting the dauphin.[19] The queen's importance as surrogate mother and

17 *Treasure*, 68.
18 Paris BN, MS. Fr. 17330, ff.131r, 134v, 138v.
19 Paris BN, MS. Fr. 17330, f.145v.; Chartier, *Chronique de Charles VII*, i, 229–32.

teacher continued in the years following her marriage, as Margaret continued to spend a great deal of her time with the queen. Similar arrangements were made for Annabella's journey to, and residence in, Savoy. Her most important mother-figure before reaching Savoy was the duchess of Burgundy, who accompanied the princess from the Low Countries and was with her when she heard the news of the deaths of her mother and sister. During her residence in Savoy, Annabella was treated as a surrogate daughter, referred to in the household accounts with the daughters of the duchess of Savoy and included on the duchess' travels.[20]

In both of the above cases, betrothed girls were sent at a young age to learn about the structure and etiquette of the courts over which they would eventually preside, but the practice of sending unbetrothed girls to foreign courts suggests that gaining familiarity with particular social behaviour was not the sole object of sending girls away from their families.[21] Unbetrothed girls were also sent to the courts of princes who arranged the girls' marriages. Eleanor Stewart was invited to the French court while her potential marriage to the king of the Romans was discussed, and stayed there for three years while an alternative alliance was sought. Her sister Joanna was not included in the initial invitation yet was welcomed to the French court and stayed there for more than a decade before returning to Scotland unmarried in spring 1458. A number of possible marriage partners were suggested for Mary of Guleders during her residence at the Burgundian court. The presence of these girls in their courts was useful to Charles VII and to the duke of Burgundy, both of whom pursued extensive marital policies but, in the late 1440s, lacked daughters to offer to potential suitors. As foster daughters of such important princes it was important for these girls to learn everything about these courts in order to maintain the prestige and honour of their courts after their marriage. It was also far easier to organise their marriages when they were resident at court and could be presented to potential suitors. The duke of Burgundy, for example, held two banquets for Scottish ambassadors in autumn 1448 which were attended by the duchess, the count of Charollais and 'damoiselles destampes de bourbon et de guelres'.[22] The importance of the French

20 Turin AS(1), Inv.16 Reg.93, ff.376v.-383v; Reg. 95, ff.134r.-138r.; Reg.98, ff.548v.-549r., 565r., 570r.; Reg.104, ff.346r.-8v.

21 Hanawalt, B., 'Female Networks for Fostering Lady Lisle's Daughters' in Parsons and Wheeler, *Medieval Mothering*, 241–2.

22 Lille ADN, B3340, Premier compte, ff. 5r., 27v., 29v.

and Burgundian courts ensured that many suitors applied to the courts for marriage alliances and, in the case of the Stewart princesses, negotiations were conducted more easily in France than in Scotland. The arrangement was not only beneficial to Charles VII and the duke of Burgundy. The girls' families were relieved of the burden of supporting them during their years in other courts and their status was enhanced by the association with the French and Burgundian courts. But the intention of these European princes was not simply to contract the best possible marriage alliance for the girls in their care. The effort and expense invested in securing such alliances was intended to have long-term consequences in the form of the relationships a potential bride established with other courts which would continue after her departure. Her experiences and the training she received while awaiting her marriage ensured that a bride would be able to utilise these ties to maximum effect. Marriage was therefore not the end result of foreign diplomacy but represented the conclusion of a girl's training for her future role and the beginning of her career.

It is significant that, regardless of whether or not a girl was betrothed when she left home, the diplomacy concluding the marriages was conducted by men in order to fulfil foreign policy objectives while the process of welcoming, caring for and training the young princesses was conducted by women. While a father could derive benefits from his daughter's marriage, the role of mothers in educating their daughters and their understanding of the multiple family loyalties and problems created by marriage – an understanding not shared by their husbands – indicates that mothers were the key figures in training girls. The fact that many of these mothers were themselves foreign brides suggests that in educating their daughters and the girls in their care about their duties and conduct they attempted to prepare them for similar experiences. These roles and experiences were thus international rather than national, and ensured that girls separated from their mothers found substitute mother-figures in the courts to which they were sent. This is not to suggest that princes were completely unmoved by the effects of their diplomacy. James I, Joan Beaufort and Margaret are reported to have shed tears at Margaret's departure for France in 1436, and their daughter developed strong affective ties with her marital family. Charles VII and Marie of Anjou are reputed to have had great affection for the daughter-in-law who had spent nine years at the French court, while the duke of Savoy claimed to lack the heart to use force to send Annabella Stewart from his court after ten years because he had fostered her for so long.[23]

Female involvement in international marital diplomacy was not limited to the spheres of welfare and education. Women could and did play an active role in marriage diplomacy, and could develop networks based on training which enhanced their own influence. Mothers and substitute mothers were aware of the relatively short time they had with their daughters – they had left their families in order to marry and several of their daughters would do the same – and may consciously have developed other, more long-term, networks of support which incorporated foster daughters and daughters-in-law. Eleanor Stewart was invited to the French court by the duchess of Burgundy at the instigation of the dauphin and Margaret in order to secure a continental marriage. Her marriage to the archduke of Austria-Tyrol in 1448 was arranged by Charles VII, and both he and his queen, Marie of Anjou, were present at the ceremony.[24] The residence of Mary of Guelders in the household of the duchess of Burgundy illustrates the potential for both foster daughters and their teachers to derive considerable benefits from the practice of fostering and training young girls in foreign courts. The duchess of Burgundy's inclusion of the foster daughters in her household in the wide variety of activities she undertook contributed to the expansion of her own network and the maximisation of her influence. The most striking example of the way in which the duchess inolved her charges in her duties is provided by her actions as mediator at the Anglo-French talks at Calais in 1439. The duchess and her fellow mediator, Cardinal Beaufort, were charged with making basic decisions regarding the timing and membership of the negotiations and expected to preside over them. The outcome of their decision-making was that negotiations took place in the duchess' tent in her presence and that of her niece, the princess of Navarre, and ten other ladies. The duchess was included in the world of war and politics in her gender-determined capacity of mediator and 'peaceweaver' and was concerned to train other women to fulfil similar duties successfully.[25] The perception that women of power were natural mediators was responsible for the duchess' nomination in 1439 and it is likely that the duchess was herself aware of the potential of that role and its possibilities for

---

23 Paris BN, MS. Fr. 17330, f.141v.; Hanawalt, 'Female Networks for Fostering', 242–3, 246–7; Barbé, *Margaret of Scotland*, 123, 132–3, 165; Paris BN, MS. Fr.18983; Macrae, 'Scotland and the Wars of the Roses', Appendix C, no.7, pp.574–6.

24 Edinburgh NAS, SP9/2; Vienna HHSA, Fam.Urk. 608.

25 *PPC*, v, 334–407; Parsons, 'Mothers, Daughters, Marriage, Power', 69.

female networking. She acted as the duke's representative at talks in Châlons in 1445 at which, in addition to her formal meetings with representatives from several European courts, she established close ties with the French queen, Marie of Anjou, and Margaret Stewart. Given that the duke of Burgundy never met his nephew, Charles VII, the relationship between the duchess and the two leading princesses of the French court was of enormous importance.[26] The likelihood that the duchess was responsible for sending copies of Christine de Pizan's *The Treasure of the City of Ladies*, a work emphasising the role and potential of princesses, to her niece, the queen of Portugal, and to another niece, Eleanor of Portugal, who married Emperor Frederick III in 1452, also suggests that her female networks had practical and political use.

The perception of marriage as a career in which an apprenticeship could be served and the role of women in training and preparing young girls for this career has significant implications for their self-awareness. The transmission of literacy, and in some cases an interest in patronage, between generations of women was a means of identifying and preserving particular values and contributed to an awareness of duty and role. The training of girls by women created networks and established a sense of the multiple identities of a medieval princess. The content of reading material emphasised the subordinate and dependent roles of women as daughters, wives and mothers, the behaviour expected of them and, in the emphasis on Mary, the latent power of maternity.[27] This awareness was consciously developed in childhood in preparation for marriage. The Stewart princesses, and James II himself, were treated largely as diplomatic pawns in the marital policies of continental princes, but they were not without power in the longer term. Potential brides had little control over their eventual marriages but were prepared as much as possible for the upheavals they faced and reminded in various ways of the power and status they acquired as a result of those marriages. The effort, expense, ceremony and public display of international marriage alliances illustrated to the participants and a wide audience the bride's importance as 'peace-weaver'.

Princesses were continuously reminded of this career as peacemaker and mediator throughout their married lives. Their role was embedded

26 Beaucourt, *Charles VII*, iv, 96; Vaughan, *Philip the Good*, 119–120; Vale, *Charles VII*, 230.
27 Jambeck, 'Patterns of Women's Literary Patronage', 228; N. Chodorow, 'Family Structure and Feminine Personality' in Rosaldo and Lamphere, *Woman, Culture, and Society*, 58; Sheingorn, '"The Wise Mother"', 78.

in their titles. In a letter expressing her consent to her daughter's marriage, Isabella Stewart called herself 'Ysabeau fille de Roy descoce duchesse de bretaigne', a title also used by her Breton subjects in a debate on the same matter. She was referred to simply as 'ysabeau descosse' by Charles VII.[28] Her sister Eleanor was addressed solely as duchess of Austria in much of her surviving correspondence, but was also referred to in other sources as 'Eleonor descosse duchesse daulterisse' and as 'Elienor de Scocia domina ac principe'. The first edition of *Pontus und Sidonia*, translated at her direction and published after her death, describes her as 'Lady Heleonora, born queen of Scotland, Archduchess of Austria'.[29] Joan Beaufort called herself 'Jehan by ye grace of God Qwein of Scotland' while the Auchinleck chronicler noted that the queen 'was callit Jane and scho was the duke of somersydis dochter'.[30] Mary of Guelders called herself 'Marie dei gracia Regina Scocie' but the Auchinleck chroincler described her as the 'Queen of Scotland, the Duke of gillerlandis dochter' and the duke of Burgundy called her his 'nepte marye de gheldres Royne descosse'.[31] Iconography also emphasised a bride's role as link between families. Several pictures in the books belonging to Isabella Stewart incorporate the Scottish and Breton arms, including portraits of the duchess wearing a dress bearing both sets of arms.[32] The Scottish and Austrian arms decorate a psalter belonging to Eleanor, and it has been argued that the initials 'P' and 'L' combined with the Scottish arms on a manuscript of Virgil indicate her ownership.[33]

The emphasis on multiple allegiances in titles and iconography acted as static and constant reminders of a princess' role within a larger family network, but the benefits of this role were also emphasised in practice. Annabella's betrothal to the count of Geneva in 1444 was promoted by Charles VII, the dauphin, and the duke of Burgundy, while the marriage contract included the duke of Brittany. With the exception of Burgundy, who did not have a direct link but had promoted Mary Stewart's marriage to the son of the lord of Veere, all of these men

28 Nantes ADLA, E12/15, E5/11, E13/1.
29 Vienna HHSA, Familien-Akten 18/II/4 f.51; Bawcutt and Henisch, 'Scots Abroad in the Fifteenth Century', 52; Stewart, 'The Austrian Connection', 138.
30 *HMC, Report*, vi, 691, no.20; 'Auch. Chron.', 162.
31 Edinburgh NLS, MS. Adv. Ch.B 73; *Charters and Documents Relating to the Collegiate Church and Hospital of the Holy Trinity*, 17; 'Auch. Chron.', 169; Lille ADN, B427/15882bis.
32 Paris BN, MS. n.a. Latin 588, f.33v.; MS. Latin 1369, f.55r.; MS. Fr. 958, f.1.
33 Köfler, 'Eleonore von Schottland', 98; Cherry, *Princes and Patrons*, 18.

were related to her by the marriages of her elder sisters, Margaret and Isabella. Annabella stayed in the care of the lady of Veere en route to Savoy in 1445 and was accompanied for part of the journey by the duchess of Burgundy. The duchess invited another sister, Eleanor, to France at the instigation of the dauphin and Margaret, and the negotiations for Eleanor's marriage involved the dukes of Brittany and Savoy. The marriage ceremony took place in the presence of the king and queen of France, and Eleanor visited her younger sister Annabella en route to Austria. The political alliance represented by the marriage of James II and Mary of Guelders was approved by France, incorporated Scotland, Burgundy, Guelders and Brittany and included a clause acknowledging the Franco–Scottish alliance, renewed by the same Scottish ambassadors only months before. The lord of Veere, father-in-law to James' sister, Mary, escorted Mary of Guelders to Scotland for her marriage in 1449. This marriage network was created largely by Charles VII and the duke of Burgundy but was constructed around the Stewart princesses. The implicit recognition of the ties between princesses was yet another reminder of their role and expanded their own networks of influence. The involvement of the duchess of Burgundy, queen of France, the lady of Veere and Margaret Stewart in negotiations demonstrates that these women were not simply pawns but could play an active role in marital policy. In addition, the success of marital diplomacy rested on the role of women such as the queen of France and duchess of Burgundy as surrogate mothers and teachers.

Even when not directly involved in diplomacy, princesses were expected to maintain communication within the network. Nowhere is this clearer in the surviving evidence than in the collection of letters to and from Eleanor Stewart. Much of this correspondence is between family members, such as the letter which seems to have been sent by her sister Mary in Veere, the three letters from Brittany – from Isabella, her daughter and son-in-law – and the five letters from her nephew, James III, and her step-brothers, James, earl of Buchan, and Andrew, bishop of Moray. Other letters from the bishops of Orkney and Aberdeen and James, Lord Hamilton illustrate that Eleanor was not contacted simply as family member but also as a kind of ambassador.[34] The letter from Hamilton, husband of Eleanor's niece Mary, reveals that he sent craftsmen to Austria for further training and secured Eleanor's favour for these men by also sending 'hors hawkis or hundis or other gudis' to

34 Innsbruck TLA, Sigm.IVa 181/4, 9, 10, 11; Urk. 9031 (1460); Sigm.IVa 181/ 3, 12, 14, 6, 2, 13, 16.

her. The bishop of Aberdeen wrote regarding the Scottish mission to Burgundy on which he and her half-brother the earl of Buchan were to serve. James III, Eleanor's nephew, had requested that the embassy visit her after completing its mission in Burgundy and the bishop wrote to explain the delay. Buchan wrote twice, once to reinforce the bishop's explanation and again, following the receipt of letters from Eleanor, to suggest that he and the bishop mediate between Burgundy and Austria to attempt to resolve their recent disgreements. The larger family network enabled the ambassadors of a third party, the Scottish king, as the nephew of a Scottish princess married to the archduke of Austria-Tyrol, to mediate between Burgundy and Austria. Eleanor had sent letters and gifts to the earl of Buchan before he wrote suggesting mediation which he stated would only take place if it were acceptable to her; her involvement seems to have been critical not only to the maintenance of communication with her Scottish family, but also to the promotion of Austrian interests in continental politics.

The earl's first letter also informed Eleanor of the good health of James III, his wife and son, and of his two brothers, the duke of Albany and earl of Mar and their interest in her wellbeing. The interest in individual health was an important part of international diplomacy. Mary of Guelders' letter to Charles VII in 1450 informs the king that she was well – possibly in response to an expression of sympathy for the premature birth and death of her first child – and promises her assistance for the king's policies. Waurin's description of the Burgundian ambassador's meeting with Mary in 1461 also illustrates the importance of preliminary enquiries about family members to the success of a mission. The queen enquired about the health and wellbeing of her uncle the duke, his son the Comte de Charollais and of 'sa belle ante la ducesse'. The ambassador addressed the queen's concerns before proceeding to a discussion of the business at hand.[35] Individuals were obviously interested in the welfare of family members and friends, but such exchanges acted as reminders of political bonds and were intended to persuade individuals to respond to the business of the embassy in a favourable manner. The fact that the actual mission of the ambassador or messenger was often communicated by the individual and was not specified in his letter of introduction was also important. The bishop of Aberdeen and earl of Buchan explained that they might be unable to visit Eleanor but sent their clerk, James Keith, in their stead. Their letters, informing Eleanor of her family's health, were presumably

35 Stevenson, *Letters and Papers*, i, 301–3; Waurin, *Anchiennes Cronicques*, ii, 302–4.

carried by him and he received further instruction and information to communicate upon his arrival. Similarly, Eleanor's letters were carried by her messenger who returned to her with further advice from Buchan not contained in his letter. The example of Eleanor's page, Jörg von Ehingen, who travelled extensively throughout Western Europe and recorded his experiences in a diary and in portraits, also indicates how information could be communicated within a larger family network.[36]

This communication played an important role in the success of European diplomacy. The evidence of embassies to Scotland of members of Joan Beaufort's family between 1426 and 1433 does not record the queen's direct participation in talks but circumstantial evidence suggests that she was at least indirectly involved. James I included his wife in political life as one of his principal counsellors, particularly in decisions relating to Margaret's marriage, and at least two of these Beaufort embassies resulted in the discussion of Anglo-Scottish marriage alliances. The queen actively maintained an interest in England and her family. She made an offering in England in 1427–8 and sent her lady-in-waiting, Margery Nortoun, to London in 1433, the same year in which she sent a gift of salmon to her mother. She sent letters to Cardinal Beaufort in 1437 regarding her husband's murder and a Scottish embassy, but the letters have unfortunately not survived. Perhaps the most notable example of strong family relationships created, but not maintained, by Joan Beaufort were those between the children of her first and second marriages. John and James Stewart appear in the accounts from 1456 and are described as brothers of the king.[37] They became the earls of Atholl and Buchan respectively, while a third brother, Andrew, became bishop of Moray, indicating their long-term favour within the royal family. The letters from Buchan and the bishop of Moray to Eleanor illustrate the way in which members of the extended family who may not have met since childhood maintained the family network. The letters Eleanor received from her niece and niece's husband, the duke of Brittany, are evidence that this network encompassed family members who may never have met at all. Mary of Guelders' role in maintaining contact with her family is better recorded. She employed several servants from the Low Countries, was attended by Elizabeth of Guelders and entertained visitors from Guelders, while the exchange of goods such as wine, bombards and horses between the duke of Burgundy and Scotland recognised the

36 Dunlop, *James Kennedy*, 364–5.
37 *ER*, vi, 115, 243, 343, 410, 633, 651.

duke's involvement in the alliance established by her marriage. The embassies sent by the king of France, the dauphin and the dukes of Burgundy, Guelders and Brittany to the queen at the beginning of the minority were intended to solicit her support for either the Lancastrians or the Yorkists, and represented the relationships each of these men had to the Stewart family. Mary of Guelders also sustained these links by sending her chamberlain to the Low Countries in 1461 and her second son, the duke of Albany, to Guelders where he lived with her family between 1460 and 1464.[38] Both Joan Beaufort and Mary of Guelders were aware of their obligations as facilitators of communication between families and fulfilled their duties.

The examination of family networks based on girls' marriages illuminates the deficiencies of the available evidence about fifteenth-century queens and princesses. Mary Stewart, for example, is virtually invisible in the record sources but the family of her husband is not. The role of the Veere household in the marriages of her siblings, James II and Annabella; the separate visits to the Veere household of Monypenny and of a Burgundian herald en route to Scotland in 1460; the visit of ambassadors from the duke of Guelders and the Scottish queen in 1461 and of Scottish heralds in 1464, are all indicative of the continuing involvement of the Veere family in matters concerning Scotland. One of Mary's half-brothers also visited Veere in November 1459.[39] The visits of heralds and ambassadors to and from Scotland may have been connected with Burgundian business or simply reflect the geographical importance of Veere in journeys to Scotland but, in view of the importance of verbal communication regarding family members, it is likely that Mary was able to maintain contact with her extended family through these visitors. Her letter to Eleanor suggests that she remained a contributing member of the larger family network based on Stewart marriages. Mary may not be visible in the record sources, but her role and importance can be inferred from the evidence regarding her family's involvement in Scottish foreign diplomacy.

A royal or noble daughter was aware of her multiple identities and roles of daughter, sister, wife and mother, and of the complex of loyalties created by these roles. She was the focus of a network of several families – her birth family, foster family and her own – and had to be capable of facilitating communication within the network and managing her various, and sometimes contradictory, identities and

38 Ditchburn, 'The Place of Guelders', 68–9.
39 Macrae, 'Scotland and the Wars of the Roses', Appendix C, no.8.

loyalties. These identities formed the basis of a princess' power and her management of them constituted the exercise of that power. The creation and management of networks of influence enabled powerful women, particularly queens, to extend their power into areas from which they had traditionally been excluded. Joan Beaufort and Mary of Guelders were included in political life as their husbands' inferior partners, particularly through the combined management of households, land resources and patronage. This involvement of the queen consort in political life ensured that upon the king's premature death she had established relationships with leading figures and officers in government which enabled the rapid succession of the king's young heir. The queen mother's continuing involvement in public life during the minority was dependent upon the stability of the government and personnel with whom she was familiar. Denied this stability, Joan Beaufort sought alternative sources of power, again through marriage and the cultivation of family networks, in order to defend herself and her son from the factions which dominated government. Mary of Guelders, on the other hand, was able to maintain a leading role in the minority government, despite some opposition, as a result of the stability of that government; the factionalism that had plagued the minority of James II did not develop strength during the minority of James III until several years after the death of the queen mother.

The ultimate result of the training of princesses by other princesses and the transmission of experiences between generations of royal and noble women was therefore an awareness of the importance and potential of their role within a masculine political world. Women were aware of their power and influence and capable of cultivating it, and their awareness was such that they did not exercise it with a view to acquiring authority for themselves but in association with, and on behalf of, others. Fifteenth-century queens and princesses lived in a male-dominated world, but their preparation for that world reveals the existence of a significant female one. This female world could never be independent of its male counterpart – de Poitiers' account of Burgundian childbirth rituals reveals that even when men were absent they determined the precedence and etiquette of their wives – but its existence and functions contributed to political life. The effort and expense invested in preparing girls for marriage and negotiating marital alliances indicate that fifteenth-century princes were aware that marriage was a career rather than an event, suggesting that, despite the relative absence of royal and noble women from the sources, their contribution to political life was obvious to their contemporaries. The study of the lives of fifteenth-century queens and princesses of Scotland illuminates the way in which court and government functioned, and is basic to an understanding of the links between Scottish and European courts.

Bibliography

Primary manuscript sources

Brussels, Archives Générales du Royaume
Trésor de Flandre, IIe Série
1449–51

Cambridge, Fitzwilliam Museum
MS. 62

Edinburgh, National Library of Scotland
Advocates 20.3.4
Ch. B 73

Edinburgh, National Archives of Scotland
Ailsa Muniments
GD25
Crawford Priory Collection
GD20
Lord Forbes Collection
GD52
Register House Charters
RH6
State Papers
SP6
SP7
SP8
SP9
SP13

Innsbruck, Landesregierungsarchiv für Tirol
Fridericiana
Lage 40
Sigmundiana
IVa
Urkunden
7494
9031

Lille, Archives Départementales du Nord
Série B, Chambre des Comptes de Lille
B308
B427
B1999
B2004
B3340
B3374
B3409–3415
B4103

London, British Library
Additional 8878
Harleian 4637 III
Royal 13.E.x

Nantes, Archives Départementales de Loire-Atlantique
Série B, Chambre des Comptes de Bretagne
B126–7
B130
Série E, Trésor des Chartes des Ducs de Bretagne
E12
E13
E16
E25
E125
E207

Paris, Archives Nationales
Série J, Trésor des Chartes
J408–9
J501–2
J677–80
Série K, Monuments Historiques
K64
K69
K1151

Paris, Bibliothèque Nationale
Dupuy
33
762
Français
958
5041
6755
10238
10370
12476
17330

Latin
  1369
  5414A
  8757
  10187
  n.a. Latin 588

Turin, Archivio di Stato (1), Sezioni Riunite
  Inventario 16, Conti delle Tesorerie Generale di Savoia
    Registri 91–105

Turin, Archivio di Stato (2), Direzione e Sezione 1
  Inventario 102, Matrimoni della Real Casa di Savoia
    Mazzo 12, 1
  Inventario 118, Trattati Antichi
    Mazzo 8, 9

Vienna, Haus-, Hof- und Staatsarchiv
  Familien-Akten
    Karton 18
  Familienurkunden
    588
    603–8
  Nederlandisches Urkunden
    1448–52

Printed primary sources and works of reference

The Acts of the Parliaments of Scotland, ed. T. Thomson and C. Innes (Edinburgh, 1814–75)

Ane Account of the Familie of Innes, ed. C. Innes (Spalding Club, 1864)

Armstrong, C.A.J., 'A Letter of James III to the Duke of Burgundy' in Armstrong, *England, France and Burgundy*, 389–402

'The Auchinleck Chronicle', printed in McGladdery, *James II*, 160–73

Bateson, M., 'The Scottish King's Household Early in the Fourteenth Century', *Scottish History Society Miscellany*, ii (1904), 31–43

Birch, W.de G., *Catalogue of Seals in the Department of Manuscripts in the British Museum* (London, 1887)

Blamires, A. et al. (eds), *Woman Defamed and Woman Defended. An Anthology of Medieval Texts* (Oxford, 1992)

Bower, W., *Scotichronicon*, ed. D.E.R. Watt (Aberdeen, 1987–1998)

Brown, P. Hume (ed.), *Early Travellers in Scotland* (Edinburgh, 1891)

The Brut or the Chronicles of England, ed. F.W.D. Brie (EETS, 1906–8)

Calendar of Documents relating to Scotland, ed. J. Bain (Edinburgh, 1881–8)

Calendar of Entries in the Papal Registers relating to Great Britain and Ireland: Papal Letters, ed. W.H. Bliss et al. (London, 1893–)

Calendar of the Patent Rolls, Henry VI, 1446–1452 (London, 1909)

Calendar of Scottish Supplications to Rome, iv, ed. A.I. Dunlop and D. MacLauchlan (Glasgow, 1983)

Calendar of State Papers and Manuscripts existing in the archives and collections of Milan, ed. A.B. Hinds (London, 1912)

Charters and Documents Relating to the Collegiate Church and Hospital of the Holy Trinity and the Trinity Hospital, Edinburgh AD. 1460–1661 (Scottish Burgh Records Society, 1871)

Chartier, J., *Chronique de Charles VII*, ed. V. de Viriville (Paris, 1858)

Chronicles of London, ed. C.L. Kingsford (Oxford, 1905)

Connolly, M., '*The Dethe of the Kynge of Scotis*: A New Edition', *SHR*, 71 (1992), 46–69

Copiale Prioratus Sanctiandree, ed. J.H. Baxter (Oxford, 1930)

Crawford, A. (ed.), *The Letters of the Queens of England 1100–1547* (Stroud, 1994)

D'Escouchy, M., *Chronique*, ed. G. du Fresne Beaucourt (Paris, 1863–4)

The Exchequer Rolls of Scotland, ed. J. Stuart et al. (Edinburgh, 1878–1908)

Extracts from the Council Register of the Burgh of Aberdeen, 1398–1570, ed. J. Stuart (Spalding Club, 1844)

Extracts from the Records of the Burgh of Edinburgh, AD 1403–1528 (Scottish Burgh Records Society, 1869)

Facsimiles of the National Manuscripts of Scotland, ed. C. Innes (London, 1867–71)

Foedera, Conventiones, Litterae et Cuiuscunque Generis Acta Publica, ed. T. Rymer (London, 1704–35)

Fordun, J., *Chronica Gentis Scotorum*, ed. W.F. Skene (Edinburgh, 1871–2)

Fraser, W., *The Douglas Book* (Edinburgh, 1885)

Gilbert of the Haye's Prose Manuscript, ed. J.H. Stevenson (Scottish Text Society, 1901, 1914)

The Golden Legend of Jacobus de Voragine, ed. and trans. G. Ryan and H. Ripperger, Reprint Edition (Salem, 1987)

Hansisches Urkundenbuch, ed. W. Stein (Halle, 1899)

Hay, W., *Lectures on Marriage*, ed. and trans. J.C. Barry (Stair Society, 1967)

The Historical Collections of a Citizen of London in the fifteenth century, ed. J. Gairdner (Camden Society New Series, 1876)

Inventaire sommaire des archives départementales de la Côte d'Or. Série B, ed. C. Rossignol and M. Garnier (Paris and Dijon, 1863–94)

Inventaire sommaire des archives départementales de Loire-Atlantique. Série E, ed. L. Maitre (Nantes, 1909)

Inventaire sommaire des archives départementales du Nord. Série B, ed. M. L'Abbé Dehaisnes and J. Finot (Lille, 1863–1906)

Kennedy, A., 'Christine de Pizan's *Epistre à la Reine* (1405)', *Revue des Langues Romans*, 92 (1988), 253–64

The Kingis Quair of James Stewart, ed. M.P. Mc Diarmid (London, 1973)

Laing, H. (ed.), *Descriptive Catalogue of Impressions From Ancient Scottish Seals, Royal, Baronial, Ecclesiastical, and Municipal (1094–1707)* (Edinburgh, 1850–66)

Legends of the Saints in the Scottish Dialect of the Fourteenth Century, ed. W.M. Metcalfe (Edinburgh, 1896)

Legge, M.D., *Anglo-Norman Letters and Petitions from All Souls MS.182* (Anglo-Norman Text Society, 1941)

Letters of Queen Margaret of Anjou, Bishop Beckington and Others, ed. C. Monro (Camden Society, 1863)

Lettres et mandements de Jean V, duc de Bretagne, ed. R. Blanchard (Nantes, 1889–95)

Liber Pluscardensis, ed. F.J.H. Skene (Edinburgh, 1877–80)

The Life and Death of King James the First of Scotland, ed. J. Stevenson (Maitland Club, 1837)

Mandements du duc François I. Répertoire, 1442–1450 (Archives Départmentales de Loire-Atlantique, no date)

Marshall, D., 'Notes on the Record Room of the City of Perth', *Proceedings of the Society of Antiquaries of Scotland*, 33 (1899), 414–40

Monstrelet, E. de, *Chronicles*, ed. and trans. T. Johnes (London, 1849)

O'Faolain, J. and Martines, L. (eds.), *Not in God's Image* (New York, 1973)

The Paston Letters, AD. 1422–1509, ed. J. Gairdner (London, 1904)

Pinkerton, J., *The History of Scotland from the Accession of the House of Stuart to that of Mary, with Appendices of Original Papers* (London, 1797)

Pizan, C. de, *The Treasure of the City of Ladies*, trans. S. Lawson (Harmondsworth, 1985)

——, *The Epistle of the Prison of Human Life with An Epistle to the Queen of France and Lament on the Evils of the Civil War*, ed. and trans. J.A. Wisman (New York, 1984)

——, *The Book of the Body Politic*, ed. and trans. K.L. Forhan (Cambridge, 1994)

——, *The Book of the City of Ladies*, trans. E.J. Richards (New York, 1982)

Poitiers, A. de, 'Les Honneurs de la Cour' in M. de la Curne de Sainte-Palaye (ed.), *Mémoires sur l'ancienne chevalerie, Considerée comme un éstablissement politique et militaire* (Paris, 1759), ii, 171–267

Proceedings and Ordinances of the Privy Council of England, ed. H. Nicolas (London, 1834–7)

Queene Elizabethes Academy, A Booke of Precedence, The Ordering of a Funerall, etc., ed. F.J. Furnivall (EETS, 1869)

Ratis Raving and Other Early Scots Poems on Morals, ed. R. Girvan (Scottish Text Society, 1939)

Records of the Earldom of Orkney, 1299–1614, ed. J.S. Clouston (Scottish History Society, 1914)

Registrum Episcopatus Aberdonensis, ed. C. Innes (Edinburgh, 1845)

Registrum Episcopatus Glasguensis, Munimenta Ecclesie Metropolitane Glasguensis, ed. C. Innes (Edinburgh, 1843)

Registrum Magni Sigilli Regum Scottorum, eds. J.M. Thomson and J.B. Paul (Edinburgh, 1882–1914)

Reports of the Royal Commission on Historical Manuscripts (London, 1870-)

Rotuli Scotiae in Turri Londinensi et in Domo Capitulari Westmonasteriensi Asservati, ed. D. Macpherson (London, 1814–19)

Stevenson, J. (ed.), *Documents Illustrative of the History of Scotland 1286–1306* (Edinburgh, 1870)

——, *Letters and Papers Illustrative of the Wars of the English in France during the Reign of Henry the Sixth* (London, 1861–4)

Stevenson, J.H. and Wood, M. (eds), *Scottish Heraldic Seals. Royal, Official, Ecclesiastical, Collegiate, Burghal, Personal* (Glasgow, 1940)

Stones, E.L.G. (ed.), *Anglo-Scottish Relations, 1174–1328, Some Selected Documents* (London, 1965)

Teulet, A. (ed.), *Inventaire chronologique des documents relatifs à l'histoire de l'Ecosse conservés aux archives du royaume à Paris* (Abbotsford Club, 1839)

Three Fifteenth-Century Chronicles, ed. J. Gairdner (Camden Society New Series, 1880)

Turgot, 'The Life of S. Margaret, Queen of Scotland' in W.M. Metcalfe (ed.), *Ancient Lives of Scottish Saints* (Paisley, 1895), 295–321

Waurin, J. de, *Anchiennes Cronicques d'Engleterre*, ed. E. Dupont (Paris, 1858–63)

——, *Recueil des Croniques et Anchiennes Istories de la Grant Bretaigne*, ed. W. and E.L.C.P. Hardy (Rolls Series, 1864–91)

Wright, T. (ed.), *Political Poems and Songs Relating to English History, Composed During the Period from the Accession of Edward III to that of Richard III* (London, 1861)

Wyntoun, Andrew of, *The Original Chronicle of Andrew of Wyntoun*, ed. F.J. Amours (Scottish Text Society, 1903–14)

Published secondary sources

Alexander, J.J.G., 'Painting and Manuscript Illumination for Royal Patrons in the Later Middle Ages' in V.J. Scattergood and J.W. Sherborne (eds), *English Court Culture in the Later Middle Ages* (New York, 1983), 141–62

Angus, W. and Dunlop, A.I., 'The Date of the Birth of James III', *SHR*, xxx (1951), 199–204

Armstrong, C.A.J., *England, France and Burgundy in the Fifteenth Century* (London, 1983)

——, 'La politique matrimoniale des ducs de Bourgogne de la maison de Valois' in Armstrong, *England, France and Burgundy*, 237–342

Axton, M., *The Queen's Two Bodies: Drama and the Elizabethan Succession* (London, 1977)

Bak, J.M., 'Roles and Functions of Queens in Árpádian and Angevin Hungary (1000–1386 AD)' in Parsons, *Medieval Queenship*, 13–24

Baker, D. (ed.), *Medieval Women: Essays Presented to Rosalind M.T. Hill on the Occasion of her Seventieth Birthday* (Oxford, 1978)

——, '"A Nursery of Saints": St Margaret of Scotland Reconsidered' in Baker, *Medieval Women*, 119–41

Balfour-Melville, E.W.M., 'The captivity of James I', *SHR* 21 (1924), 45–53

——, 'The Later Captivity and Release of James I', *SHR* 21 (1924), 89–100

——, 'James I at Windsor', *SHR* 25 (1928), 226–8

——, *James I, King of Scots: 1406–1437* (London, 1936)

Barbé, L.A., *Margaret of Scotland and the Dauphin Louis* (London, 1917)

——, *Sidelights on the History, Industries and Social Life of Scotland* (London, 1919)

——, 'A Stuart Duchess of Brittany' in Barbé, *Sidelights on the History*, 1–45

——, 'A Scots Soldier of Fortune', in Barbé, *Sidelights on the History*, 61–7

——, 'A Scottish Claim to a French Province', in Barbé, *Sidelights on the History*, 69–75

Barrow, G.W.S., *Robert Bruce and the Community of the Realm* (third edition, Edinburgh, 1988)

——, 'A Kingdom in Crisis: Scotland and the Maid of Norway', *SHR*, 69 (1990), 120–41

Bawcutt, P., '"My bright buke": Women and their Books in Medieval and Renaissance Scotland' in J. Wogan-Browne et al. (eds), *Medieval Women: Texts and Contexts in Late Medieval Britain. Essays for Felicity Riddy* (Turnhout, 2000), 17–34

Bawcutt, P. and Henisch, B., 'Scots Abroad in the Fifteenth Century: the Princesses Margaret, Isabella and Eleanor' in Ewan and Meikle, *Women in Scotland*, 45–55

Baxter, J.H., 'The Marriage of James II', *SHR* 25 (1928), 69–72

Beaucourt, G. du Fresne de, *Histoire de Charles VII* (Paris, 1881–91)

Bedos-Rezak, B., 'Women, Seals and Power in Medieval France, 1150–1350' in Erler and Kowaleski, *Women and Power*, 61–82

——, 'Medieval Women in French Sigillographic Sources' in Rosenthal, *Medieval Women and the Sources of Medieval History*, 1–36

Behrens, B., 'Treatises on the Ambassador Written in the Fifteenth and Early Sixteenth Centuries', *EHR*, li (1936), 616–27

Bell, S.G., 'Medieval Women Book Owners: Arbiters of Lay Piety and Ambassadors of Culture' in Erler and Kowaleski, *Women and Power*, 149–87

Bernard, R.B., 'The Intellectual Circle of Isabel of Portugal, Duchess of Burgundy, and the Portuguese Translation of *Le Livre des Trois Vertus*' in McLeod, *The Reception of Christine de Pizan*, 43–58

Billings, R.W., *The Baronial and Ecclesiastical Antiquities of Scotland* (Edinburgh, 1845–52)

Bird, P., 'Images of Women in the Old Testament' in Ruether, *Religion and Sexism*, 71–7

Bloch, R.H., *Medieval Misogyny and the Invention of Western Romantic Love* (Chicago, 1991)

Blumenfeld-Kosinski, R., 'Christine de Pizan and the Misogynistic Tradition', *Romanic Review*, 81 (1990), 279–90

Boardman, S., *The Early Stewart Kings: Robert II and Robert III* (East Linton, 1996)

Boffey, J., 'Women authors and women's literacy in fourteenth- and fifteenth-century England' in Meale, *Women and Literature*, 159–82

Bornstein, D. (ed.), *Ideals for Women and the Works of Christine de Pizan* (Detroit, 1981)

Boyer, M.N., 'Status and Travel Stipends in Fourteenth-century France', *Speculum*, xxxix (1964), 45–52

Brabant, M. (ed.), *Politics, Gender, and Genre. The Political Thought of Christine de Pizan* (Boulder, 1992)

Bradley, P.J., 'Henry V's Scottish policy – a study in realpolitik' in J.S. Hamilton and P.J. Bradley (eds), *Documenting the past. Essays in medieval history presented to George Peddy Cuttino* (Woodbridge/Wolfeboro, 1989), 177–95

Brandenbarg, T., 'St Anne and her family. The veneration of St Anne in connection with concepts of marriage and the family in the early-modern period' in L. Dresen-Coenders (ed.), *Saints and She-Devils: Images of Women in the 15th and 16th Centuries* (London, 1987), 101–27

Brown, A.L., 'The Scottish "Establishment" in the Later Fifteenth Century', *Juridical Review*, xxiii (1978), 89–105

Brown, E.A.R., 'The political repercussions of family ties in the early fourteenth century: the marriage of Edward II of England and Isabelle of France', *Speculum*, 63 (1988), 573–95

Brown, J.M. (ed.), *Scottish Society in the Fifteenth Century* (London, 1977)

——, 'The Exercise of Power' in Brown, *Scottish Society*, 33–65

Brown, M., '"That Old Serpent and Ancient of Evil Days": Walter, Earl of Atholl and the Death of James I', *SHR*, 71 (1992), 23–45

——, *James I* (Edinburgh, 1994)

——, 'Scotland Tamed? Kings and Magnates in Late Medieval Scotland: a review of recent work', *Innes Review*, xlv no.2 (1994), 120–46

——, *The Black Douglases* (East Linton, 1998)

——, '"Vile Times": Walter Bower's Last Book and the Minority of James II', *SHR*, 79 (2000), 165–88

Brundage, J.A., *Law, Sex, and Christian Society in Medieval Europe* (Chicago, 1987)

——, 'Widows and Remarriage: Moral Conflicts and Their Resolution in Classical Canon Law' in Walker, *Wife and Widow*, 17–26

——, 'The Merry Widow's Serious Sister: Remarriage in Classical Canon Law' in R.R. Edward and V. Ziegler (eds), *Matrons and Marginal Women in Medieval Society* (Woodbridge, 1995), 33–48

Bullough, V.L., 'Medieval Medical and Scientific Views of Women', *Viator*, 4 (1973), 485–501

Burns, J.H., *Scottish Churchmen and the Council of Basle* (Glasgow, 1962)

——, *Lordship, Kingship, and Empire. The Idea of Monarchy 1400–1525 (The Carlyle Lectures 1988)* (Oxford, 1992)

Bynum, C., '" … And Woman His Humanity": Female Imagery in the Religious Writing of the Later Middle Ages' in C. Bynum, S. Harrell and P. Richman (eds), *Gender and Religion: On the Complexity of Symbols* (Boston, 1986), 257–88

Campbell, P.G.C., 'Christine de Pisan en Angleterre', *Revue de Littérature Comparée*, 5 (1925), 659–70

Carpenter, J. and MacLean, S.B. (eds), *Power of the Weak. Studies on Medieval Women* (Urbana, 1995)

Casey, K., 'The Cheshire Cat: Reconstructing the Experience of Medieval Women' in B.A. Carroll (ed.), *Liberating Woman's History: Theoretical and Critical Essays* (Urbana, 1976), 224–49

Cherry, A., *Princes, Poets and Patrons: the Stuarts and Scotland* (Edinburgh, 1987)

Chevalier, B., 'Les Ecossais dans les armées de Charles VII jusqu'à la bataille de Verneuil', *Jeanne d'Arc. Une époque, un rayonnment* (Paris, 1982), 85–94

Chodorow, N., 'Family Structure and Feminine Personality' in Rosaldo and Lamphere, *Woman, Culture, and Society*, 43–66

Clive, E.M., *The Law of Husband and Wife in Scotland* (Edinburgh, 1982)

Collier, J.F., 'Women in Politics' in Rosaldo and Lamphere, *Woman, Culture, and Society*, 89–96

Contamine, P., 'Scottish soldiers in France in the second half of the fifteenth century: mercenaries, immigrants or Frenchmen in the making?' in G.G. Simpson (ed.), *The Scottish Soldier Abroad 1247–1967* (Edinburgh, 1992), 16–30

Crawford, A., 'The King's Burden? – the Consequences of Royal Marriage in Fifteenth-century England' in R.A. Griffiths (ed.), *Patronage The Crown and the Provinces in later medieval England* (Stroud, 1981), 33–56

——, 'The Piety of Late Medieval English Queens' in C. Barron and C. Harper-Bill (eds), *The Church in Pre-Reformation Society: Essays in Honour of F.R.H. Du Boulay* (Woodbridge, 1985), 48–57

Danbury, E., 'Images of English Queens in the Later Middle Ages', *The Historian*, 46 (Summer 1995), 3–9

Delaney, S., 'Mothers to Think Back Through: Who are They? The Ambiguous Example of Christine de Pizan' in L. Finke and M. Shichtman (eds), *Medieval Texts and Contemporary Readers* (Ithaca, 1987)

——, 'History, Politics, and Christine Studies: A Polemical Reply' in Brabant, *Politics, Gender and Genre*, 193–207

Ditchburn, D., 'The Place of Guelders in Scottish Foreign Policy, c.1449–c.1542' in G.G.Simpson (ed.), *Scotland and the Low Countries, 1124–1994* (East Linton, 1996), 59–75

Donahue, C., 'The Canon Law on the Formation of Marriage and Social Practice in the Later Middle Ages', *Journal of Family History*, 8 (1983), 144–58

——, 'The policy of Alexander the Third's consent theory of marriage' in S. Kuttner (ed.), *Proceedings of the Fourth International Congress of Medieval Canon Law* (Vatican City, 1976), 251–81

Dow, B.H., *The Varying Attitude toward Women in French Literature of the Fifteenth Century: The Opening Years* (New York, 1936)

Dowden. J., *The Bishops of Scotland* (Glasgow, 1912)

Downie, F.A., '"La voie quelle menace tenir": Annabella Stewart, Scotland, and the European Marriage Market, 1444–56', *SHR*, lxxviii (1999), 170–191

——, 'And they lived happily ever after? Medieval queenship and marriage in Scotland, 1424–1449' in T. Brotherstone, D. Simonton and O. Walsh (eds), *Gendering Scottish History: An International Approach* (Glasgow, 1999), 129–41

——, 'Queenship in Late Medieval Scotland' in M. Brown and R. Tanner (eds), *Scottish Kingship 1306–1488: Essays in Honour of Norman Macdougall* (forthcoming)

Duby, G., *Medieval Marriage: Two Models from Twelfth-Century France* (Baltimore, 1978)

——, *The Knight, the Lady and the Priest. The Making of Modern Marriage in Medieval France* (London, 1984)

Dunbar, A.H., *Scottish Kings 1005–1625* (second edition, Edinburgh, 1906)

Dunbar, J.G., *Scottish Royal Palaces. The Architecture of the Royal Residences during the Late Medieval and Early Renaissance Periods* (East Linton, 1999)

Duncan, A.A.M., *Scotland: The Making of the Kingdom* (Edinburgh, 1975)

——, 'The community of the realm of Scotland and Robert Bruce: a review', *SHR*, xlv (1976), 184–201

——, *James I, King of Scots 1424–1437* (Glasgow, 1984)

Dunlop, A.I., *Scots abroad in the fifteenth century*, Historical Association Pamphlet (London, 1942)

——, *The Life and Times of James Kennedy, Bishop of St. Andrews* (Edinburgh, 1950)

Dunn, D., 'Margaret of Anjou, Queen Consort of Henry VI: A Reassessment of her Role, 1445–53' in R.E. Archer (ed.), *Crown, Government and People in the Fifteenth Century* (Stroud, 1995), 107–43

Durkan, J., 'The Observant Franciscan Province in Scotland', *Innes Review*, xxxv (1984), 51–7

Durkan, J. and Ross, A., *Early Scottish Libraries* (Glasgow, 1961)

Eales, R., 'The Game of Chess: An Aspect of Medieval Knightly Culture' in C. Harper and R. Harvey (eds), *The Ideals and Practice of Medieval Knighthood, I: Papers from the First and Second Strawberry Hill Conferences* (Woodbridge, 1986), 12–34

Eames, P., 'Furniture in England, France and the Netherlands from the Twelfth to the Fifteenth Century', *Furniture History*, xiii (1977), 1–303

Enright, M.J., 'King James and His Island: An Archaic Kingship Belief?', *SHR*, 55 (1976), 29–40

Erler, M. and Kowaleski, M. (eds), *Women and Power in the Middle Ages* (Athens, Georgia, 1988)

Ewan, E., 'A realm of one's own? The place of medieval and early modern women in Scottish history' in T. Brotherstone, D. Simonton and O. Walsh (eds), *Gendering Scottish History: An International Approach* (Glasgow, 1999), 19–36

Ewan, E. and Meikle, M.M. (eds), *Women in Scotland, c.1100–c.1750* (East Linton, 1999)

Facinger, M., 'A Study of Medieval Queenship: Capetian France, 987–1237', *Studies in Medieval and Renaissance History*, 5 (1968), 1–48

Farmer, S., 'Persuasive Voices: Clerical Images of Medieval Wives', *Speculum*, 61 (1986), 517–43

Ferguson, M.W., Quilligan, M. and Vickers, N.J. (eds), *Rewriting the Renaissance. The Discourses of Sexual Difference in Early Modern Europe* (Chicago, 1986)

Ferrante, J.M., *Women as Image in Medieval Literature from the Twelfth Century to Dante* (New York, 1975)

——, 'The Education of Women in the Middle Ages in Theory, Fact and Fantasy' in P.H. Labalme (ed.), *Beyond Their Sex: Learned Women of the European Past* (New York, 1984), 9–42

——, 'Public Postures and Private Maneuvers: Roles Medieval Women Play' in Erler and Kowaleski, *Women and Power*, 213–29

Ferrier, J.M., *French Prose Writers of the Fourteenth and Fifteenth Centuries* (Oxford, 1966)

Fradenburg, L.O., *City, Marriage, Tournament. Arts of Rule in Late Medieval Scotland* (Madison, 1991)

——, (ed.), *Women and Sovereignty* (Edinburgh, 1992)

——, 'Troubled Times: Margaret Tudor and the Historians' in S. Mapstone and J. Wood (eds), *The Rose and the Thistle: Essays on the Culture of Late Medieval and Renaissance Scotland* (East Linton, 1998), 38–58

Gabriel, A.L., 'The Educational Ideas of Christine de Pisan', *Journal of the History of Ideas*, 16 (1955), 3–21

Gibson, G.M., 'Blessing from Sun and Moon: Churching as Women's Theatre' in B.A. Hanawalt and D. Wallace (eds), *Bodies and Disciplines: Intersections of Literature and History in Fifteenth-Century England* (Minneapolis, 1996), 139–54

Glente, K. and Winther-Jensen, L. (eds), *Female Power in the Middle Ages* (Copenhagen, 1989)

Gold, P.S., *The Lady and the Virgin. Image, Attitude, and Experience in Twelfth-Century France* (Chicago, 1985)

Goody, J., *The Development of the Family and Marriage in Europe* (Cambridge, 1983)

Gottlieb, B., 'The Problem of Feminism in the Fifteenth Century' in J. Kirshner and S. Wemple (eds), *Women of the Medieval World: Essays in Honor of John H. Mundy* (Oxford, 1985), 337–64

Grant, A., *Independence and Nationhood: Scotland, 1306–1469* (London, 1984)

——, 'Crown and Nobility in Late Medieval Britain' in R.A. Mason (ed.), *Scotland and England, 1286–1815* (Edinburgh, 1987), 34–59

Griffiths, R.A., 'Queen Katherine of Valois and a Missing Statute of the Realm', *Law Quarterly Review*, xciii (1977), 248–58

——, *The Reign of King Henry VI. The exercise of royal authority 1422–1461* (London, 1981)

Guichenon, S., *Histoire Généalogique de la Royale Maison de Savoye*, nouvelle édition (Turin, 1778–80)

Hanawalt, B.A., 'Lady Honor Lisle's Networks of Influence' in Erler and Kowaleski, *Women and Power*, 188–212

——, 'Female Networks for Fostering Lady Lisle's Daughters' in Parsons and Wheeler, *Medieval Mothering*, 239–58

Harriss, G.L., *Cardinal Beaufort* (Oxford, 1988)

Haskell, A.S., 'The Paston Women on Marriage in Fifteenth-Century England', *Viator*, 4 (1973), 459–71

Helle, K., 'Norwegian Foreign Policy and the Maid of Norway', *SHR*, 69 (1990), 142–56

Herlihy, D., 'The Medieval Marriage Market' in D.B.J. Randall (ed.), *Medieval and Renaissance Studies*, 6 (Durham, NC, 1976), 3–27

Hindman, S., *Christine de Pizan's 'Epistre Orthéa': painting and politics at the court of Charles VI* (Toronto, 1986)

Huneycutt, L., 'Medieval Queenship', *History Today*, 39 (June 1989), 16–22

——, 'The Idea of the Perfect Princess: *The Life of Saint Margaret* in the Reign of Matilda II', *Anglo-Norman Studies*, 12 (1989), 81–97

——, 'Intercession and the High-Medieval Queen: The Esther Topos' in Carpenter and MacLean, *Power of the Weak*, 126–46

——, 'Public Lives, Private Ties: Royal Mothers in England and Scotland, 1070–1204' in Parsons and Wheeler, *Medieval Mothering*, 295–311

Jambeck, K.K., 'Patterns of Women's Literary Patronage: England, 1200-ca.1475' in McCash, *Cultural Patronage of Medieval Women*, 228–65

Jeay, M., 'Sexuality and Family in Fifteenth-Century France: Are Literary Sources a Mask or a Mirror?', *Journal of Family History*, 4 (1979), 328–45

Jones, M.K. and Underwood, M.G., *The King's Mother. Lady Margaret Beaufort, Countess of Richmond and Derby* (Cambridge, 1993)

Jordan, C., 'Woman's Rule in Sixteenth-Century British Political Thought', *Renaissance Quarterly*, 40 (1987), 421–51

——, 'Boccaccio's Infamous Women: Gender and Civic Virtue in the *De Mulieribus Claris*' in C. Levin and J. Watson (eds), *Ambiguous Realities: Women in the Middle Ages and Renaissance* (Detroit, 1987), 25–47

——, *Renaissance Feminism. Literary Texts and Political Models* (Ithaca, 1990)

Jori, I., *Genealogia Sabauda* (Bologna, 1942)

Kantorowicz, E., *The King's Two Bodies: A Study in Medieval Political Theology* (Princeton, 1957)

Kelly, H.A., *Love and Marriage in the Age of Chaucer* (Ithaca, 1975)

Kelly, J., 'Did Women Have a Renaissance?' in R. Bridenthal and C. Koonz (eds), *Becoming Visible. Women in European History* (Boston, 1977), 137–64

——, 'Early Feminist Theory and the Querelle des femmes, 1400–1789', *Signs*, 8 (1982), 4–28

Kendall, P.M., *Louis XI* (London, 1971)

Köfler, M., 'Eleonore von Schottland' in M. Köfler and S. Caramelle, *Die Beiden Frauen des Erzerhogs Sigmund von Osterreich-Tirol* (Innsbruck, 1982), 15–114

Krieger, L., 'The Idea of Authority in the West', *AHR*, 82 (1977), 249–70

Laidlaw, J.C., 'Christine de Pizan, the Earl of Salisbury and Henry IV', *French Studies*, 36 (1982), 130–43

Laing, D., 'Remarks on the Character of Mary of Gueldres, Consort of King James the Second of Scotland; in connexion with an attempt to determine the Place of her Interment in Trinity College Church, Edinburgh', *Proceedings of the Society of Antiquaries of Scotland*, iv (1860–2), 566–77

Lamphere, L., 'Strategies, Cooperation, and Conflict Among Women in Domestic Groups' in Rosaldo and Lamphere, *Woman, Culture, and Society*, 97–112

Laynesmith, J.L., *The Last Medieval Queens. English Queenship 1445–1503* (Oxford, 2004)

Lee, P.A., 'Reflections of Power: Margaret of Anjou and the Dark Side of Queenship', *Renaissance Quarterly*, 39 (1986), 183–217

Looten, C., 'Isabelle de Portugal, duchesse de Bourgogne et comtesse de Flandre, 1397–1471', *Revue de Littérature Comparée*, xviii (1938), 5–22

Lyall, R.J., 'The Court as a Cultural Centre', *History Today*, 34 (1984), 27–33

——, 'The Medieval Scottish Coronation Service: some seventeenth-century evidence', *Innes Review*, 28 (1977), 3–21

——, 'Books and Book Owners in Fifteenth-Century Scotland', in J. Griffiths and D. Pearsall (eds), *Book Production and Publishing in Britain, 1375–1475* (Cambridge, 1989), 239–56

Lynn, T.B., 'The Ditié de Jeanne d'Arc: Its Political, Feminist and Aesthetic Significance', *Fifteenth Century Studies*, 1 (1978), 149–57

McCash, J.H. (ed.), *The Cultural Patronage of Medieval Women* (Athens, Georgia, 1996)

——, 'The Cultural Patronage of Medieval Women: An Overview' in McCash, *Cultural Patronage of Medieval Women*, 1–49

McCracken, P., *The Romance of Adultery: Queenship and Sexual Transgression in Old French Literature* (Philadelphia, 1998)

McDiarmid, M.P., 'The Kingship of the Scots in Their Writers', *Scottish Literary Journal*, vi, 5–18

Macdougall, N., *James III. A Political Study* (Edinburgh, 1982)

——, 'Bishop James Kennedy of St Andrews: a reassessment of his political career' in N. Macdougall (ed.), *Church, Politics and Society: Scotland 1408–1929* (Edinburgh, 1983), 1–22

——, *James IV* (Edinburgh, 1989)

Macfarlane, L.J., *William Elphinstone and the Kingdom of Scotland, 1431–1514* (Aberdeen, 1985)

McGladdery, C., *James II* (Edinburgh, 1990)

McLeod, G.K. (ed.), *The Reception of Christine de Pizan From the Fifteenth Through the Nineteenth Centuries* (Lewiston, 1991)

McLoughlin, E.C., 'Equality of Souls, Inequality of Sexes: Woman in Medieval Theology' in R.R. Reuther (ed.), *Religion and Sexism: Images of Women in the Jewish and Christian Traditions* (New York, 1974), 213–66

McNamara, J. and Wemple, S.F., 'Sanctity and Power: the Dual Pursuit of Medieval Women' in Morewedge, *The Role of Woman in the Middle Ages*, 90–118

——, 'The Power of Women Through the Family in Medieval Europe, 500–1100' in Erler and Kowaleski, *Women and Power*, 83–101

McNeill, P.G.B., 'The Scottish Regency', *Juridical Review*, xii (1967), 127–48

MacQueen, J., 'Tradition and the Interpretation of *The Kingis Quair*', *The Review of English Studies*, New Series xii (1961), 117–31

Macrae, C.T., 'The English Council and Scotland in 1430', *EHR*, 54 (1939), 415–25

McCartney, E., 'The King's Mother and Royal Prerogative in Early Sixteenth-Century France' in Parsons, *Medieval Queenship*, 117–41

——, 'Ceremonies and Privileges of Office: Queenship in Late Medieval France' in Carpenter and MacLean, *Power of the Weak*, 178–219

McRoberts, D., 'The Rosary in Scotland', *Innes Review*, 23 (1972), 81–6

Marshall, R.K., *Virgins and Viragos: A History of Women in Scotland from 1080 to 1980* (London, 1980)

——, *Scottish Queens, 1073–1714* (East Linton, 2003)

Marwick, J.D., *The History of the Collegiate Church and Hospital of the Holy Trinity and the Trinity Hospital, Edinburgh 1460–1661*, Scottish Burgh Records Society (Edinburgh, 1911)

Mason, R.A., 'Kingship, Tyranny and the Right to Resist in Fifteenth Century Scotland', *SHR*, lxvi (1987), 125–51

Maurer, H.E., *Margaret of Anjou. Queenship and Power in Late Medieval England* (Woodbridge, 2003)

Meale, C.M., (ed.), *Women and Literature in Britain, 1150–1500* (Cambridge, 1996)

——, ' " ... alle the bokes that I haue of latyn, englisch, and frensch": laywomen and their books in late medieval England' in Meale, *Women and Literature*, 128–58

Mombello, G., 'Christine de Pizan and the House of Savoy' in E.J. Richards (ed.), *Reinterpreting Christine de Pizan* (Athens, Georgia, 1992), 187–204

Michel, F.M., *Les Ecossais en France, les Français en Ecosse* (London, 1862)

Mill, A.J., *Medieval Plays in Scotland* (London, 1927)

Mirrer, L. (ed.), *Upon My Husband's Death. Widows in the Literature and Histories of Medieval Europe* (Ann Arbor, 1992)

Morewedge, R.T. (ed.), *The Role of Woman in the Middle Ages* (London, 1975)

Morice, Dom H., *Mémoires pour servir de preuves à l'histoire Ecclesiastique et Civile de Bretagne* (Paris, 1974)

Myers, A.R., *Crown, Household and Parliament in Fifteenth Century England*, ed. C.H. Clough (London, 1985)

——, 'The Captivity of a Royal Witch: The Household Accounts of Queen Joan of Navarre, 1419–21', in Myers, *Crown, Household and Parliament*, 93–133

——, 'The Household of Queen Margaret of Anjou' in Myers, *Crown, Household and Parliament*, 135–209

——, 'The Household of Queen Elizabeth Woodville, 1466–7' in Myers, *Crown, Household and Parliament*, 251–318

Neilson, G., 'The Submission of the Lord of the Isles to James I: its Feudal Symbolism', *The Scottish Antiquary*, xv (1901), 113–22

Nicholson, R., *Scotland: The Later Middle Ages* (Edinburgh, 1974)

Nijsten, G., *In the Shadow of Burgundy. The Court of Guelders in the Late Middle Ages* (Cambridge, 2004)

Noonan, J.T., 'Power to Choose', *Viator*, 4 (1973), 419–34

Ortner, S.B., 'Is Female to Male as Nature is to Culture?' in Rosaldo and Lamphere, *Woman, Culture, and Society*, 67–87

Parsons, J.C. 'Ritual and Symbol in the English Medieval Queenship to 1500' in Fradenburg, *Women and Sovereignty*, 60–77

——, (ed.), *Medieval Queenship* (Stroud, 1994)

——, 'Introduction: Family, Sex, and Power: The Rhythms of Medieval Queenship' in Parsons, *Medieval Queenship*, 1–11

——, 'Mothers, Daughters, Marriage, Power: Some Plantagenet Evidence, 1150–1500' in Parsons, *Medieval Queenship*, 63–78

——, 'The Queen's Intercession in Thirteenth-Century England' in Carpenter and MacLean, *Power of the Weak*, 147–77

——, 'The Pregnant Queen as Counsellor and the Medieval Construction of Motherhood' in Parsons and Wheeler, *Medieval Mothering*, 39–61

——, 'Of Queens, Courts, and Books: Reflections on the Literary Patronage of Thirteenth-Century Plantagenet Queens' in McCash, *Cultural Patronage of Medieval Women*, 175–201

Parsons, J.C. and Wheeler, B. (eds), *Medieval Mothering* (New York, 1996)

Parsons, T., 'On the Concept of Influence', *Public Opinion Quarterly*, 27 (1963), 37–62

Paton, G.C.H.(ed.), *An Introduction to Scottish Legal History*, Stair Society vol.20 (Edinburgh, 1958)

Perroy, E., *The Hundred Years War* (London, 1965)

Phillippy, P.A., 'Establishing Authority: Boccaccio's *De claris mulieribus* and Christine de Pizan's *Livre de la cité des dames*', *Romanic Review*, 77 (1986), 167–94

Pigeaud, R., 'Woman as Temptress: Urban Morality in the 15th Century' in L. Dresen-Coenders (ed.), *Saints and She-Devils: Images of Women in the 15th and 16th Centuries* (London, 1987), 39–58

Pinkerton, J., *The History of Scotland from the Accession of the House of Stuart to that of Mary, with Appendices of Original Papers* (London, 1797)

Poulet, A., 'Capetian Women and the Regency: the Genesis of a Vocation' in Parsons, *Medieval Queenship*, 93–116

Pratt, R.A., 'Jankyn's Book of Wikked Wyves: Medieval Antimatrimonial Propaganda in the Universities', *Annuale Medievale*, 3 (1962), 5–27

Preston, J., 'Fortunys Exiltree: A Study of *The Kingis Quair*', *The Review of English Studies*, New Series vii (1956), 339–47

Prestwich, M., 'Edward I and the Maid of Norway', *SHR*, 69 (1990), 157–74

Queller, D.E., *The Office of the Ambassador in the Middle Ages* (Princeton, 1967)

Quilligan, M., *The Allegory of Female Authority. Christine de Pizan's 'Cité des Dames'* (Ithaca, 1991)

Rait, R.S.(ed.), *Five Stuart Princesses* (London, 1902)

Reid, N., 'Margaret Maid of Norway and Scottish Queenship', *Reading Medieval Studies*, viii (1982), 75–96

Reno, C., 'Christine de Pizan: At Best a Contradictory Figure?' in Brabant, *Politics, Gender, and Genre*, 171–91

Riis, T., *Should Auld Acquaintance Be Forgot ... Scottish-Danish Relations c.1450–1707* (Odense, 1988)

Rogers, K.M., *The Troublesome Helpmate: A History of Misogyny in Literature* (Seattle, 1966)

Rosaldo, M.Z. and Lamphere, L. (eds), *Women, Culture, and Society* (Stanford, 1974)

Rose, M.B. (ed.), *Women in the Middle Ages and the Renaissance: Literary and Historical Perspectives* (Syracuse, 1986)

Rosenthal, J.T. 'Aristocratic Cultural Patronage and Book Bequests, 1350–1500', *Bulletin of the John Rylands University Library of Manchester*, 64 (1982), 522–48

——, 'Aristocratic Marriage and the English Peerage, 1350–1500: Social Institution and Personal Bond', *Journal of Medieval History*, 10 (1984), 181–94

——, (ed.), *Medieval Women and the Sources of Medieval History* (Athens, Georgia, 1990)

——, 'Fifteenth-Century Widows and Widowhood: Bereavement, Reintegration and Life Choices' in Walker, *Wife and Widow*, 33–58

Ruether, R.R. (ed.), *Religion and Sexism: Images of Women in the Jewish and Christian Traditions* (New York, 1974)

Sayles, G.O., 'The royal marriages act, 1428', *Law Quarterly Review*, 94 (1978), 188–92

Scalingi, P.L., 'The Sceptre or the Distaff: the Question of Female Sovereignty, 1516–1607', *The Historian*, 41 (1978), 59–75

Scanlan, J.D., 'Husband and Wife: Pre-Reformation Canon Law of Marriage of the Officials' Courts' in Paton, *An Introduction to Scottish Legal History*, 69–81

Schilfgaarde, A.P. van, *Zegels en Genealogische Gegevens van de Graven en Hertogen van Gelre, Graven van Zulphen* (Arnhem, 1967)

Schmitt, C.B., 'Theophrastus in the Middle Ages', *Viator*, 2 (1971), 251–70

Scott, J.W., 'Gender: A Useful Category of Historical Analysis', *AHR*, vol.91 no.5 (Dec. 1986), 1053–75

Scott, M., 'A Burgundian Visit to Scotland in 1449', *Costume*, xxi (1987), 16–25

Seton, B., 'The Distaff Side', *SHR*, 27 (1919–20), 272–86

Shahar, S., *The Fourth Estate: A History of Women in the Middle Ages* (London, 1983)

Sheingorn, P., '"The Wise Mother": The Image of St Anne Teaching the Virgin Mary', *Gesta*, 32 (1993), 69–80

Smith, S.L., *The Power of Women. A Topos in Medieval Art and Literature* (Philadelphia, 1995)

Sommé, M., 'La jeunesse de Charles le Téméraire d'après les comptes de la cour de Bourgogne', *Revue du Nord*, 64 (1982), 731–50

Southern, R.W., *The Making of the Middle Ages* (New Haven, 1953)

Stafford, P., 'Sons and Mothers: Family Politics in the Early Middle Ages' in Baker, *Medieval Women*, 79–100

——, *Queens, Concubines and Dowagers. The King's Wife in the Early Middle Ages* (London, 1983)

——, 'The Portayal of Royal Women in England, Mid-Tenth to Mid-Twelfth Centuries' in Parsons, *Medieval Queenship*, 143–67

Stahl, A.M., 'Coinage in the Name of Medieval Women' in Rosenthal, *Medieval Women and the Sources of Medieval History*, 321–41

Staniland, K., 'Royal Entry into the World' in D. Williams (ed.), *England in the Fifteenth Century: Proceedings of the 1986 Harlaxton Symposium* (Woodbridge, 1987), 297–313

Stewart, A.M., 'The Austrian Connection c.1450–1483: Eleonora and the Inter-textuality of *Pontus und Sidonia*' in J.D. McClure and M.R.G. Spiller (eds), *Bryght Lanternis. Essays on the Language and Literature of Medieval and Renaissance Scotland* (Aberdeen, 1989), 129–49

Strohm, P., 'Queens as Intercessors' in P. Strohm, *Hochon's Arrow. The Social Imagination of Fourteenth-Century Texts* (Princeton, 1992), 95–120

Tanner, R. *The Late Medieval Scottish Parliament: Politics and the Three Estates, 1424–1488* (East Linton, 2001)

Thompson, E.M., *The Carthusian Order in England* (London, 1930)

Tolley, T., 'Hugo van der Goes's Altarpiece for Trinity College Church in Edinburgh and Mary of Guelders, Queen of Scotland' in J. Higgitt (ed.), *Medieval Art and Architecture in the Diocese of St Andrews* (Leeds, 1994), 213–31

Trévédy, J., 'Trois duchesses douairières de Bretagne', *Bulletin Archéologique de l'Association Bretonne*, Troisième Série, 27 (1909), 3–49

Turner, J.G., *One Flesh: Paradisal Marriage and Sexual Relations in the Age of Milton* (Oxford, 1987)

Tytler, P.F., *The History of Scotland from the Accession of Alexander III to the Union* (Edinburgh, 1864)

Vale, M.G.A., *Charles VII* (London, 1974)

Vaughan, R., *Philip the Good* (London, 1970)

Walker, S.S. (ed.), *Wife and Widow in Medieval England* (Ann Arbor, 1993)

Warner, M., *Alone of All Her Sex: The Myth and Cult of the Virgin Mary* (New York, 1976)

Watson, G.W., 'Wolfart van Borssele, Earl of Buchan', *The Genealogist*, new series, xiv, 10–11 and xvi, 136

Watt, D.E.R., 'The Minority of Alexander III of Scotland', *Transactions of the Royal Historical Society*, xxi (1971), 1–24

——, 'The Papacy and Scotland in the Fifteenth Century', *The Church, Politics and Patronage in the Fifteenth Century*, ed. R.B. Dobson (Gloucester, 1984), 115–32

Weber, M., *The Theory of Social and Economic Organisation*, trans. A.M. Henderson and T. Parsons (New York, 1947)

Webster, B., 'Scotland Without a King, 1329–41' in A. Grant and K.J. Stringer (eds), *Medieval Scotland: crown, lordship and community* (Edinburgh, 1993), 223–38

Weiss, R., 'The Earliest Account of the Murder of James I of Scotland', *EHR*, 52 (1937), 479–91

Willard, C.C., 'A Portuguese Translation of Christine de Pisan's *Livre des trois vertus*', *Publications of the Modern Language Association*, 78 (1963), 459–64

——, 'An Autograph Manuscript of Christine de Pizan?', *Studi Francesi*, 9 (1965), 452–7

——, 'The Manuscript Tradition of the *Livre des Trois Vertus* and Christine de Pizan's Audience', *Journal of the History of Ideas*, 27 (1966), 433–44

——, 'A fifteenth-century view of woman's role in medieval society. Christine de Pisan's *Livre des Trois Vertus*' in Morewedge, *The Role of Woman in the Middle Ages*, 90–120

——, *Christine de Pizan. Her Life and Works* (New York, 1984)

——, 'The Patronage of Isabel of Portugal' in McCash, *Cultural Patronage of Medieval Women*, 306–20

Wilson, D., 'Notes of the Search for the Tomb of the Royal Foundress of the College Church of the Holy Trinity at Edinburgh', *Proceedings of the Society of Antiquaries of Scotland*, iv (1860–2), 554–65

Wood, C.T., *Joan of Arc and Richard III: Sex, Saints and Government in the Middle Ages* (Oxford, 1988)

——, 'The First Two Queens Elizabeth, 1464–1503' in Fradenburg, *Women and Sovereignty*, 60–77

Wormald, J., 'Taming the Magnates?' in K.J. Stringer (ed.), *Essays on the Nobility of Medieval Scotland* (Edinburgh, 1985), 270–80

Unpublished theses

Brown, M.H., 'Crown-Magnate Relations in the Personal Rule of James I' (unpublished PhD thesis, University of St Andrews, 1991)

Crawford, B.E., 'The Earls of Orkney-Caithness and their relations with Norway and Scotland: 1158–1470' (unpublished PhD thesis, University of St Andrews, 1971)

Chamberlayne, J.L., 'English queenship, 1445–1503' (unpublished DPhil thesis, York University, 1999)

Macrae, C., 'Scotland and the Wars of the Roses' (unpublished DPhil thesis, Oxford University, 1939)

Mooney, C.L., 'Queenship in Fifteenth-Century France' (unpublished PhD thesis, Ohio State University, 1977)

Stevenson, A.W.K., 'Trade between Scotland and the Low Countries in the Later Middle Ages' (unpublished PhD thesis, University of Aberdeen, 1982)

Index

Abelard, Peter 82
Abercorn 110
Aberdeen: bishop 165, 196;
    Candlemas 1441 77; customs 120;
    and Joan Beaufort 153; queens'
    dowers 103, 104, 107, 143
Aitkyne (barber) 96
Albert, duke of Austria 54, 61, 62,
    69–70, 71
Alexander II, king of Scots 28, 134
Alexander III, king of Scots 28, 86,
    134–5
Alnwick 163
Amadeus VIII, duke of Savoy 19,
    54–5, 56, 57. See also Felix V, anti-
    pope
Amadeus IX, duke of Savoy 19
Angus, earls of See Douglas, William,
    James and George
Annabella Drummond, queen of Scot-
    land 23, 24, 87–8, 103, 122
Anne, Saint 77, 185
Anne of Bohemia, queen of England
    97, 122
Anne of Brittany, queen of France 19
Anne of Cyprus, duchess of Savoy 128
Appin of Dull 103, 104, 105, 113
'Appoyntement': (1439) 142, 151, 155;
    (1452) 110
Aristotle 22, 131
Armagnacs 15, 63
Arnold, duke of Guelders 60, 66,
    67–8, 71–2, 73, 169, 181 n97
Arras conference (1435) 45, 46, 48, 54,
    68, 69

Atholl: earldom of 73, 105, 109, 110;
    earls of See Stewart, Walter and
    John
Auchinleck Chronicle: James II's
    minority 142; James III's minority
    170; on Mary of Guelders 93–4,
    170, 171, 172, 175, 176, 194; on
    queens 22; on royal births 125–8,
    131
Austria: alliances 61, 70; dukes of See
    Albert and Sigismund; marriage
    strategies 62–4, 196
Ayr: customs 116

Balfour, Andrew 117
Balfour, John 118, 177
Balfour, Michael 177–8
Balliol, Edward 87
Bamburgh 163
baptisms 130, 131, 199
Basel, Council of (1441) 55
Bathsheba 9, 16
Beaufort, Edmund, count of Mortain
    41–2
Beaufort, Henry, Cardinal 34, 39, 41,
    42, 68, 120, 142, 192, 197
Beaufort, Joan, countess of Westmore-
    land 187
Beaufort, John, earl of Somerset 33
Beaufort, Thomas, duke of Exeter 34,
    37, 120
Beaufort family 197; marriage policy
    33–4
Bedford, John, duke of 20, 46
Berclay, Alexander 120

218